Chef John Folse's

Plantation Celebrations

Chef John Folse's Plantation Celebrations

Recipes From Our Louisiana Mansions

By

Chef John D. Folse, CEC, AAC

Chef John Folse & Company

Gonzales, Louisiana

Library of Congress Catalog Card Number: 93-074150

ISBN 0-9625152-2-1

First Printing: January 1994
Second Printing: September 1994
Third Printing: July 1996
Fourth Printing: July 1997
Fifth Printing: May 2000
Sixth Printing: February 2007

Printed in Canada

Additional copies available from:

Chef John Folse & Company
2517 S. Philippe Avenue
Gonzales, LA 70737
(225) 644-6000
or via the Internet at
http://www.jfolse.com

Also Available:

The Evolution of Cajun & Creole Cuisine

Chef John Folse's Louisiana Sampler

Something Old & Something New

Hot Beignets & Warm Boudoirs

The Encyclopedia of Cajun & Creole Cuisine

Table of contents

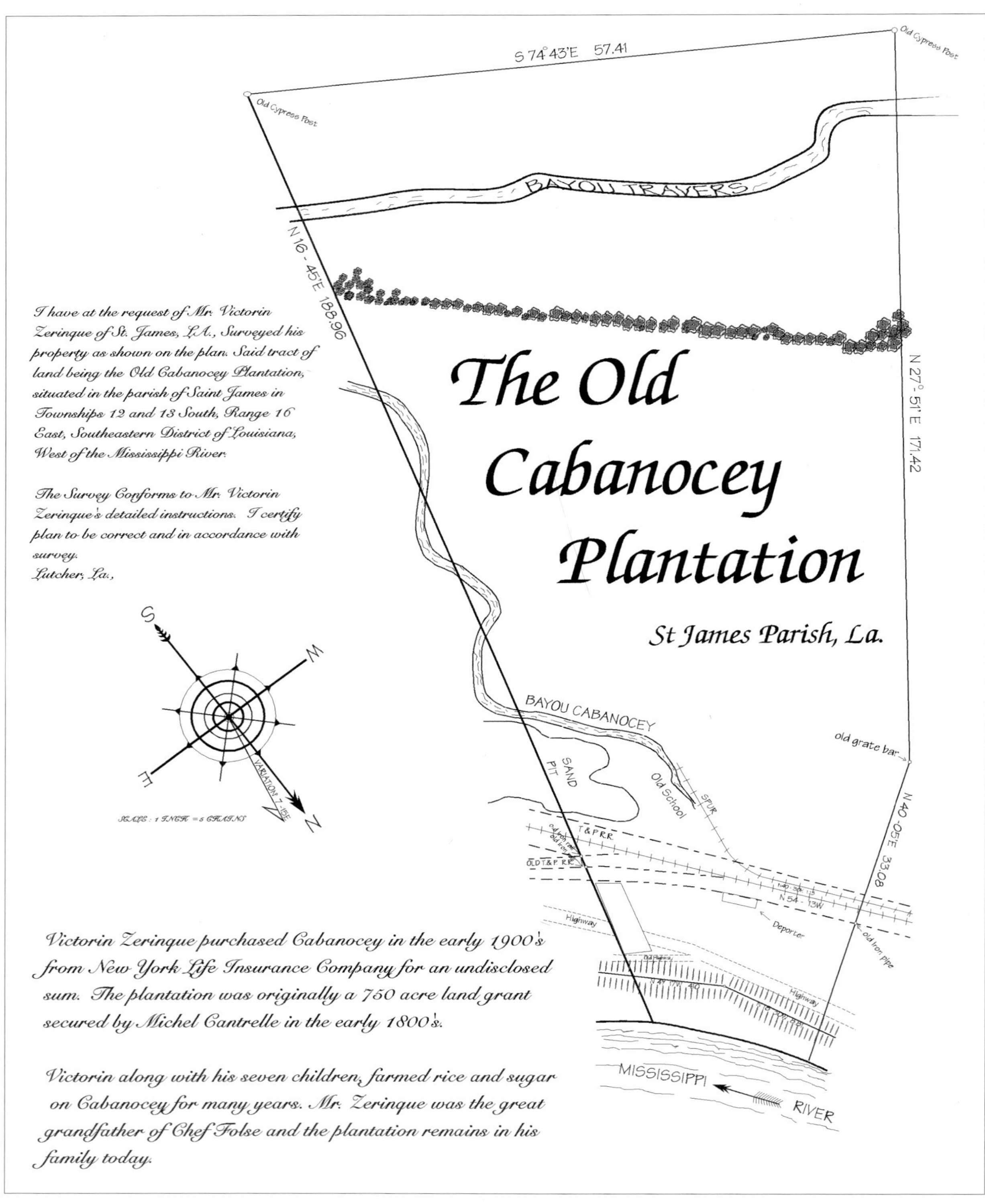
S 74°43'E 57.41
Old Cypress Post
Old Cypress Post
BAYOU TRAVERS
N 16 - 45'E 188.96
N 27°- 51'E 171.42
The Old Cabanocey Plantation
St James Parish, La.
I have at the request of Mr. Victorin Zerinque of St. James, LA., Surveyed his property as shown on the plan. Said tract of land being the Old Cabanocey Plantation, situated in the parish of Saint James in Townships 12 and 13 South, Range 16 East, Southeastern District of Louisiana, West of the Mississippi River.
The Survey Conforms to Mr. Victorin Zerinque's detailed instructions. I certify plan to be correct and in accordance with survey.
Lutcher, La.,
S
W
E
N
VARIATION 7-15E
SCALE: 1 INCH = 5 CHAINS
BAYOU CABANOCEY
old grate bar
SAND PIT
Old School
SPUR
N 40-05'E 33.08
T&P R.R.
OLD T&P R.R.
Highway
Deporter
old iron pipe
Highway
MISSISSIPPI
RIVER
Victorin Zerinque purchased Cabanocey in the early 1900's from New York Life Insurance Company for an undisclosed sum. The plantation was originally a 750 acre land grant secured by Michel Cantrelle in the early 1800's.
Victorin along with his seven children, farmed rice and sugar on Cabanocey for many years. Mr. Zerinque was the great grandfather of Chef Folse and the plantation remains in his family today.

Foreword

I was born on Cabanocey Plantation in St. James Parish, Louisiana. Although I didn't know it at the time, just to be born there made a person part of history. I was by no means part of a great plantation family like the Romans, Cantrelles, Bringiers or Kenners. Quite the contrary, I came at a time when men were land poor. The plantations were gifts from our grandfathers and fathers before, handed down from one generation to another. In many cases, a French Creole or Antebellum mansion was considered an albatross for the family who inherited it. We certainly did not consider it part of a great legacy.

My great grandfather, Victorin Zeringue, purchased Cabanocey in the early 1900s. With over 750 acres, he and his wife, Marie Eveline Robert, thought they were destined for greatness. If anything, they were great landowners. Oh, they made a good living and in those days, that was a triumph. Victorin and Evelie went on to have many children, one of them my grandfather, Albert. Albert married Regina Waguespack and together they produced six more heirs to Cabanocey. One of them, my mother, Therese, married Royley Folse and eight more heirs were born.

Where will the story of Cabanocey end? As a great poet wrote, "No man ever owns land. He merely borrows it for a short while and then returns it to the maker". This is true of all parcels regardless of size, but certainly for the tens of thousands of acres borrowed by the planters. In these next few pages, I will not attempt to predict the future of these lands and buildings. Instead, we will take a good look into the past. Who were these planters? Why did they come to Louisiana and from where? What purpose did they serve in history and more importantly, what foods did they create? I guess we should begin with the river.

On April 9, 1682 Robert Cavalier Sieur de LaSalle accepted the task of exploration of the Mississippi River for France. He was a great military leader and had much experience with the Indians of North America because of his many campaigns. He had listened in awe to their stories of a river called Malbenchi, "the great one". He had been told that this large body of water flowed to the west. Thinking that all wealth came from the Orient, he felt that by traveling this river, he could find the Pacific Ocean and set up the most strategic port city on the continent. Once established, France could control the flow of the enormous wealth from China throughout the North American continent. He and his men set sail only to become disenchanted when they realized that the river flowed south. They decided to return north but first they planted the French flag, established the land for Louis XIV and called it Louisiana. Sixteen years later, King Louis, determined to explore and settle this land, called upon two of his most able adventurers, the brothers Bienville and Iberville. Pierre LeMoine Sieur d'Iberville had not only the respect of the king, but also had never lost a land or naval battle. Their flotilla consisted of two small man-of-war ships and several coastal vessels. Their mission was to chart the mouth of the Mississippi River and befriend the Indians of Louisiana. They were to establish trade for two important commodities - salt and furs. This salt was not used for cooking, but for the preservation of hides for shipment to France. As their ships approached the shoreline near present day Grand Isle, they saw a large number of raccoons roaming the beach. Thinking they were cats, they called the area "Cat Island". On March 3rd while following the shoreline in six small boats, a violent storm came up. Iberville gave command for all boats to head into the rock formation on the shoreline. As the small boats hit the shore, expecting to be destroyed on the rocks, they were pleasantly surprised to find that they were large pillows of mud and not stone. The boats were saved. Iberville cupped his hands, tasted the water and smiled. It was fresh water and by an act of God, he had miraculously found the mouth of the river. They settled in for the night at a place they named "Mardi Gras Point", after realizing that it was Fat Tuesday, the day before Ash Wednesday. Two days later, after traveling upriver and battling high winds and strong currents, the group settled at a large clearing between the river and a lake that led to the Gulf of Mexico. The Indians called this spot "Chinchuba". They ate an evening meal of alligator and buffalo and were so impressed with the site that Bienville founded the city of New Orleans on this very spot.

When Iberville and Bienville reported their success in the new world, Louis decided it was time to colonize the territory. By 1710, the aristocrats of French society were beginning to arrive from Paris seeking adventure and fortune in Louisiana. They brought with them a knowledge of French cooking techniques and a desire to learn the use of local ingredients. These French kitchens produced such dishes as coq au vin, etouffee, sauce piquante, pommes souffles and cassoulets. Their greatest gift to Louisiana, however, was the result of a desire for their native bouillabaisse. Since the ingredients for this Mediterranean soup were not available in bayou country, a new dish emerged from the black iron pots of the French - gumbo. This soup incorporated the local seafoods with the dark brown roux and a new vegetable from Africa, kin gumbo, which we know today as okra.

In 1762, after defeat in the Seven Years War, France gave Louisiana to Spain to keep from losing it to England. It took Spain seven years to claim Louisiana and though they did, the inhabitants remained loyal to France. But it was not long before the locals began using saffron, allspice, cloves and chili peppers brought over by the Spanish from South and Central America. The Spanish introduced other ingredients common in Louisiana cooking today such as kidney beans, black beans, garbanzo beans and pinto beans. They also gave us coffee and chicory. Their most precious gift, however, emerged from a desire to recreate their famous rice dish, paella. Once again, unable to get access to the ingredients necessary to create the dish, they substituted local items. By replacing lobster with ham and adding local fresh vegetables and rice, jambalaya was produced.

The Africans arrived in Louisiana from the English colonies. Forced into slave labor on the early plantations and in the Creole homes of New Orleans, these men and women contributed much to our developing cuisine. With their vast knowledge of "making do" and living off the land, as they did in Africa, they became experts in our early kitchens. They brought from their homeland black-eyed peas or "congre", watermelon seeds and a traditional dish, Gumbo Z'herbs. From the congo, this stew was made of seven different greens without meat, and was enjoyed by New Orleanians on Good Friday during the Lenten season. Indisputably, the greatest contribution of the Africans to Creole cuisine was okra, the key ingredient in our premier soup, gumbo. The seeds from the okra plant were sewn into the lining of their clothes and transported to Louisiana. By the mid to late 1700s, the English, Germans, Acadians and Italians had begun to arrive adding even more diversity to our ever changing culture and cuisine. It was because of these nations coming to lay claim to a new world and their yearning for a better lifestyle once here, that the great plantation era of Louisiana was born.

These early settlers, discovering the rich lands bordering the Mississippi River, quickly began to move out of the city of New Orleans. They obtained large land grants with only one stipulation - that they build a home and plant a crop within one year. After a single generation, the people from these many nations began to intermarry producing the Creoles. Though many scholars refer to the Creole as an offspring from the marriage between the Spanish and French, most agree that the Creoles represented all nations who came to New Orleans. With the turn of the century, these families grew in size and importance and by 1830, the antebellum era was upon us. The plan of a typical plantation home was simple. It had to be on or near the river with large white columns supporting the roof and galleries. Normally, giant oaks or magnolias were planted and often the home was flanked by outbuildings on either side such as garconnieres and pigeonaires. Behind the house there were thousands of acres of sugar cane or cotton with cotton gins or sugar mills to process these crops. With the homes and the acreage came the slaves - a reality as significant as the river itself. They came against their own free will, torn from their homelands to toil for another. In some cases, they were mistreated. While in others, they found kindness and respect. The plantation owners saw them as commodities, and provided their basic needs. Often, after years of faithful service, they were set free. The only good thing to be said of slavery is that it provided the workers with constant, though wageless, employment, a place to live and food to eat. Like communism, the slave system denied equality. But unlike communism, it did not channel all of the energies of its workers into its destruction.

The plantation owners of the 1850s enjoyed a lifestyle unlike any since the time of Rome. Their wealth was immeasurable and three good crops could produce a millionaire. It was said that by 1855, there were more millionaires to be found between Natchez and New Orleans than in the rest of the seventy-five year old republic. New Orleans was by far the largest port in the nation, though only fifty years old, and Louisiana's population was already at one million. The great white mansions lined the east and west banks of the Mississippi River like cypress trees lined the bayous. Fortunes were created every night and entrepreneurs by the thousands flocked to South Louisiana. Though cotton production was lucrative, sugar cane offered even greater wealth to the planter. Though the risk of operating a successful plantation was great, it was considered small compared to the payback. It was a self-sufficient kingdom governed by "the Master". The plantation produced its own food, clothing, shelter and labor. It was a nation within a nation, often with nearly 5,000 individuals living within its compound.

The plantation owners and their families became well educated and well traveled. With their new-found wealth, nothing was more important than food and entertainment. This new lifestyle dictated the addition of ballrooms and dining rooms to the big houses to accommodate their guests. Specialty ingredients were sought after to prepare elaborate feasts. The swamp floor, the Gulf of Mexico and the Mississippi River became their outdoor pantries. Every imaginable ingredient became accessible to the plantation cooks. The cuisine that developed in Louisiana during this period was the most important ever to develop in America. This was the cuisine of the Cajuns and Creoles. The intermarriage of nations and the combination of their culinary styles created our Louisiana cooking. How did this unique cuisine affect all of us in Louisiana and in the world today? The purpose of this book is to answer this question. Hopefully, you will quickly see that what was created then has influenced every pot in America today. These were the greatest of cooks. They established a new cuisine in a new land with ingredients never before seen. Then came the war!

The Civil War and the abolition of slavery ravaged the south and this plantation lifestyle. The fields could not be tended, horses could not be fed and the great white mansions became burdens. Cattle and chickens roamed where grand balls once took place. Many houses were destroyed by the Union army or the carpetbaggers. Under Louisiana's Napoleonic Law, these large land grants were divided and divided again. Because of absentee ownership, many of these "temples to the past" fell prey to abandonment, neglect and time. Today, along the river, only a few of these great plantation manors remain. With infused capital from new owners, a renewed interest in our past and with the help of large Louisiana corporations, those still standing will be here forever as a tribute to a once glorious past. Now, let's cook!

The photographer

Ron Manville

Ron has been a corporate and commercial photographer for ten years in and around New England. Born in Virginia, he is a graduate of the Rochester Institute of Technology.

In 1992 he, along with Chef James Griffin, formed YUM, Inc., a company specializing in food photography and styling.

He works in all formats from 35mm to 4x5 in a variety of styles both on location and in his 2000 square foot studio.

Plantation Celebrations is the fourth cookbook he has photographed.

YUM, Inc. is the collaboration between the artistic minds of the photographer and the chef. YUM has served clients on location, in the studio and internationally. Their client list spans the commercial, editorial and cookbook markets. One of their foremost clients is the *National Culinary Review*, the monthly trade publication of the American Culinary Federation. In addition to working toward their own line of cookbooks, food graphics and food stocks, YUM has a close association with the culinary program of Johnson and Wales University. For further information or a color brochure on YUM, write P.O. Box 9116, Pawtucket, Rhode Island, 02862 or call (401) 722-3313.

The food stylists

Chefs Jim and Christine Griffin

James is an assistant professor at Johnson and Wales University and a member of the 1992 and 1996 U.S. Culinary Teams. Having been awarded gold medals at culinary competitions in the United States and Europe, Jim is recognized internationally as a true culinary professional.

Along with his many accolades, James holds a Master of Science degree in Hospitality Administration and is co-owner of YUM, Inc.

Christine is also an assistant professor at Johnson and Wales and has been awarded gold medals at American Culinary Federation events and the 1988 Culinary Olympics in Frankfurt, Germany. In 1991, she won a gold medal at A Taste of Ireland competition held in Dublin.

Christine holds a Master of Science degree in Management Technology and teaches specialized courses in nutritional cuisine at Johnson and Wales.

Christine and Jim were married in August of 1992.

The designer

William Pitts

Strangely enough, I am a Mississippian who knows little about Louisiana - culture, cuisine, or otherwise. The production of this book has been one more course in my post-graduate education.

The field of graphic arts has changed considerably since my graduation from Delta State University with a Bachelor of Fine Arts in Commercial Design, and the years following have been a continual striving toward self education in my field.

My introduction to the computer in 1985 steered me in a new direction from the one in which I was headed after college. Manual paste-up gave way to electronic precision, turning what once was an arduous process into an enjoyable one. The possibilities for page layout as well as illustration were staggering for one who had been schooled in the conventional methods. I was hooked.

I started my own commercial design company in the summer of 1992 in Jackson after having worked for a service bureau for three and one-half years, and have since branched out into book publishing, video box design, magazine layout, architectural rendering, medical procedure manuals, technical illustrations, and soft drink logo designs.

Among other books, I have collaborated in the design and production of a textbook entitled *Mississippi: The Study of Our State.* I have also designed and electronically laid out *A Priceless Heritage: The Story of Mississippi Power Company*, a corporate history.

I hope that I have preserved intact the flavor and regional atmosphere that John has so appetizingly captured with his recipes and commentary. If the concerted design elements of Ron, Jim, Christine, and myself are in any way analogous to the components of John's recipes, then we're happy. I have enjoyed designing *Plantation Celebrations.*

The book

The text for the book was composed on an Ultra 386 portable computer . The book itself was designed and typeset on a Macintosh IIci using Aldus PageMaker v. 4.2 (my upgrade to version 5.0 hadn't arrived in time). The endsheet map was drawn using Adobe Illustrator v. 5.0.

The text type is Simoncini Garamond, with Present for initial caps. Headlines and subheads are set in Bernhard Modern, and Tiffany Italic and Demi Italic.

Hanson Graphics of New Orleans generated the duotones that appear throughout the book.

Friesen Printers of Canada provided four color separations, film output and, of course, the printing.

Text paper is 80 lb. Jenson Gloss Book, the endsheets are 100 lb. White Offset and the cover is 80 lb. Jenson Gloss Book laminated over 100 point board.

"A Taste of Louisiana"
Chef John Folse
SILVER OAK

The author

Chef John Folse, CEC, AAC

Chef John Folse is the owner and executive chef of his Louisiana based corporations. His Lafitte's Landing Restaurant in Donaldsonville, is recognized as one of the finest restaurants in and around New Orleans. White Oak Plantation, in Baton Rouge, houses his catering and events management company. Louisiana's Premier Products, his cook and chill plant in New Orleans, manufactures soups, sauces, entrees and meats for foodservice and retail establishments across the country. Chef Folse is the author of numerous books and publications available in bookstores nationally.

John is respected around the world as an authority on Cajun and Creole cuisine and culture. He hosts his own national television cooking show, "A Taste of Louisiana" on PBS. In addition, his syndicated radio show, "Stirrin' It Up!," can be heard on many stations nationwide. He has taken his famous "Taste of Louisiana" from Hollywood to the Great Wall of China, opening promotional Louisiana restaurants in Hong Kong, Japan, Beijing, London, Paris, Rome, Bogota, Taipei and Seoul. In 1987, Chef Folse was selected as "Louisiana Restaurateur of the Year" by the Louisiana Restaurant Association and in November of 1988, the Louisiana Sales and Marketing Executives named him "Louisiana's Marketing Ambassador to the World." In 1988, Chef Folse made international headlines by opening his "Lafitte's Landing East" in Moscow during the presidential summit between Ronald Reagan and Mikhail Gorbachev. This opening represented the first time an American Restaurant had operated on Soviet soil. Immediately following this venture, John hosted ten Soviet chefs for the first Soviet American Culinary Exchange. In 1989, Chef Folse was invited to create the first ever Vatican State Dinner in Rome, and while there had a private audience with Pope John Paul II. In 1990, Chef Folse was named the "National Chef of the Year" by the American Culinary Federation, the highest honor bestowed upon an American chef. His Lafitte's Landing Restaurant was inducted into the "Fine Dining Hall of Fame," in 1989, and received the DiRoNA (Distinguished Restaurants of North America) award in 1996.

Chef Folse is the recipient of numerous culinary awards and recognitions, and has been honored by local, state and international governments for his continuing efforts to showcase America's regional cooking around the world. His most prestigious acknowledgement to date was Nicholls State University's decision to name their new culinary program in his honor. An Associate of Science in Culinary Arts degree program began in January of 1996, and a Bachelor of Science in Culinary Arts degree program began in January of 1997. Nicholls State, his Alma Mater, is located in Thibodaux, Louisiana. For additional information on our organization you may locate us on the Internet at http://www.jfolse.com

Photo credit: Jose Garcia

Dedication

There are many people who deserve my heartfelt thanks and gratitude. First, I must begin with the early plantation owners. The men and women, with adventure in their hearts and the burning desire for a better life in an otherwise hostile new territory, created an era unlike any since the time of Rome.

I pay special tribute to the African-Americans, the slaves, torn from their homelands against their will to toil for another's wealth and glory. They were the laborers whose sweat and tears cleared the land and built the mansions. Though they existed in pain, they created like no others. It is from their hands that much of the food on these pages originated.

To the individuals, foundations and corporations who own the plantations today, I say thank you for your cooperation in my efforts to produce this book.

To my wife, **Laulie**, who once again not only edited every word of this book but also gave me a year and a half without complaint to finish the project. It's her expertise that makes my rambling sentences appear perfect in the completed text.

To my Administrative Assistant, **Pamela Castel**, whose dedication to each of my projects is incomparable. Whether at her desk, on the road, in the studio or on a laptop computer, her commitment can never be measured.

To the chefs of Lafitte's Landing Restaurant and White Oak Plantation - **Martin Klier**, **Steve Zucker**, **Mike Dardenne**, **Terry McDonner**, **Donnie Bergeron** and **Frank Harris**. Without their culinary assistance, you could not view these beautiful photographs.

To **Si Brown and my good friends at Bruce Foods Corporation** in New Iberia, Louisiana, who not only sponsor my "A Taste of Louisiana" series on PBS, but also manufacture Louisiana Gold Pepper Sauce. Without it, I could cook absolutely nothing!

To **Albertson's Incorporated**, who supplied every bit of food product necessary to test the recipes, produce the photography and create the television series.

To **Charley Steen of the world famous Steen's Cane Syrup mill** in Abbeville, Louisiana, who produces Louisiana Cane Syrup - the one ingredient that I find so significant in Cajun and Creole cuisine.

Finally, to all of you who treat us as family as we travel throughout Louisiana. I only wish that every one could experience this fabulous Southern hospitality.

Chapter One

Rouxs, Stocks, Sauces, etc.

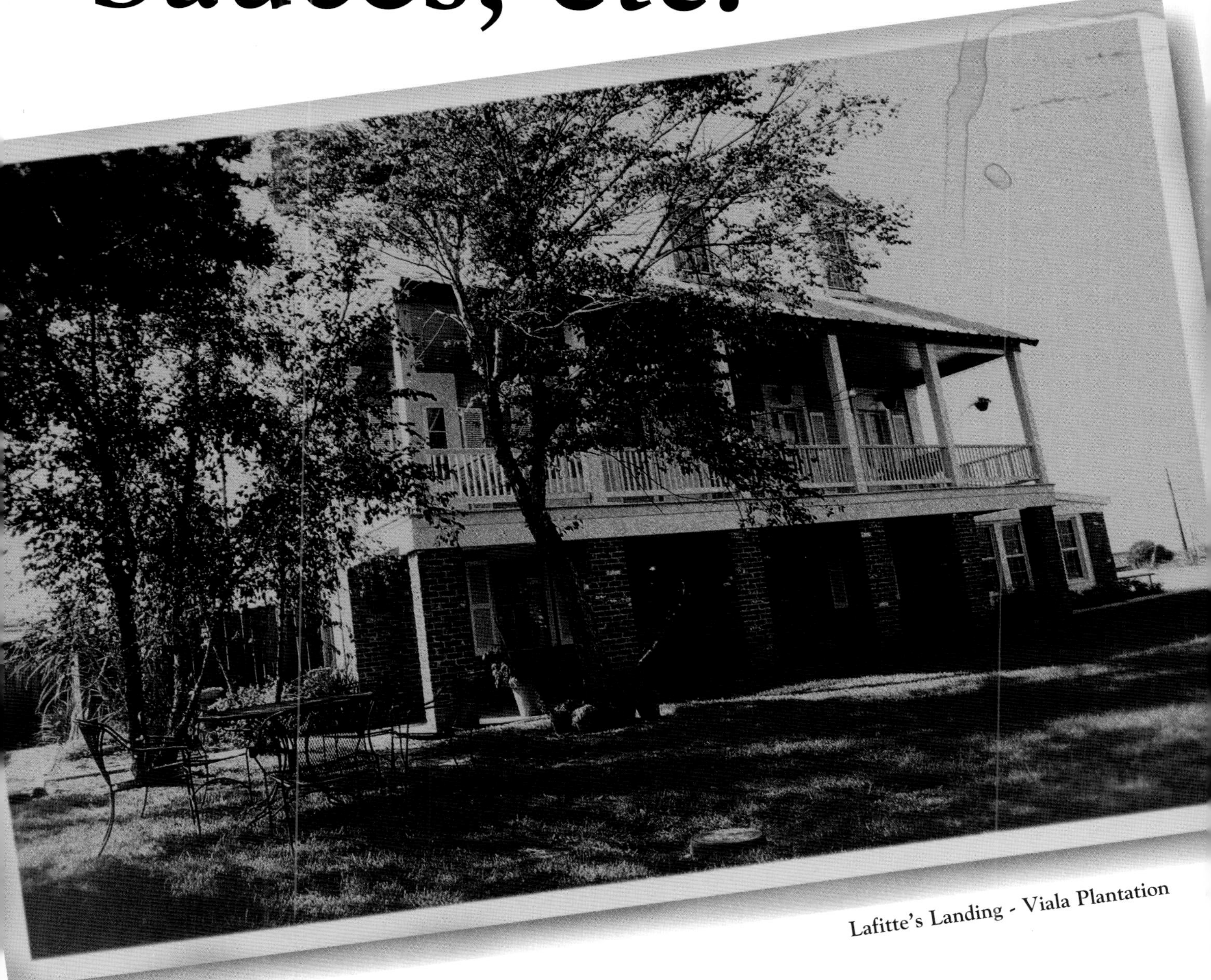

Lafitte's Landing - Viala Plantation

Viala Plantation - Lafitte's Landing

"A Pirate's Lair"

Almost 200 years ago, a legend was born. Its name was Jean Lafitte. The name of the legend is about all that historians can agree upon. Some say he was born in 1782. Others point to the year 1780. Was it in France or the West Indies? Does anybody really know? There is disagreement about his birthdate, birthplace, marriage (or marriages) and even the time and place of his death. But there is no disagreement that Jean Lafitte was one of the most colorful characters in the history of Louisiana. He was denounced as a pirate, a scoundrel and a smuggler. He was admired as a corsair, a privateer and gentlemen rover. Poets sighed for the man who committed "a thousand villainies and a single heroism", assisting the Americans at the Battle of New Orleans.

In 1797, Donaldsonville was a small frontier settlement. The Acadians had arrived here from Nova Scotia only ten years before. This area seemed the perfect location for Dumas St. Martin and J. P. Viala to build their raised Acadian cottage. In the heart of this thriving settlement, Bayou Lafourche flowed from the Mississippi River and emptied into the Gulf of Mexico. Being totally navigable, it was referred to as the longest highway in bayou country. It was for this reason that the Pirate, Jean Lafitte, chose Donaldsonville and this home to store his contraband and allow his two young children to dwell. Local legend states that it was in this very building that Emma Viala, granddaughter of the builder, married Jean Pierre, son of the infamous pirate, in the early 1800s.

St. Martin and Viala constructed their home of virgin cypress harvested from the property. Their 700 acre land grant was issued for the cultivation of indigo. This blue dye had been contracted for shipment to the Prussian Army for military uniforms. Indigo was the major money crop in this area prior to cotton and sugar. In the late 1950s, the home fell into a state of disrepair. It was then purchased and restored by the Hymel family who lived in the house until the 1960s.

Prior to being demolished, Earl "Tubby" Ewen, an LSU football great of the 1920s, purchased the home. He moved it to its present site at the western approach to the Sunshine Bridge in 1964. It was converted into a restaurant by Ewen and later run by Mike Person, his grandson. Chef John Folse acquired the restaurant in 1978 and once again restored the property to its original condition.

To reach Viala Plantation, take I-10 from Baton Rouge or New Orleans. Take Exit 182 to the Sunshine Bridge. 504-473-1232.

Chinese Sassafras Wood Carving, Taiwan

At left, Lafitte's Pepper Seared Lamb Chops (page 209)

Stocks in Cajun and Creole Cooking

As both Cajun and Creole cuisines are descended from their French classical and regional ancestors, I must place major emphasis on the importance of stocks in our cooking. What early Creole home would have been complete without the aroma of a constantly simmering stock pot filled with fish, shellfish or game bones.

Soups, sauces, marinades, sautes and braises all have as their essential base, a good, hearty and flavorful stock. Naturally, the bond between classical French stock principles and Creole cuisine is more recognizable than that of its Cajun cousin. In Cajun cuisine, to simmer ingredients that give flavor in a rich hearty liquid and then toss the ingredients out the back door would go against the grain of the hardworking Cajun. No, the Cajuns cooked anything they could hunt, trap or fish in a black iron pot, and the natural stock remained as the gravy. But the principles of Creole and classical stocks remained. Whole cuts of meat and plenty of seasoning vegetables went into the pot, but remained to become a part of the dish itself.

The evolution of crawfish bisque, from its classical origin, shows this development in Cajun cuisine. "Bisque d' ecrivisses" was a pureed crawfish soup in classical French cuisine. It was flavored with consomme and a mirepoix of seasoning vegetables, thickened with rice, strained and finished with cream. The dish was then garnished with stuffed crawfish heads. In Cajun cuisine, this dish finds its finest expression, but nothing is strained out! The vegetables remain and the dark Cajun roux gives the soup a character never touched in classical French cooking.

Courtbouillon is another example of the differences in French and Cajun cuisines. In classical cuisine, a courtbouillon consists of seasoning vegetables and spices, simmered in water producing a flavorful poaching liquid for fish and other seafood. In South Louisiana, this becomes a dish in and of itself, as in Redfish Courtbouillon. The fish is cooked with vegetables and spices to create a sauce of inexpressible flavor with no loss or waste.

Many dishes in Cajun cuisine are this way. A sauce is created right in the pot without the fuss and waste of classical or even Creole cooking. Sauce Piquante quickly comes to mind. I've tasted Venison Sauce Piquante in my native St. James Parish that had the rich velvety character of an Espagnole Sauce simmered all day by the chef of a French nobleman.

So remember, as we take this journey through Cajun and Creole cuisines, that the principles of stocks are essential.

Whether we make a hunter sauce from a game stock to grace a stuffed loin of venison or braise a rabbit as we create a "Lapin Sauce Piquante", in Cajun and Creole cooking the stock makes the difference. Here, old world principles have been adapted and local indigenous ingredients have been substituted to produce a cuisine that is truly American.

Stock Techniques

Stocks have four major ingredients: Bones, mirepoix (aromatic vegetables), bouquet garni (spices and herbs), and liquid (water, wine and/or stock).

1. Bones

Stocks can be made from any bones that you have in your kitchen. For a white stock, as in white veal stock, fish stock or chicken stock, simply wash the bones of blood and break or cut them into manageable pieces, exposing any marrow. For dark stocks, such as brown veal stock, game stock or duck stock, brown bones well. A light coating of oil can aid in this process. Well browned bones add rich color and flavor to the stock. However, do not burn or char them, as this will make a bitter stock.

2. Mirepoix

Onions, shallots, scallions, leeks, celery, garlic, carrots, mushroom trimmings and tomatoes can all be used to infuse aromatic flavor into your stock, depending on what you have available in your kitchen. NEVER use bell pepper, cabbage, cauliflower or related vegetables as these make a stock bitter and/or overpower it. For brown stocks, the mirepoix can be added to the bones as they brown. For white stocks, they can be slightly sweated by sauteing before hand in butter. Size of cut depends on cooking time. For long stocks (beef, veal and game), larger pieces are fine. For quicker stocks (chicken, fish and shellfish), smaller sizes are required.

3. Bouquet Garni

Black peppercorns, parsley, whole thyme, bay leaf and cloves can be either tied up in a leek or in a cheese cloth and placed in the liquid. In the case of stocks that cook more than an hour or two, the bouquet garni should be added during the last hour and a half.

4. Liquid

The whole purpose of a stock is to extract the color, flavor, nutrients and gelatin from the bones. Cold water is the mainstay in this process. It can be supplemented with either red or white wine as well. A double strength stock can be made by starting your stock with a previously made one that has been strained, cooled and skimmed of all fat. Cold liquid is used to draw the flavor out of the bones. In the preparation of green vegetables like asparagus, hot water or steam is used and cooking time is shortened to lock in flavor, color and nutrients. So therefore, in stocks, we use cold water and long cooking time in order to draw the flavor out. NEVER add salt to the water. When the stock simmers, the salt remains as the volume reduces and the stock will prove too salty. Stocks should be simmered slowly and skimmed of all impurities and fat which rise to the surface. This will produce a hearty, flavorful and clear stock.

The Roux

Stocks may be thickened by means of reductions, eggs, butter, vegetable purees, cream, foie gras, various starches and even blood. In classical French cuisine, the roux is the primary thickening agent. Equal parts of butter and flour are well blended over heat to create a roux. This process may produce rouxs of different colors and thickening capabilities depending on the cook's need. In Cajun and Creole cuisine, the roux has been raised to a new dimension never before experienced in other forms of cooking.

Butter, lard, peanut oil, bacon fat and even duck fat have been used in combination with flour to produce as many taste and color variations as there are cooks in South Louisiana. In classical cuisine, the brown roux is used for brown sauce, the blonde roux for veloutes and the white roux for bechamels. In Creole cuisine, a brown roux is made from butter or bacon fat and is used to thicken gumbos and stews requiring a lighter touch. The Cajuns, on the other hand, are the originators of the most unique rouxs in modern cookery.

The Cajun dark brown roux is best made with vegetable oil, although in the past, it was thought imperative that only animal fat be used. The flour and oil are cooked together until the roux reaches a caramel color. This roux has less thickening power, however, due to the fact that the darker the roux gets, the more the starch compound which thickens liquid breaks down. Thus, the thickening capabilities of the dark roux are diminished. The dark brown roux is the secret to traditional Cajun food because of the richness and depth it adds to the dish. Butter is used in classical and Creole rouxs, however, the Cajuns use only vegetable oil or lard to produce their lighter colored rouxs. Tan in appearance, these light rouxs are used primarily with vegetables and light meat dishes.

Nothing in Cajun country has a greater aroma than a light brown roux simmering with onions, celery, bell pepper and garlic. On many occasions, growing up in South Louisiana, my hunger was satisfied with a touch of this vegetable seasoned roux spread on a piece of French bread.

Certain gumbos are further thickened, in Bayou country, with either okra or file powder. Considering the variations in cooking time and fats or oils, the number of different roux possibilities are infinite. I will attempt to delineate six such rouxs, three used in classical cuisine, one used in Creole cooking and two that are strictly Cajun.

LAGNIAPPE

Lagniappe, "a little something extra", was always given to customers after a purchase in the stores of early New Orleans. This gave special pleasure to children since normally the lagniappe was a piece of candy. No matter how small the purchase, the merchant always added "something for nothing". It seems that the term originated five centuries ago in Normandy and Brittany. Grains like oat, wheat and barley when sold were spread on a woven cloth known in French as a "nappe". When the seller emptied the contents of the cloth into the buyer's receptacle, there were always a few grains clinging to the cloth. To compensate for this loss, the seller would take one or two handfuls from his stock and throw it into the buyers bin and say, "pour la nappe", for the cloth. The custom continued and today in Louisiana that little something extra, lagniappe, is often extended even in a cookbook.

The Roux

THE BROWN BUTTER ROUX:

1/2 cup butter
1/2 cup flour

In a heavy bottom saute pan, melt butter over medium high heat. Using a wire whisk, add flour, stirring constantly until flour becomes light brown. You must continue whisking during the cooking process, as flour will tend to scorch as the browning process proceeds. Should black specks appear in the roux, discard and begin again. This volume of roux will thicken three cups of stock to sauce consistency.

THE BLONDE BUTTER ROUX:

1/2 cup butter
1/2 cup flour

In a heavy bottom saute pan, melt butter over medium high heat. Proceed exactly as in the brown roux recipe, however, only cook to the pale gold state. This roux is popular in Creole cooking and will thicken three cups of stock to a sauce consistency.

THE WHITE BUTTER ROUX:

1/2 cup butter
1/2 cup flour

In a heavy bottom saute pan, melt butter over medium high heat. Proceed exactly as in the blonde roux recipe, however, only cook until the flour and butter are well blended and bubbly. Do not brown. This classical style roux is popular in Creole cooking and will thicken three cups of stock to a sauce consistency.

THE CREOLE ROUX:

The Creole roux can be made with lightly salted butter, bacon drippings or lard. As with everything regarding food in Louisiana, whenever someone attempts to reduce this wealth of food lore to written material, an argument breaks out. Let's just say that Creole rouxs vary in color the same as classical and Cajun ones. The Creoles, however, did have in their larder butter for the roux, whereas any butter a Cajun may have had would have been saved for a biscuit or cornbread and never put in the black iron pot for a roux.

If a comparison statement can be made, it would be that generally speaking, the Creole roux is darker in color than the classical French brown roux it descended from but not as dark as the Cajun dark roux.

The Roux

THE LIGHT BROWN CAJUN ROUX:

1 cup oil
1 cup flour

In a black iron pot or skillet, heat the oil over medium high heat to approximately 300 degrees F. Using a wire whisk, slowly add the flour, stirring constantly until the roux is peanut butter in color, approximately two minutes. This roux is normally used to thicken vegetable dishes such as corn maque choux (shrimp, corn and tomato stew) or butter beans with ham. If using this roux to thicken an etouffee, it will thicken approximately two quarts of liquid. If used to thicken seafood gumbo, it will thicken approximately two and a half quarts of stock.

THE DARK BROWN CAJUN ROUX:

1 cup oil
1 cup flour

Proceed as you would in the light brown Cajun roux recipe but continue cooking until the roux is the color of a light caramel. This roux should almost be twice as dark as the light brown roux but not as dark as chocolate. You should remember that the darker the roux gets, the less thickening power it holds and the roux tends to become bitter. This roux is used most often in sauce piquantes, crawfish bisques and game gumbos. However, it is perfectly normal to use the dark brown roux in any dish in Cajun cooking.

This roux gives food such a rich character that I sometimes make shrimp and corn bisque with it, as well as a river road seafood gumbo that will knock your socks off. Slow cooking is essential to achieve that dark, rich color. There's always been considerable debate over the origin of the dark brown cajun roux. I've always contended that because the Cajuns cooked in black iron pots over open fires using lard as a base, the dark roux was discovered by accident when the fire got too hot and the flour over-browned. With their lean pantries in mind, the Cajuns kept the roux instead of discarding it. They enjoyed the flavor and kept doing it that way. It developed during the Cajuns' less affluent years as a means of enriching a soup or stew with flavor when the larder was not as full but the number of chairs at the table were many.

Either way, if properly done, the dark Cajun roux enriches food with color and flavor that is so fantastic it could only be Cajun.

The Roux

Table of Sauce and Soup Consistencies Using The Roux of Cajun and Creole Cooking

THE BUTTER BASE ROUXS (THE CLASSICAL AND CREOLE ROUXS)

1 cup butter
1 cup flour

This recipe will thicken the following:

- 6 cups stock to a thick white sauce consistency.
- 8 cups stock to a concentrated soup consistency.
- 10 cups stock to a thick soup consistency.
- 12 cups stock to a perfect Louisiana gumbo consistency.
- 14 cups stock to a light gumbo consistency.

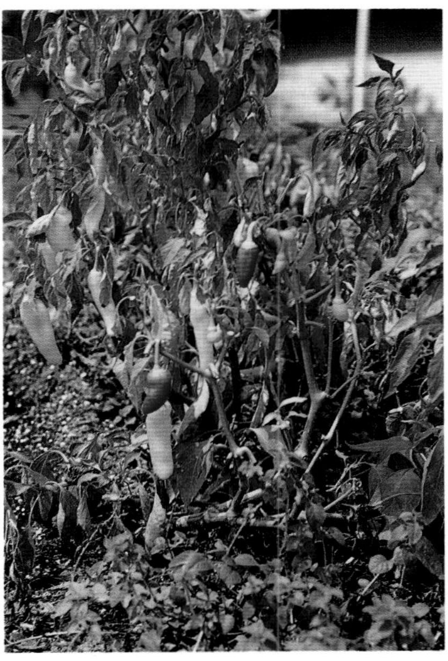

Peppers from the Herb Garden

THE OIL BASE ROUXS (THE CAJUN ROUXS)

1 cup vegetable oil
1 cup flour

Cooked at 300 degrees F. for three to five minutes, this recipe will thicken the following:

- 6 cups stock to a thick brown sauce consistency.
- 8 cups stock to a thick gumbo consistency.
- 10 cups stock to a perfect Louisiana gumbo consistency.
- 12 cups stock to a light gumbo consistency.

It should be noted that the butter or oil base rouxs may be made well in advance, cooled, separated into half cup portions and placed in the refrigerator or freezer. The roux will keep well for months and always be available to you should an emergency arise.

BEEF, VEAL OR GAME STOCK

PREP TIME: 6 Hours
MAKES: 2 Quarts

INGREDIENTS:

3 pounds marrow bones
3 pounds shin of beef
3 large onions, unpeeled and quartered
3 carrots, peeled and sliced
3 celery stalks, peeled and sliced
3 heads garlic, sliced in half to expose pods
2 bay leaves
4 sprigs parsley
15 black peppercorns
1 tsp whole thyme
1-1/2 gallons water
3 cups dry red wine

METHOD:

Preheat oven to 400 degrees F. Have your butcher select and save three pounds of beef or veal marrow bones and three pounds of an inexpensive shin meat or stew meat of beef. Place bones and shin meat in roasting pan and bake until golden brown, approximately thirty minutes. Place browned bones, meat and all remaining ingredients in a three gallon stock pot. Bring to a rolling boil, reduce to simmer and cook for six hours adding water if necessary to retain volume. During this cooking process, skim off all impurities that rise to the surface of the pot. Remove pot from heat and strain stock through fine cheese cloth or strainer. Allow stock to rest for fifteen minutes and skim off all oil that rises to the top. Return stock to a low boil and reduce to two quarts.

GAME STOCK:

To create the basic game stock, proceed exactly as you would for the beef or veal stock. The difference, however, is that you must substitute three pounds of duck, rabbit, venison or other wild game bones into the stock pot in place of the veal or beef bones. Other than the shellfish stock, game stock is used more often in Cajun and Creole cuisine than any other sauce base.

Changes

Oak Alley Plantation

Oak Alley Plantation

"Grandeur Under the Oaks"

Whenever I consider the ingredients necessary for a picnic, a couple of things come to mind. First, you need some food. It need not be elaborate, just simple things like plantation fried chicken, carrot salad Bon Sejour and a platter of jelly rolls. Naturally, you need friends to enjoy it with and the perfect setting. I always look for lush green surroundings, running water, and if I'm lucky, a 400 year-old oak tree to shade my blanket. Well, without a doubt, Oak Alley Plantation is not only the most picturesque picnic spot in Louisiana, but there are also twenty-eight live oaks from which to choose.

In the late 1600s, an unknown French settler transplanted twenty-eight live oaks in a double alley from the river to his small cabin. Since he was a trapper, he felt the oak alley would alert travelers on the Mississippi to his cabin. These twenty-eight oaks, eighty feet apart, are today over 300 years old and in full-grown splendor.

Jacques Roman, brother of a governor of Louisiana, built his mansion in 1836 at the end of this alley on the site of the trapper's cabin. He originally named the home Bon Sejour, meaning good rest. Riverboat captains re-named the home Oak Alley after the magnificent trees. Built in the Greek revival style, the home is surrounded by twenty-eight Doric columns eight feet in circumference. The pale pink color was obtained by mixing crushed brick with the plaster.

The Dining Room at Oak Alley

The gardens surrounding the house contain seasonal flowers and shrubs, as well as an all important vegetable garden. Most homes of the nineteenth century were relatively self sufficient and functioned remarkably well as such. Slaves at Oak Alley were encouraged to experiment with horticulture whenever possible. As a result, Antoine, a slave of Roman, developed the world famous paper-shelled pecan here at Oak Alley. After the Civil War, Roman's fortune failed. The family left the plantation in 1866. In 1925, the Andrew Stewart family bought the home and acreage and began restoration. Today, the property is run by a non-profit foundation.

To reach Oak Alley, take I-10 east from Baton Rouge or west from New Orleans to Exit 182. Cross the Sunshine Bridge and take Highway 18 toward Vacherie. 504-265-2151.

At left, clockwise from bottom left, Plantation Fried Chicken with Garlic and Herbs (page 184), Jelly Roll (page 298), Carrot Salad (page 124), and Stuffed Celery Sticks (page 57)

FISH STOCK

PREP TIME: 1 Hour MAKES: 2 Quarts

INGREDIENTS:

2 pounds fish bones, heads included
2 diced onions
2 diced carrots
2 diced celery stalks
6 cloves diced garlic
4 sprigs parsley
2 bay leaves
1 tsp dry thyme
6 black peppercorns
1 lemon, sliced
1 gallon cold water
3 cups dry white wine

METHOD:

Ask your seafood supplier to reserve two pounds of white fish bones and heads or two pounds of whole inexpensive white fish for this stock. Combine all ingredients in a two gallon stock pot. Bring to a rolling boil, reduce to simmer and cook for forty-five minutes. During the cooking process, skim off all impurities that rise to the surface. Add water if necessary to retain volume. Strain through fine cheese cloth or strainer. Return stock to a low boil and reduce to two quarts.

Viala Plantation - Lafitte's Landing Restaurant

SHELLFISH STOCK

PREP TIME: 1 Hour MAKES: 2 Quarts

COMMENT:

The shellfish stock is the most utilized stock in Cajun and Creole cooking simply because it is the base for most of our soups and gumbos.

INGREDIENTS:

1 pound crab shells
1 pound shrimp shells, with heads
1 pound crawfish shells, with heads
2 onions, diced
2 carrots, diced
2 celery stalks, diced
6 cloves garlic, diced
4 sprigs parsley
2 bay leaves
1 tsp dried thyme
6 black peppercorns
1 sliced lemon
1 gallon cold water
2 cups dry white wine

METHOD:

Have your seafood supplier select one pound each of crab, shrimp and crawfish shells, including the heads if possible. Do not rinse the shells prior to beginning the stock. In the rinsing process, all fats are removed and herein lies the secret to a good shellfish stock. Combine all ingredients in a two gallon stock pot. Bring to a rolling boil, reduce to simmer and cook for one hour. During the cooking process, skim off all impurities that rise to the surface. Add water if necessary to retain appropriate volume. Strain stock through fine cheese cloth or strainer. Return stock to a low boil and reduce to two quarts.

CHICKEN STOCK

PREP TIME: 1 Hour MAKES: 2 Quarts

INGREDIENTS:

2 pounds chicken bones
2 pounds chicken necks, wings and gizzards
2 onions, finely chopped
2 carrots, peeled and thinly sliced
6 cloves diced garlic
2 celery stalks, finely chopped
2 bay leaves
2 sprigs parsley
1 tsp dry thyme
12 whole black peppercorns
1 gallon cold water
2 cups dry white wine

METHOD:

Have your butcher select two pounds of chicken bones and two pounds of chicken necks, wings and gizzards for this stock. Place all ingredients in a two gallon stock pot. Bring to a rolling boil, reduce to simmer and cook for one hour. During the cooking process, skim off all impurities that rise to the surface. Strain through fine cheese cloth or strainer and allow stock to rest for thirty minutes. Skim off all oil that rises to the surface of the stock. Return stock to a low boil and reduce to two quarts.

Viala Plantation - Lafitte's Landing Restaurant

DEMI-GLACE

PREP TIME: 1 Hour MAKES: 1 Quart

COMMENT:

Demi-glace is an essential sauce in classical cuisine. I have incorporated this sauce into most of the dishes created at Lafitte's Landing Restaurant.

INGREDIENTS:

2 quarts beef, veal or game stock (see recipe)
1/2 cup white roux (see recipe)
1 ounce tomato sauce

METHOD:

Equally divide the stock into two heavy bottom sauce pans and bring to a low boil. Using a wire whisk, add one half cup white roux into one of the sauce pans, stirring constantly as mixture thickens. Into the thickened mixture, blend tomato sauce. What you have just created is known in classical cooking as an espagnole sauce. If this sauce is not full-flavored, you may wish to add a mirepoix or bouquet garni. (see stock technique) Continue simmering while skimming all impurities that rise to the surface. As the espagnole sauce reduces, replace the volume with the stock from the second pot until all has been incorporated. Strain through cheese cloth or fine strainer. You may wish to add an ounce of sherry or brandy for increased flavor.

MEAT GLAZE

PREP TIME: 1 Hour MAKES: 1 Cup

INGREDIENT:

1 quart beef or veal stock

METHOD:

Meat glaze or "glace de viande" is produced by reducing a rich, clear beef or veal stock to such a point that it napes or coats the back of a spoon. This is done by simmering the stock over medium to medium high heat in a heavy bottom sauce pan. As the stock reduces, you may transfer it from time to time to a smaller pot, straining it each time through cheese cloth. This syrupy mixture becomes firm and rubbery in texture upon refrigeration and coats meat giving it sheen and additional flavor. It also is used to enhance soups and sauces, and can be added to a Gastrique to give rich body to fine butter sauces. Glazes may also be made from chicken, duck, fish and game stocks and are known in classical cooking as glace de volaille (chicken), glace de canard (duck), glace de poisson (fish) and glace de gibier (game). Meat glazes may be kept refrigerated for weeks at a time.

Viala Plantation - Lafitte's Landing Restaurant

VELOUTE

PREP TIME: 45 Minutes MAKES: 2 Quarts

INGREDIENTS:

2 quarts chicken or fish stock (see recipe)
1/2 cup white roux (see recipe)
salt and white pepper to taste

METHOD:

In a heavy bottom sauce pan, bring stock to a low boil. Reduce to simmer and using a wire whisk, blend roux into the hot stock. Continue to whip until mixture is smooth and slightly thickened. Season to taste using salt and white pepper. Reduce heat to low and cook veloute approximately thirty minutes, skimming all impurities that rise to the surface. The veloute is the base for all great cream soups and flavored white sauces. It is the most practical of all mother sauces and is created with relative ease. In classical cuisine, the veloute is defined as an ordinary white stock. However, in Creole cooking, the roux is added to the white stock prior to calling it a veloute.

HOLLANDAISE SAUCE

PREP TIME: 15 Minutes MAKES: 1 Cup

INGREDIENTS:

8 ounces unsalted butter
3 tbsps red wine vinegar
1/2 cup dry white wine
1 tsp lemon juice
dash of Louisiana Gold Pepper Sauce
3 egg yolks
salt and white pepper to taste

METHOD:

In a small sauce pan, melt butter over medium high heat. Once melted, remove from heat and cool slightly. In a separate saute pan, add vinegar, wine, lemon juice and Louisiana Gold. Place over medium heat and reduce to approximately one half volume. Remove from heat and keep warm. In a stainless steel bowl, whip egg yolks with vinegar mixture. Place over double boiler and whip constantly using a wire whisk until egg mixture is double in volume, smooth and creamy. Do not allow mixture to overheat as eggs will scramble. Remove from heat and add melted butter in a slow steady stream, whisking constantly. If the sauce is too thick, add a few drops of warm water while whisking. Season to taste using salt and pepper and add additional lemon juice if necessary. This sauce is best when served immediately. If allowed to cool, the butter will harden.

Viala Plantation - Lafitte's Landing Restaurant

BEARNAISE SAUCE

PREP TIME: 15 Minutes MAKES: 1 Cup

INGREDIENTS:

8 ounces butter
3 tbsps tarragon vinegar
1/2 cup white wine
1 tsp lemon juice
dash of Louisiana Gold Pepper Sauce
1 tbsp chopped tarragon
1 tsp chopped green onions
1 tsp finely chopped parsley
3 egg yolks
salt and cayenne pepper to taste

METHOD:

In a small saute pan, melt butter over medium high heat. Once melted, set aside and cool slightly. In a separate saute pan, add vinegar, white wine, lemon juice, Louisiana Gold, tarragon, green onions and parsley. Bring to a slight boil, whisking constantly, and reduce liquid by one half volume. In a stainless steel bowl, whisk egg yolks with vinegar mixture and stir until well blended. Place bowl over a sauce pan of boiling water and whisk constantly until egg mixture has doubled in volume and is smooth and creamy. Be careful not to overheat as eggs will scramble. Remove bowl from sauce pan and add melted butter in a slow steady steam, whipping constantly until all is incorporated. If the sauce should become too thick, add a few drops of warm water. Season to taste using salt and pepper and add additional lemon juice if necessary. This sauce is best when served immediately. If allowed to cool, the butter will harden.

BECHAMEL SAUCE

PREP TIME: 30 Minutes *MAKES: 1 Quart*

INGREDIENTS:

1 quart milk
1 small onion, diced
3 whole cloves
pinch of thyme
6 whole peppercorns
2 small bay leaves
1/2 cup white roux (see recipe)
salt and white pepper to taste
pinch of nutmeg

METHOD:

In a heavy bottom sauce pan, heat milk over medium high heat. Add onion, cloves, thyme, peppercorns and bay leaves and continue to scald milk with seasonings for approximately twenty minutes. Do not boil. Strain scalded milk through fine cheese cloth into another sauce pan. Bring back to a low boil and add roux, whisking constantly with a wire whip until all is incorporated. Continue to whisk until mixture achieves a nice white sauce consistency. Be careful that sauce does not scorch. When thickened, remove from heat and season to taste using salt, pepper and nutmeg. This sauce is the primary ingredient for all creamed vegetable casseroles and au gratin dishes. For more flavor in the bechamel, you may wish to add a small amount of chicken or fish stock as in the veloutes.

Viala Plantation - Lafitte's Landing Restaurant

NANTUA SAUCE

PREP TIME: 1 Hour *MAKES: 2 Quarts*

COMMENT:

Technically speaking, this sauce is in the bechamel family and is made by adding cream and crawfish butter to a basic white sauce. We have developed a sauce here in South Louisiana that is more closely akin to a veloute.

INGREDIENTS:

2 pounds crawfish shells, heads included
2 cups chopped onions
1 cup chopped celery
1 cup chopped carrots
6 cloves diced garlic
2 bay leaves
1 tsp dried thyme
15 whole peppercorns
1 gallon cold water
2 cups dry white wine
1/2 cup tomato sauce
1/2 cup white roux (see recipe)
1 pint heavy whipping cream
1/2 ounce brandy
salt and white pepper to taste

METHOD:

In a two gallon stock pot over medium high heat, combine crawfish shells and heads, onion, celery, carrots, garlic, bay leaves, thyme, peppercorns, water, and wine. Bring to a low boil, reduce heat to simmer and cook thirty minutes. During the cooking process, skim off all impurities that rise to the surface. When cooked, strain stock through fine cheese cloth or strainer. Discard all stock ingredients and return hot stock to the pot. Bring to a low boil and reduce to approximately two quarts. Add tomato sauce and white roux, whisking constantly until roux is well blended and the sauce is slightly thickened. Reduce heat to simmer and cook fifteen minutes. Add heavy whipping cream and brandy and season to taste using salt and pepper. Strain sauce for a second time through fine cheese cloth or strainer, adjust seasonings and allow to cool.

BEURRE BLANC

PREP TIME: 15 Minutes *MAKES: 1 Cup*

COMMENT:

This sauce comes to us from the regional cuisine of Brittany. The city of Nantes, on the Loire, is famed for serving this sauce with pike and Loire shad. Today in Louisiana, beurre blanc lends itself to many exciting variations.

INGREDIENTS:

1/2 cup dry white wine
2 tbsps white vinegar
1 tsp lemon juice
1 tsp finely diced shallots
1 clove diced garlic
1 tbsp sliced green onions
8 ounces chipped, unsalted butter
salt and white pepper to taste
1 tsp finely chopped parsley

METHOD:

In a heavy bottom saute pan over medium high heat, combine wine, vinegar, lemon juice, shallots, garlic and green onions. Stir constantly until liquid is reduced to approximately two tablespoons. At this point, the mixture is commonly known as a gastique. Reduce heat to low and add chipped butter, a few pieces at a time, swirling pan constantly. Do not stir with a metal spoon or whip, as hot spots may develop and butter will separate. Continue to add chipped butter, swirling pan constantly, until all has been incorporated. Remove from heat and season to taste using salt and white pepper. Garnish with chopped parsley.

Viala Plantation - Lafitte's Landing Restaurant

BEURRE CAJUN

PREP TIME: 15 Minutes *MAKES: 1 Cup*

INGREDIENTS:

1/4 cup crawfish tails with fat
1/2 cup dry white wine
1 tbsp lemon juice
1 clove diced garlic
1 tbsp sliced green onions
1/4 cup finely sliced andouille
dash of Louisiana Gold Pepper Sauce
8 ounces chipped, unsalted butter
salt and cayenne pepper to taste

METHOD:

In a saute pan over medium high heat, combine crawfish tails, wine, lemon juice, garlic, green onions, andouille and Louisiana Gold. Saute approximately three to five minutes or until all liquids in pan are reduced by one half volume. Add chipped butter, a few pieces at a time, swirling pan constantly. Do not stir with a metal spoon or wire whisk as hot spots will develop in the pan and butter will separate. Continue to add butter, a few pieces at a time, swirling pan, until all is incorporated. Remove from heat and season to taste using salt and cayenne pepper. This sauce is excellent when served over pan sauteed or charbroiled fish.

BEURRE CREOLE

PREP TIME: 15 Minutes MAKES: 1 Cup

INGREDIENTS:

1/2 cup dry white wine
2 tbsps lemon juice
1/4 cup jumbo lump crabmeat
1/4 cup diced tomatoes
1 clove diced garlic
1 tbsp sliced green onions
1 tsp tomato sauce
8 ounces chipped, unsalted butter
dash of Louisiana Gold Pepper Sauce
salt and cayenne pepper to taste

METHOD:

In a saute pan over medium high heat, combine wine, lemon juice, crabmeat, tomatoes, garlic and green onions. Saute approximately three minutes or until juices are rendered into the pan. Add tomato sauce, blend well into mixture and continue to cook until all juices have been reduced to approximately two tablespoons. Slowly add chipped butter, a few pats at a time, while swirling pan constantly. Do not use a metal spoon or wire whisk as hot spots may develop and butter will separate. Continue adding butter while swirling pan until all has been incorporated. Season to taste using Louisiana Gold, salt and pepper. This sauce is excellent over broiled or sauted fish or grilled shrimp.

Viala Plantation - Lafitte's Landing Restaurant

BEURRE ROUGE

PREP TIME: 15 Minutes MAKES: 1 Cup

INGREDIENTS:

1/2 cup dry red wine
1 tbsp red wine vinegar
1 clove diced garlic
1 tbsp sliced green onions
8 ounces unsalted, chipped butter
dash of Louisiana Gold Pepper Sauce
salt and cayenne pepper to taste

METHOD:

In a saute pan over medium high heat, combine red wine, vinegar, garlic and green onions. Bring to a low boil and reduce until approximately two tablespoons of liquid remain. Add chipped butter, a few pats at a time, swirling pan constantly. Do not use a metal cooking spoon or wire whisk as hot spots will develop and butter will separate. Continue to add butter, swirling pan constantly, until all has been incorporated. Season to taste using Louisiana Gold, salt and cayenne pepper. This sauce is excellent over grilled fish or light meats.

Viala Plantation - Lafitte's Landing Restaurant

BEURRE POIVRE VERT I

PREP TIME: 15 Minutes *MAKES: 1 Cup*

INGREDIENTS:

3 tbsps green peppercorn liquid
1/2 cup dry white wine
2 tbsps lemon juice
2 cloves diced garlic
1 tbsp sliced green onions
2 tbsps green peppercorns
8 ounces unsalted, chipped butter
dash of Louisiana Gold Pepper Sauce
salt to taste

METHOD:

In a saute pan over medium high heat, combine peppercorn liquid, wine, lemon juice, garlic and green onions. Bring to a low boil and add green peppercorns. Continue to saute until liquid is reduced to approximately two tablespoons. Slowly add chipped butter, a few pats at a time, swirling pan constantly. Do not use a metal spoon or wire whisk as hot spots will develop and butter will separate. Continue to add butter, swirling pan, until all has been incorporated. Remove from heat and season to taste using Louisiana Gold and salt. This sauce is excellent when served with fish or veal.

Viala Plantation - Lafitte's Landing Restaurant

BEURRE POIVRE VERT II

PREP TIME: 15 Minutes *MAKES: 1 Cup*

INGREDIENTS:

1/2 cup dry red wine
2 tbsps red wine vinegar
2 tbsps green peppercorn liquid
2 cloves diced garlic
1 tbsp sliced green onions
2 tbsps green peppercorns
2 tbsps meat glaze (see recipe)
8 ounces unsalted, chipped butter
dash of Louisiana Gold Pepper Sauce
salt to taste

METHOD:

In a heavy bottom saute pan over medium high heat, combine wine, vinegar, peppercorn liquid, garlic and green onions. Bring to a low boil and add peppercorns and meat glaze. Continue to saute, stirring occasionally, until liquid has reduced to approximately three tablespoons. Slowly add chipped butter, a few pats at a time, swirling pan constantly. Do not use a metal spoon or wire whisk as hot spots will develop and butter will separate. Continue to add butter, swirling pan, until all has been incorporated. Remove from heat and season to taste using Louisiana Gold and salt. This sauce is excellent over grilled tuna or veal dishes.

BEURRE CITRON

PREP TIME: 15 Minutes *MAKES: 1 Cup*

INGREDIENTS:

1/2 cup dry white wine
3 tbsps lemon juice
2 tbsps orange juice
1 tbsp lime juice
2 cloves diced garlic
1 tbsp sliced green onions
8 ounces unsalted, chipped butter
dash of Louisiana Gold Pepper Sauce
salt and cayenne pepper to taste

METHOD:

In a saute pan over medium high heat, combine wine, juices, garlic and green onions. Bring to a low boil and saute until liquid is reduced to approximately three tablespoons. Add chipped butter, a few pats at a time, swirling pan constantly. Do not use a metal spoon or wire whisk as hot spots will develop and butter will separate. Continue to add butter, swirling pan, until all has been incorporated. Season to taste using Louisiana Gold, salt and cayenne pepper. This sauce is excellent over broiled or poached fish.

Viala Plantation - Lafitte's Landing Restaurant

CRAWFISH BUTTER

PREP TIME: 15 Minutes *MAKES: 1 1/2 Cups*

COMMENT:

Crawfish butter is ideal for adding that unique Cajun and Creole flavor to any classical butter sauce. Simply place one tablespoon of this compound butter into any beurre blanc based sauce and miracles happen.

INGREDIENTS:

1/4 cup butter
1/2 cup chopped onions
1/4 cup chopped celery
1/4 cup chopped carrots
2 cloves minced garlic
1/2 pound live, whole crawfish
1/4 cup brandy
1/2 pound chilled unsalted butter

METHOD:

In a heavy bottom saute pan, melt butter over medium high heat. Saute onions, celery, carrots and garlic three to five minutes or until vegetables are wilted. Add crawfish, cover and swirl pan approximately two minutes or until crawfish are pink in color. Simmer for three minutes. Deglaze with brandy being careful as brandy will ignite. Place all ingredients in a food processor with a metal blade and blend on high until well chopped. Remove mixture and chill. Once well chilled, add butter to the crawfish mixture. Blend crawfish flavor well into the softened butter. Force mixture through a fine screen sieve to remove all foreign debris and shells. Place in ceramic or plastic container, cover and chill.

BORDELAISE SAUCE

PREP TIME: 15 Minutes
MAKES: 1 Cup
COMMENT:

Bordelaise, in the city of New Orleans, has a completely different look and taste than the bordelaise of classical cuisine. Bordelaise means "the sauce from Bordeaux". In classical cooking, the sauce begins with a red wine reduction. Originally, however, the sauce was made with white bordeaux and the key ingredient added during reduction was bone marrow. Often times, the sauce was garnished with rounds of marrow. The Creoles of early New Orleans, making do with what was available, changed this sauce completely and this is their version.

INGREDIENTS:

3/4 cup butter
3 tbsps olive oil
1/4 cup diced garlic
1 tsp cracked black peppercorns
1/4 cup sliced green onions
1 ounce red bordeaux wine
1 tbsp chopped pimentos
1/4 cup chopped parsley
salt to taste
dash of Louisiana Gold Pepper Sauce

Simmering Crawfish Stock

METHOD:

In a heavy bottom saute pan, melt butter and olive oil over medium high heat. Add garlic, black peppercorns and green onions. Saute approximately two to three minutes or until vegetables are wilted. Be careful not to over-brown the garlic, as this will give the sauce a bitter taste. Deglaze with red wine and add pimentos and parsley. Season to taste using salt and Louisiana Gold. Remove from heat.

Changes

REMOULADE SAUCE

PREP TIME: 15 Minutes

MAKES: 2 Cups

COMMENT:

The recipe for the remoulade sauce of the River Road is found in the appetizer section of this book. I have taken this opportunity to give you a second version, the Creole style, which is thought to be the original Louisiana version.

INGREDIENTS:

1 cup olive oil
1/4 cup red wine vinegar
3/4 cup Creole mustard
1/2 cup sliced green onions
1/4 cup chopped parsley
1/4 cup diced celery
1 tbsp diced garlic
1 tbsp paprika
salt to taste
Louisiana Gold Pepper Sauce to taste

METHOD:

In a large ceramic mixing bowl, combine olive oil, vinegar and Creole mustard. Using a wire whisk, blend well until all ingredients are well incorporated. Add green onions, parsley, celery and garlic. Continue mixing until all seasonings are well blended. Add paprika for color and season to taste using salt and Louisiana Gold. Place in the refrigerator, covered with clear wrap, and allow to sit overnight. You may wish to serve a generous portion of this sauce over shrimp, lump crabmeat or salad.

Changes

Madewood Plantation

Rice
Sugar
Flour

Madewood Plantation

"Queen of the Bayous"

When architects were summoned to lay out the design and floor plan of a great Louisiana plantation home, certain factors had to be considered. The size of the family dictated the number of bedrooms. If the family entertained a lot or had daughters, a formal ballroom would be needed. Clothes closets were always omitted, simply because a tax was levied on each room with a door. By leaving these out, the family saved money and armoires were used in their places. There was one room considered quite common today that was always missing from plantation floor plans. Though very rare in homes until 1890, this plantation had two such rooms. I imagine they created quite a stir back then. To my knowledge, Madewood was the first plantation on Bayou Lafourche with indoor bathrooms.

This magnificent Greek revival mansion was designed by the noted New Orleans architect, Henry Howard. Located on Bayou Lafourche, the home was built in 1840 by Colonel Thomas Pugh. It took four years to cut, plank and plane the pine and cypress trees prior to construction, thus the name - Madewood. Over sixty thousand hand-made bricks were used, creating walls over twenty inches thick. The foundation was designed of a solid slablike stylobate in the Greek temple fashion. The facade features six fluted Ionic columns and diamond-shaped balusters surround the gallery. Colonel Pugh died of yellow fever prior to the completion of the home, but his widow, Eliza, directed the balance of the work.

The Music Room

The interior of the home features fourteen foot ceilings with ornate medallions and chandeliers. The window frames, cornices and doors are finished in the faux-bois, "false wood", technique. The beautifully carved, curved stairway is suspended in mid air and is unsupported by visible means. On the main floor, one finds a library, music room, double parlors and a beautiful ballroom which is also used as the family dining room. The old kitchen, located in the rear, is attached to the main house by a thick wall of brick and mortar for protection from fire.

The home changed hands only twice before being purchased in 1964 for $70,000 by the Harold Marshall family. Today, the home is owned by Keith Marshall and his wife, Millie.

To reach Madewood, take I-10 from Baton Rouge or New Orleans to Exit 182. Follow Highway 70 to Louisiana Highway 308 to the town of Napoleonville. 504-369-7151.

At left, clockwise from bottom left, Baked Pumpkin Lafourche (page 138), The Perfect Salad (page 116), and Thelma Parker's Shrimp Pie (page 222)

LOUISIANA TARTAR SAUCE

PREP TIME: 15 Minutes **MAKES: 2 Cups**

COMMENT:

Tarter sauce is normally served with all fried seafood dishes in South Louisiana. You may wish to try this sauce as a dip for garfish beignets or as a topping for a seafood terrine.

INGREDIENTS:

1-1/2 cups heavy duty mayonnaise
2 tbsps lemon juice
1/4 cup chopped pimento olives
1/4 cup chopped sweet pickles
1 tbsp sweet pickle juice
1/4 cup chopped parsley
1/4 cup chopped capers
1 tbsp sliced green onions
salt to taste
Louisiana Gold Pepper Sauce to taste

METHOD:

In a large ceramic bowl, combine mayonnaise and lemon juice. Using a wire whisk, blend until well incorporated. Add olives, pickles, pickle juice, parsley, capers and green onions. Fold all seasoning ingredients into the mayonnaise until mixture is evenly blended. Season to taste using salt and Louisiana Gold. If you prefer a more tart taste, add a little lemon juice or white vinegar. If a sweeter taste is preferred, add more sweet pickle juice or a touch of sugar. Cover with clear wrap and refrigerate overnight for flavors to develop.

LOUISIANA SEAFOOD COCKTAIL SAUCE

PREP TIME: 15 Minutes **MAKES: 2 Cups**

COMMENT:

Cocktail sauce is one of the seafood sauces found primarily in the city of New Orleans. This sauce has many variations but most are tomato ketchup based and spiced with a touch of horseradish.

INGREDIENTS:

1 cup tomato sauce
1/4 cup ketchup
2 tbsps red wine vinegar
3 tbsps Worcestershire
1 tbsp horseradish
1/4 cup chopped bell pepper
1/4 cup chopped celery
1 tbsp diced garlic
salt to taste
Louisiana Gold Pepper Sauce to taste

METHOD:

In a large ceramic bowl, combine tomato sauce, ketchup, vinegar, Worcestershire and horseradish. Using a wire whip, blend until all ingredients are well incorporated. Add bell pepper, celery and garlic. Season to taste using salt and Louisiana Gold. Continue to blend until all seasonings are evenly mixed throughout the sauce. Adjust seasonings to taste should a more sweet or tart flavor be desired. Cover and refrigerate overnight for flavors to develop. This sauce is always served with boiled seafood.

Viala Plantation - Lafitte's Landing Restaurant

MARCHAND DE VIN

PREP TIME: 30 Minutes MAKES: 2 Cups

COMMENT:

The wine merchant sauce is probably the most famous of the New Orleans sauces. Though the original version in classical cooking employed bone marrow, we have elected to remove this ingredient in the Creole version.

INGREDIENTS:

1/4 cup butter
1/4 cup finely minced ham
1/2 cup finely sliced green onions
1/4 cup finely minced garlic
2 tbsps finely minced onions
1/2 cup dry red wine
1 cup demi-glace (see recipe)
1 tsp salt
1/4 tsp cayenne pepper
pinch of cracked black pepper

METHOD:

In a heavy bottom saute pan, melt butter over medium high heat. Saute ham, green onions, garlic and onions three to five minutes or until vegetables are wilted. Deglaze with red wine and reduce to one half volume. Add demi-glace and return mixture to a simmer. Season to taste using salt, cayenne pepper and cracked black pepper. Continue to reduce until sauce is slightly thickened and all flavors are well incorporated. This sauce is best served over any sauteed or grilled meat or veal.

Viala Plantation - Lafitte's Landing Restaurant

BROWN MEUNIERE SAUCE

PREP TIME: 15 Minutes MAKES: 1 Cup

COMMENT:

The brown meuniere sauce is the most popular sauce at Lafitte's Landing Restaurant. Its tart taste and rich flavor goes well with both meat and fish. However, many exciting variations may be made using meuniere as the mother sauce.

INGREDIENTS:

4 ounces demi-glace
2 ounces dry white wine
1 ounce lemon juice
1/2 pound cold, unsalted butter
salt and cayenne pepper to taste

METHOD:

In a saute pan over medium high heat, combine demi-glace, wine and lemon juice. Using a wire whisk, stir until all ingredients are well blended. Bring to a low boil and reduce until the liquids are about one half in volume. Slowly whisk in cold butter, a few pats at a time, swirling pan constantly while butter is incorporating. Pan must be swirling constantly as hot spots will develop and the butter will break down. Continue to add butter, swirling constantly, until all is incorporated. Season to taste using salt and cayenne pepper and keep warm. Since this is a basic butter sauce, it cannot be reheated as butter will melt and separate. If allowed to chill, it will return to the solid state.

LOUISIANA STYLE HUNTER SAUCE

PREP TIME: 30 Minutes
MAKES: 2 Cups
COMMENT:

This is the most complex flavor derived from a demi-glace. The sauce is dependent on the concentration of wild game flavor in the stock. I recommend this sauce with all venison and roasted wild duck dishes.

INGREDIENTS:

1/4 cup butter
1/4 cup diced wild Louisiana mushrooms
1/4 cup sliced green onions
1 tbsp diced garlic
1/4 cup diced ripe tomatoes
1 ounce dry red wine
1 ounce brandy
1 cup game demi-glace
1 tbsp chopped parsley
salt and cracked black pepper to taste

Andouille, Hams and Ducks in the Smokehouse at Viala

METHOD:

As previously mentioned, this is the most complex of demi-glace flavorings. Similar to the Grand Veneur or Royal Hunt Sauce, the Louisiana Hunter Sauce can turn any simple roasted game into a culinary masterpiece. Take the time to accomplish the game stock and this sauce will be quite simple.

In a heavy bottom sauce pan, melt butter over medium high heat. Add mushrooms, green onions, garlic and tomatoes. Saute for three to five minutes or until vegetables are wilted. Deglaze with red wine and brandy. Reduce heat to simmer and cook until volume is one half. Add game demi-glace and parsley and season to taste using salt and cracked black pepper. Simmer for approximately five minutes or until the sauce is slightly thickened and full-flavored.

HINT: Refer to the demi-glace recipe and make demi-glace from two quarts of rich game stock. This should yield one quart of rich full bodied game demi-glace.

Changes

Viala Plantation - Lafitte's Landing Restaurant

CREME FRAICHE

PREP TIME: 12 Hours *MAKES: 1 Cup*

COMMENT:

Creme Fraiche is similar to heavy buttermilk or sour cream. We use this unique cream to finish many of our demi-glace based sauces. Not only does it tend to smooth out the flavor but it also gives the sauce a nice tangy bite.

INGREDIENTS:

8 ounces heavy whipping cream
3 tsps buttermilk

METHOD:

In a ceramic bowl, combine cream and buttermilk. Cover with clean cloth and let set at room temperature for eight to twelve hours. Most cooks will combine the cream with the buttermilk and place the mixture on a pantry shelf overnight. The finished creme fraiche should be placed in a covered container and stored in the refrigerator. You may also wish to use this sauce as you would heavy whipping cream or sour cream.

Longue Vue Gardens

HORSERADISH CREOLE CREAM

PREP TIME: 15 Minutes *SERVES: 6*

COMMENT:

There are many horseradish-based sauces around today but I know of no other that incorporates Creole style mustard in its recipe. I have often used this sauce with oysters on the half shell and smoked shrimp, however, it is always an accompaniment to my corned beef and cabbage dinner.

INGREDIENTS:

1/2 cup prepared horseradish
1 cup mayonnaise
2 tbsps Creole style mustard
1 tsp minced garlic
1 tbsp chopped parsley
pinch of sugar
3/4 cup heavy whipping cream
salt and cracked black pepper to taste
dash of Louisiana Gold Pepper Sauce

METHOD:

In a large mixing bowl, combine horseradish, mayonnaise and mustard. Using a wire whisk, blend all ingredients thoroughly. Add garlic, parsley and sugar and continue to whip until all ingredients are well blended. Season to taste using salt, pepper and Louisiana Gold. In a separate metal bowl, whip the heavy whipping cream until soft peaks form. Using a wooden spoon, gently fold the whipped cream into the horseradish mixture. Adjust seasonings if necessary and transfer to a serving bowl.

Chretien Point Plantation

PLANTER'S PUNCH

PREP TIME: 10 Minutes *MAKES: 1 Drink*

COMMENT:

This drink was undoubtedly named in jest of the Southern planters who loved having a drink or two while trying to conceal the contents of the glass. This rum "punch" was consumed daily as was the mint julep. However, like the champagne mimosa, this drink was often found on the breakfast table.

INGREDIENTS:

12 ounce stemmed wine glass
1 1/2 ounces light rum
1/2 ounce grapefruit juice
1/2 ounce orange juice
1/2 ounce grenadine
1/2 ounce dark rum
slice orange and cherry

METHOD:

Into a cocktail shaker, pour light rum, grapefruit juice, orange juice and grenadine. Shake vigorously for one minute. Fill wine glass with ice cubes and pour drink mixture over the ice. Float dark rum on top of drink and garnish with a slice of orange and cherry. I feel that this drink was more popular in plantation country than the mint julep simply because the large plantations had grapefruit and orange orchards to supply the main ingredients.

Boscobel Cottage

MINT JULEP

PREP TIME: 10 Minutes *MAKES: 1 Drink*

COMMENT:

This southern cooler was extremely popular during the plantation era. The mint fragrance gives the drink an extremely refreshing aroma which makes it perfect for those hot southern afternoons.

INGREDIENTS:

1-9 ounce old fashioned glass
6 mint leaves
2 tsps powdered sugar
1 ounce bourbon
1 ounce Southern Comfort
1 ounce simple syrup
1 cup crushed ice
1 sprig fresh mint

METHOD:

Place mint leaves in the bottom of old fashioned glass along with powdered sugar. Using a muddler, crush mint leaves into powdered sugar. Add bourbon, Southern Comfort, simple syrup and crushed ice. Using an iced tea spoon, blend all ingredients well into the mint-sugar mixture. Garnish with fresh mint sprig and serve with a straw. This cocktail should be stirred long enough for frost to form on the outside of the glass. It has been said that the early planters would only drink mint juleps from silver tumblers.

Chapter Two
Appetizers

Longue Vue Plantation

Longue Vue Gardens

"A Grand City Estate"

When Edgar Stern, a well known cotton broker, and his wife, Edith, heir to the Sears fortune, built their Greek revival mansion just outside New Orleans, their friends referred to it as a "grand city estate". In furnishing the home, absolutely nothing was spared, from the finest of English and French antiques to the very best in Oriental carpeting. They surrounded their showplace with twenty-three working fountains and eight acres of impeccable gardens designed after some of the most famous in the world. In New Orleans, the Sterns were one of the wealthiest families in the city, but also the most generous. It was their generosity that gave us Dillard University and Flint Goodridge Teaching Hospital. These two projects of Edgar Stern were the best known African American institutions in the city. Mrs. Stern was also heavily involved in philanthropic causes. Her most popular was Newcomb College Nursery School.

Longue Vue remains as it was when the Stern family lived in it. The home contains all of its original furnishings including collections of modern art, needlework and creamware from Wedgewood, Leeds and other continental potteries. The old and the new are gracefully joined together here, offering something of interest to all who appreciate the finer things in life.

The Dolphin Fountain, circa 1500, one of twenty-three at Longue Vue

The gardens which surround the estate both compliment and enhance it. The plan is laid out with one large formal garden surrounded by several smaller ones. Longue Vue features beautifully manicured lawns with oaks, magnolias, camellias, azaleas and crepe myrtles as permanent plantings. The largest garden, the Spanish court, echoes the fourteenth century Generalife gardens of the Alhambra in Granada, Spain. Fountains and mosaic sidewalks contribute to this Moorish-Spanish flavor. Other gardens include the Pan, Portico, Walled, Yellow, Canal, Pond and the Wild garden which is, as its name implies, an informal planting of Louisiana trees and shrubs.

The classic beauty of the home and the ever changing gardens create in Longue Vue a tranquil union of architecture, arts and horticulture. It is a unique memorial to a way of life that no longer exists.

To reach Longue Vue, take I-10 to New Orleans. Exit on City Park Avenue and travel toward the river to 7 Bamboo Road. 504-488-5488.

At left, clockwise from bottom left, Oyster Stuffed Artichoke Bottoms (page 36), Corned Beef and Cabbage (page 201), and Shrimp, Crab and Okra Gumbo (page 89)

OYSTER STUFFED ARTICHOKE BOTTOMS

PREP TIME: 1 Hour
SERVES: 6
COMMENT:

One of the most famous soups in South Louisiana is oyster and artichoke bisque. It seems that these two flavors are often married in Louisiana cuisine. Here is just another example of the flavor of oysters and spinach used to fill artichokes presented as an appetizer.

INGREDIENTS:

12 artichoke bottoms, fresh or canned
1 cup chopped oysters
1/4 cup butter
1/2 cup minced onions
1/2 cup minced celery
1/4 cup minced red bell pepper
1 tbsp diced garlic
3 cups cooked spinach
1/4 cup tomato ketchup
salt and cracked pepper to taste
Louisiana Gold Pepper Sauce to taste
1/2 ounce herbsaint or anise
1/2 cup seasoned Italian bread crumbs
1/4 pound butter
1 ounce sherry
2 tbsps chopped parsley

METHOD:

Preheat oven to 350 degrees F. If the artichoke bottoms are canned, soak in cold water for one hour prior to use to remove the brine, vinegar taste. In a heavy bottom black iron skillet, melt butter over medium high heat. Add onions, celery, bell pepper and garlic. Saute three to five minutes or until vegetables are wilted. Chop the cooked spinach very fine and add to the sauteing vegetables. Blend well and add oysters. Stir until all ingredients are well incorporated. Simmer five minutes and add ketchup, salt, pepper and Louisiana Gold. Lower heat to simmer and cook ten to fifteen additional minutes. Add herbsaint, blend into the spinach mixture and remove from heat. Sprinkle in bread crumbs and allow the mixture to cool slightly. Once cooled, stuff the center of each artichoke bottom with the oyster mixture. Place the artichokes in a large baking pan and top with melted butter and sherry. Sprinkle with parsley and bake uncovered for fifteen to twenty minutes. Serve two artichokes with a spoon of sherry butter sauce. You may wish to place one whole oyster on the bottom of the artichoke prior to stuffing with the spinach mixture.

Changes

POINT HOUMAS GRILLED OYSTERS

PREP TIME: 1 Hour
SERVES: 6
COMMENT:

Often, there are references to the use of oysters as a main ingredient at many Louisiana plantations. Obviously, there was a great supply from the Gulf of Mexico, and the Mississippi River provided the transportation necessary to get them to the table. There are many historical references to oysters being served at Houmas House and this is one such dish.

INGREDIENTS:

36 fresh shucked oysters, reserve shells
1/4 pound butter
1/4 cup olive oil
1/4 cup minced onions
1/4 cup minced celery
1/4 cup minced red bell pepper
1 tbsp diced garlic
1/4 cup lemon juice
dash of Worcestershire Sauce
pinch of fresh thyme
pinch of basil
pinch of oregano
salt and cracked pepper to taste
Louisiana Gold Pepper Sauce to taste
1 cup grated Parmesan cheese
1/2 cup chopped parsley

METHOD:

I recommend using a backyard barbecue pit for this dish. The grill seems to impart a unique flavor to the oysters, however, the recipe works fine in a conventional oven. Scrub the oyster shells well to remove all grit and sand and place on a cookie sheet. Place shells on the grill to heat thoroughly for approximately five minutes. While shells are heating, melt butter in a heavy bottom black iron skillet over medium high heat. Add olive oil, onions, celery, bell pepper and garlic. Saute three to five minutes or until vegetables are wilted. Add lemon juice, Worcestershire Sauce, thyme, basil and oregano. The dried herbs will work well in this recipe. Season lightly with salt, pepper and Louisiana Gold. Place raw oysters in the hot shells and top with one teaspoon of the sauce and a sprinkle of cheese. Grill for three to four minutes or until oysters begin to curl. Garnish with chopped parsley and serve hot off the grill.

Changes

___

___

___

___

LAGNIAPPE

Oysters are a very perishable seafood and I often wondered with the lack of quality transportation, how oysters made it to so many inland plantations. It seems that the fresh oysters were chilled in ice at the docks then wrapped in newspaper, saw dust and even damp moss. The oysters were then loaded onto wagons, insulated once again with the use of a heavy tarp and then hauled to the plantations. There is even reference to Abraham Lincoln hosting an oyster shucking party on the lawn of the White House, bringing them in from the Chesapeake Bay by horse and wagon.

SMOKED OYSTER SPREAD

PREP TIME: 30 Minutes
MAKES: 3 cups
COMMENT:

Margaret Shaffer, owner of Ardoyne Plantation, often surprised me with one of her favorite recipes. I remember the afternoon I spent with her, sitting at the kitchen table, thumbing through an old handwritten book of family recipes. It was here that I found this smoked oyster spread.

INGREDIENTS:

1-4 ounce can smoked oysters, drained and chopped
1-8 ounce package softened cream cheese
1 1/2 cups mayonnaise
1/4 cup chopped green olives
1 tsp diced garlic
1/4 cup finely chopped parsley
1 tbsp lemon juice
salt to taste
Louisiana Gold Pepper Sauce to taste
lemon wedge for garnish

METHOD:

In a large mixing bowl, combine cream cheese, mayonnaise, green olives, garlic and parsley. Using a wire whisk, stir until all ingredients are well blended. Add chopped oysters and lemon juice and continue to blend into the mixture. Season to taste using salt and Louisiana Gold. Place the spread in a small serving dish and garnish with chopped parsley and a wedge of lemon. Place in the center of a large serving platter and surround with garlic croutons, crackers or fresh vegetables. NOTE: I find that this dish develops a more intense flavor when prepared one day ahead.

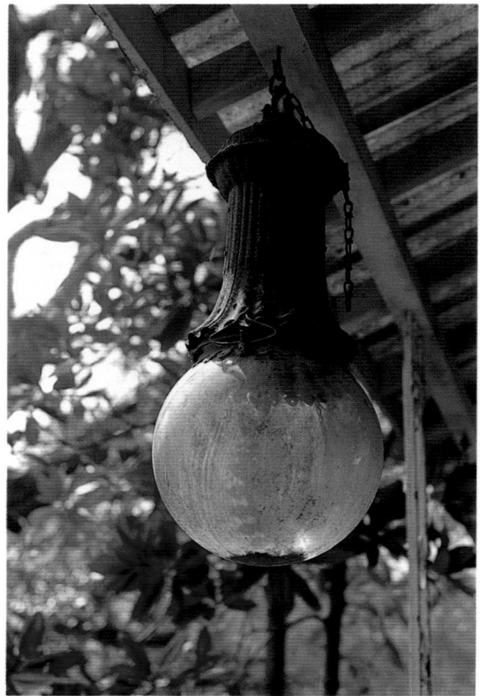

Kerosene Mule Barn Lamp

Changes

GARLICKY SHRIMP LAFOURCHE

PREP TIME: 1 Hour
SERVES: 6
COMMENT:

Madewood is often called the "Queen of the Bayou" because of its location on the banks of Bayou Lafourche. There is no dispute that the Cajuns in this area love the flavor of garlic and this dish would not be the same without it.

INGREDIENTS:

24 jumbo shrimp
12 cloves minced garlic
1 cup claw crabmeat
1/4 pound butter
1/2 cup minced onions
1/4 cup minced celery
1/4 cup minced red bell pepper
1/4 cup sliced green onions
1/4 cup chopped parsley
1 tbsp chopped basil
1 tsp chopped thyme
1 egg, beaten
1/2 cup seasoned Italian bread crumbs
salt and cracked pepper to taste
Louisiana Gold Pepper Sauce to taste
1 cup white wine
1/2 cup melted butter
paprika for color
1/4 cup chopped parsley

METHOD:

I refer to jumbo shrimp as ten to twelve shrimp to the pound, head on. However, since this dish is made with headless shrimp, you should try to seek out fifteen to twenty count to the pound. Preheat oven to 375 degrees F. Peel, devein and butterfly the shrimp, leaving the tail section on for presentation purposes. In a heavy bottom saute pan, melt butter over medium high heat. Add onions, celery, bell pepper and garlic. Saute three to five minutes or until vegetables are wilted. Add crabmeat and continue to saute three to five additional minutes. Sprinkle in green onions, parsley, basil and thyme. Season to taste using salt, cracked pepper and Louisiana Gold. Remove from heat and allow to cool slightly. Blend in egg and bread crumbs. Place the shrimp on a large baking sheet and stuff with the crabmeat mixture. Pour in the white wine and drizzle melted butter over shrimp. Dust with paprika and parsley. Bake ten to twelve minutes or until shrimp are pink and stuffing is heated thoroughly. Serve immediately with white wine/butter sauce.

Changes

BOILED SHRIMP PATE WITH HERBED MAYONNAISE

PREP TIME: 1 1/2 Hours
SERVES: 6-8
COMMENT:

Many creative dishes came about by using leftovers from crab, crawfish and shrimp boils. I can think of boiled crawfish potato salad, boiled crabmeat cakes and this wonderful boiled shrimp pate.

INGREDIENTS:

1 pound boiled shrimp, peeled
1/4 cup minced onions
1/4 cup minced celery
1/4 cup minced red bell pepper
1 tbsp minced garlic
2/3 cup dry white wine
pinch of thyme
pinch of basil
1 egg, beaten
salt and cracked pepper to taste
Louisiana Gold Pepper Sauce to taste
6 tbsps softened butter

METHOD:

If you do not have shrimp left over from a recent boil, prepare fresh shrimp in the following manner. Season two quarts of water with salt, cracked pepper, one lemon, one small onion, cubed, two bay leaves and one tablespoon chopped garlic. Add a tablespoon of liquid crab boil and simmer all ingredients for thirty minutes. Add shrimp and cook only until they turn pink, curl and begin to float, approximately three to five minutes. Remove, cool under cold tap water and set aside. Preheat oven to 350 degrees F. In a food processor fitted with a metal blade, add shrimp, onions, celery, bell pepper, garlic and white wine. Using the pulse switch, blend two to three times until shrimp are finely ground. Add thyme, basil and egg and continue pulsing two to three more times. Season to taste using salt, pepper and Louisiana Gold. Add butter and pulse to incorporate all ingredients well. Pour the pate mixture into a greased, one quart baking mold. Place the mold into a larger baking pan filled with water. The water should reach halfway up the side of the baking mold. Cook in this water bath for fifty minutes to one hour or until pate is set. Remove from oven and chill overnight. To create the herbed mayonnaise, blend one tablespoon each of chopped purple basil, chopped green basil, thyme and cracked pepper with one cup of mayonnaise. Mix well and allow to sit approximately one hour. To serve, unmold and place the pate in the center of a large serving platter. Fill a hollowed red bell pepper with the herbed mayonnaise and place this next to the mold. Surround with garlic croutons or toast points.

LAGNIAPPE

Social events involving food are common around the country today. The New England Clam Bake, the Texas Barbecue and the famous Pacific Northwest Salmon Bake are just a few. Though they are all exciting and fun to attend, none is quite as special as the Louisiana shrimp, crawfish or crab boil. From choosing the proper seasonings for the pot, to adding the corn, potatoes, sausage and even artichokes in the Italian community, these boils get everyone involved. So next time you're in bayou country, if you happen to see a crowd gathering around a large black iron pot under a shade tree, stop on in. It's a seafood boil and there's nothing like it.

Changes

Magnolia Plantation

Magnolia Plantation

"When Cotton Was King"

When Ambrose LeComte built his plantation home on the Cane River, he positioned it under a grove of magnolia trees. It was the largest home in the area with not only twenty-eight rooms and twin galleries, but also its own Catholic Chapel still in use today. Included on the property were brick slave cabins, a rarity at that time, and a mule driven cotton press. This press was state-of-the-art back then, and is one of only two left standing in America today. When Union General Nathaniel Banks came through after the Battle of Mansfield, he burned the home to the ground. In 1896, the home was completely restored on its original foundation.

Magnolia is still framed by the magnificent 150 year old trees that lend their name to the plantation. This two and a half story structure was built on a French land grant issued to Jean Baptiste LeComte, II. The plantation is a complex which consists of an overseer's house, a pigeonnier, a community store, several barns and a blacksmith's shop. In 1852, Matthew Hertzog, son-in-law of Ambrose, assumed management of the plantation. Upon Matthew's death, his son ran the plantation for over fifty years. On 2,192 acres, the Hertzog family raised cotton, soy-beans and cattle. Through the years, the plantation has been known for its successful racing stables. Ambrose LeComte's "Flying Dutchman" won the St. Charles Hotel handicap at the New Orleans - Old Metairie Racetrack in 1850. The horse lies buried between the oaks on the plantation. Another famous horse, "LeComte", was sold to a European dealer who took it by steamboat to France. The horse died before reaching shore and today the town of Lecompte, near Alexandria, is named after this horse.

A Peacock in the Barnyard

Today, the plantation home is occupied by Betty Hertzog, great granddaughter of the builder. It is still a working plantation.

To reach Magnolia, take I-49 North to the Highway 119 exit, south of Natchitoches. 318-379-2221.

At left, clockwise from bottom left, Tomato Basil Pie (page 155), Cane River Pound Cake (page 280), and Rolled Vegetable Meatloaf (page 199)

CRAWFISH AND CUCUMBER DIP WITH VEGETABLE BASKET

PREP TIME: 1 Hour
MAKES: 3 Cups
COMMENT:

There are many that would think that vegetable-type appetizers are new. Believe me, they have been around for hundreds of years. This particular version, using crawfish as a flavoring, just goes to show how imaginative the early plantation cooks were.

INGREDIENTS:

1 cup crawfish tails
1 cup diced cucumber, unpeeled
8 ounces Philadelphia cream cheese
1/2 cup mayonnaise
1/4 cup minced onions
1/4 cup minced red bell pepper
1/4 cup minced garlic
1 tbsp chopped parsley
1 tbsp chopped mint
1 tsp chopped dill
1 tsp chopped thyme
1 tbsp lemon juice
salt and cracked pepper to taste
Louisiana Gold Pepper Sauce to taste

METHOD:

This dip will be ideal for any raw vegetables or chips. I recommend carrots, zucchini, summer squash, celery, radishes and even poached mushrooms. However, let your imagination be your guide. In the bowl of a food processor fitted with a metal blade, combine crawfish, cucumber, cream cheese and mayonnaise. Blend on high speed one to two minutes or until all is well processed. Add onions, bell pepper, garlic, parsley, mint, dill and thyme. Continue to process until flavors are well blended. Add lemon juice and season to taste using salt, pepper and Louisiana Gold. Remove from processor and place in a covered bowl. Set aside and allow flavors to develop for a few hours. To serve, you may wish to hollow out a large purple cabbage or cauliflower and fill it with the dip. Surround with chilled vegetables.

Changes

SPICY PLANTATION SEAFOOD DIP

PREP TIME: 1 Hour
SERVES: 12-20
COMMENT:

The abundance of shellfish in Louisiana's bayous created a need to combine many different varieties in one dish. Here, more than in any other part of the country, you will see the marriage of meats and vegetables to seafoods time and again.

INGREDIENTS:

1/2 pound jumbo lump crabmeat
1/2 pound cooked crawfish tails, chopped
1/2 pound cooked shrimp, chopped
1/4 pound butter
1/4 cup diced onions
1/4 cup diced celery
1/4 cup diced red bell pepper
1/4 cup diced yellow bell pepper
1/4 cup diced garlic
1/4 cup diced tasso ham
1/4 cup sliced green onions
1/4 cup chopped parsley
1 tbsp chopped fresh dill
1-8 ounce pkg cream cheese, softened
1 cup mayonnaise
Worcestershire Sauce to taste
salt and cracked pepper to taste
Louisiana Gold Pepper Sauce to taste
juice of one lemon

METHOD:

It is acceptable to substitute any local seafood when making this dish. Often, I have used one and a half pounds of either of the seafoods, as opposed to the combination of the three, and the recipe was just as good. Either way will work just perfect. In a heavy bottom saute pan, melt butter over medium high heat. Add onions, celery, bell peppers, garlic and tasso. Saute three to five minutes or until vegetables are wilted. Add crawfish, shrimp, green onions and parsley. Continue to saute three to five minutes. Remove from heat and allow to cool. In a large mixing bowl, combine seafood mixture with dill, cream cheese, mayonnaise and Worcestershire Sauce. Using a wire whisk, blend all ingredients well into the mayonnaise mixture. Season to taste using salt, pepper, Louisiana Gold and lemon juice. Gently fold in the lump crab and adjust seasonings, if necessary. Pour seafood dip into a decorative fish mold and serve with a basket of assorted crackers.

Changes

GENERAL JACKSON'S CRABMEAT FRITTERS

PREP TIME: 1 Hour
MAKES: 16
COMMENT:

When General Jackson arrived in the city to fight the Battle of New Orleans, his biggest problem wasn't the British. It was his stomach. It seems the rich food of Louisiana soon had the General in an uproar and he needed something with a little more delicate flavor. Crabmeat turned out to be the perfect remedy.

INGREDIENTS:

1 pound jumbo lump crabmeat
1/4 cup butter
1/4 cup minced onions
1/4 cup minced celery
1/4 cup minced red bell pepper
1/4 cup minced yellow bell pepper
1 tbsp diced garlic
1/4 cup sliced green onions
1 tbsp chopped parsley
1 tsp chopped basil
1 tsp chopped thyme
2 eggs, beaten
1 tbsp mayonnaise
1 tbsp Creole mustard
salt and cracked pepper to taste
Louisiana Gold Pepper Sauce to taste
juice of 1/2 lemon
1 cup seasoned Italian bread crumbs
oil for deep frying

METHOD:

In a heavy bottom black iron skillet, melt butter over medium high heat. Add onions, celery, bell peppers and garlic. Saute three to five minutes or until vegetables are wilted. Add lump crabmeat, blending well into the vegetable mixture. Sprinkle in green onions, parsley, basil and thyme. Continue to saute an additional three to five minutes. Remove from heat and allow to cool slightly. Add eggs, mayonnaise and Creole mustard. Blend well into the mixture and season to taste using salt, pepper, Louisiana Gold and lemon juice. Once blended, sprinkle in just enough bread crumbs to hold the mixture together and chill for approximately one hour. In a homestyle deep fryer, such as Fry Daddy, preheat oil according to manufacturer's directions. If no fryer is available, place three inches of oil in a black iron dutch oven and heat to 375 degrees F. Form the mixture into sixteen crab fritters, approximately two inches in length. Coat in additional bread crumbs and deep fry five to seven minutes or until golden brown. I recommend serving these fritters with tartar or remoulade sauce (see recipe).

Changes

PECAN HERBED CHICKEN STRIPS

PREP TIME: 30 Minutes

SERVES: 8-10

COMMENT:

It just seems natural that the cottage boasting the state champion pecan tree should have at the same time created this pecan flavored chicken dish. This recipe proves once more the versatility of the Louisiana pecan. I have tried substituting almonds and walnuts in this dish and they seem to work fine but the flavor isn't quite as pronounced with these nuts.

INGREDIENTS:

4 chicken breast halves
2 cups finely chopped pecans
2 tbsps chopped basil
1 tbsp chopped thyme
1 tbsp chopped sage
1/4 cup corn starch
1 tsp sugar
2 tbsps sherry
salt and cracked pepper to taste
Louisiana Gold Pepper Sauce to taste
2 egg whites
oil for deep frying

The Resting Horse of Boscobel

METHOD:

In a homestyle deep fryer, such as Fry Daddy, heat oil according to manufacturer's directions. If using a black iron dutch oven, heat to 375 degrees F. Skin and debone the chicken breasts. Using a sharp boning knife, slice the breasts into three quarter inch strips. Set aside. In a large mixing bowl, combine basil, thyme, sage, corn starch and sugar. Blend well to mix all dry ingredients. Add sherry, salt, pepper, Louisiana Gold and egg whites. Using a wire whisk, blend until whites are frothy but not whipped. Place pecans on a cookie sheet or pie pan. Dip the chicken into egg white batter and coat with pecans. Deep fry until golden brown. This dish may be served with a sweet mustard dipping sauce made by combining one half cup Creole mustard with one fourth cup Louisiana cane syrup.

Changes

TERRINE OF CHICKEN WITH TARRAGON MAYONNAISE

PREP TIME: 1 Hour

SERVES: 20

COMMENT:

The English plantation owners often created light flavored terrines that were excellent when served chilled with an accompanying sauce. No dish is more subtle yet full flavored than a glace of chicken. Here it is further enhanced with the addition of tarragon in the mayonnaise.

INGREDIENTS:

5 chicken breasts
1 diced carrot
1 small onion, quartered
1 diced celery stalk
1 bay leaf
10 peppercorns
1 cup minced onions
1 cup minced celery
1/2 cup minced red bell pepper
1/2 cup minced yellow bell pepper
1 tbsp diced garlic
1/4 cup sliced green onions
1/4 cup chopped parsley
salt and cracked pepper to taste
Louisiana Gold Pepper Sauce to taste
4-1/4 ounce packages unflavored gelatin
1 cup mayonnaise
2 tbsps chopped tarragon
1 tbsp chopped parsley
1 tsp diced garlic
1 tsp lemon juice

METHOD:

Remove skin and place chicken breasts in a stock pot with carrot, onion, celery, bay leaf and peppercorns. Add enough water to cover the breasts by one inch. Season the water lightly with salt and pepper and bring to a low boil over medium heat. Once the chicken is tender and falling from the bone, remove from the poaching liquid. Strain and reserve one quart of the chicken stock. Debone the chicken and chop fine with a French knife. Degrease the poaching liquid and place it in a two quart sauce pan. Bring the stock to simmer and add onions, celery, bell peppers and garlic. Continue to simmer for ten minutes or until vegetables are wilted. Add green onions and parsley and adjust seasonings in the stock using salt, pepper and Louisiana Gold. Remove vegetable stock from heat and allow to cool slightly. Blend in gelatin. Place the chopped chicken in a rectangular terrine mold. Ladle in enough of the stock and seasonings to fill the terrine. Using a teaspoon, stir the ingredients to incorporate throughout the mold. Cover with clear wrap and refrigerate overnight. When ready to serve, unmold the terrine in the center of a large serving platter and garnish with tarragon mayonnaise. To make the tarragon mayonnaise, combine mayonnaise, tarragon, parsley, garlic and lemon juice and season to taste using salt and Louisiana Gold. This sauce is best when made one to two days ahead of time and refrigerated in an air tight container.

Changes

CHICKEN LIVER PÂTÉ

PREP TIME: 1 Hour
MAKES: 5 cups
COMMENT:

As a young boy growing up in South Louisiana, I have vivid memories of Sunday dinners at Mamere Zeringue's house. The main course was always roasted chicken, French-style, always crispy skin and juicy as could be on the inside. My favorite two pieces were the wing and liver. No wonder I am a fan of this pâté!

INGREDIENTS:

2 pounds fresh chicken livers
1/2 cup butter
1/4 cup diced onions
1/4 cup diced celery
1 tsp diced garlic
1/4 cup finely sliced green onions
1/2 cup brandy
1/2 cup heavy whipping cream
salt and cracked pepper to taste
pinch of allspice
pinch of ground thyme
Louisiana Gold Pepper Sauce to taste
1 cup melted butter

METHOD:

In a large saute pan, melt butter over medium high heat. Add onions, celery, garlic and green onions. Saute three to five minutes or until vegetables are wilted. Add chicken livers and continue to saute, stirring occasionally to keep vegetables from scorching. Cook until chicken livers are done, approximately fifteen minutes. Remove pan from heat and pour in brandy.

NOTE: *Be careful as alcohol will ignite and burn a few minutes until flame extinguishes itself.*

Allow liquids to reduce by approximately one half volume. Spoon the liver mixture into the container of a food processor fitted with a metal cutting blade. Pulse one minute. Add heavy whipping cream, salt, pepper, allspice, thyme and Louisiana Gold. Continue to blend and add butter. Remove from processor and spoon pâté mixture into lightly oiled five-cup souffle mold. Cover with clear wrap and chill in the refrigerator a minimum of four hours, preferably overnight. When ready to use, unmold, place in the center of a large serving platter and surround with garlic croutons, crackers or toast points. You may wish to garnish the pâté with orange zest and fresh parsley.

Changes

CARAMELIZED VIDALIA ONION DIP

PREP TIME: 1 Hour
SERVES: 10-12
COMMENT:

It's apparent to me that dips and spreads, both hot and cold, were very common at early Louisiana plantations. This probably came about because of the need to entertain often, but at the same time, these dishes could be prepared quickly and easily. This onion dip is one of my personal favorites.

INGREDIENTS:

2 large vidalia onions, quartered and thinly sliced
2 tbsps butter
2 tbsps vegetable oil
1/4 cup chopped red bell pepper
1/4 cup chopped yellow bell pepper
1/4 cup diced garlic
1 cup sour cream
1 cup mayonnaise
1/4 cup sliced green onions
1 tbsp chopped parsley
1 tbsp chopped purple basil
1 tsp chopped thyme
salt and cracked pepper to taste
Louisiana Gold Pepper Sauce to taste

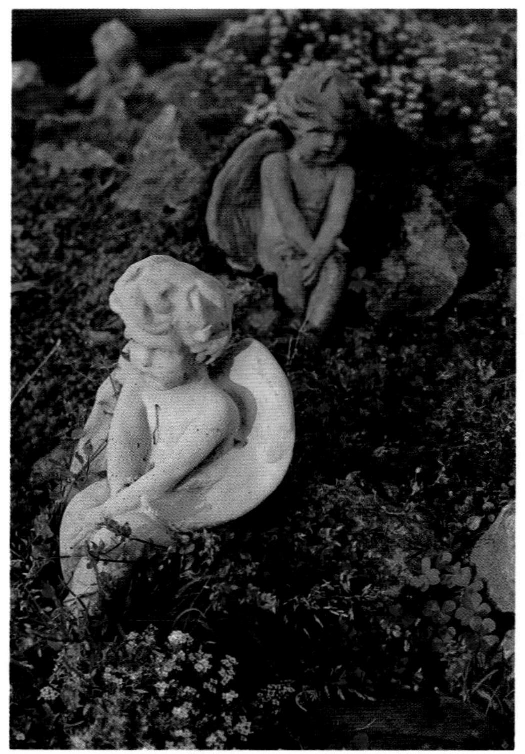

Angelic Faces at Magnolia Ridge

METHOD:

In a heavy bottom saute pan, heat butter and oil over medium high heat. Saute onions until caramelized and golden brown, approximately thirty to forty-five minutes. It is important to stir the onions constantly to keep them from scorching or burning. This slow caramelizing process will guarantee a sweet flavor in the dip. Add bell peppers and garlic and continue to saute three to five minutes. Remove from heat and allow to cool. Pour onions into a large mixing bowl and add sour cream, mayonnaise, green onions, parsley, basil and thyme. Blend well into the onion mixture and season to taste using salt, pepper and Louisiana Gold. Pour the onion dip into a decorative bowl and place in the center of a large serving platter. Surround the bowl with garlic croutons, crackers or chips.

Changes

SHREVE'S TOWN BAKED MUSHROOMS

PREP TIME: 1 Hour
SERVES: 6
COMMENT:

After a large log jam on the Red River was destroyed, river traffic allowed the small Shreve's Town to become a major port. Steamboat traffic increased greatly and this frontier town soon became known as Shreveport. This au gratin style crabmeat dish emerged from the kitchens of North Louisiana.

INGREDIENTS:

36 large button mushrooms, stemmed
1 pound jumbo lump crabmeat
1/4 pound butter
1/4 cup minced onions
1/4 cup minced celery
1/4 cup minced red bell pepper
1/4 cup minced garlic
1/4 cup finely diced andouille sausage
3 tbsps flour
1 1/4 cups milk
1/4 cup sliced green onions
1/2 ounce sherry
pinch of nutmeg
salt and cracked pepper to taste
Louisiana Gold Pepper Sauce to taste
1/2 cup grated Parmesan cheese
paprika for color
6 ounces sherry

METHOD:

Preheat oven to 350 degrees F. Wash the mushrooms under cold running water to remove any grit and sand from the cavity left when the stem was removed. Poach in lightly salted water two to three minutes. Place mushrooms, stem side down, on a drain cloth to remove all excess liquid. While mushrooms are draining, melt butter in a black iron dutch oven over medium high heat. Add onions, celery, bell pepper, garlic and andouille. Saute three to five minutes or until vegetables are wilted. Sprinkle in flour and using a wire whisk, blend well into the vegetable mixture. Slowly pour in milk, stirring constantly. Bring to a low boil. Add crabmeat, green onions, sherry and nutmeg. Blend well into the mixture and season to taste using salt, pepper and Louisiana Gold. Continue to cook until crabmeat is heated thoroughly and well coated with the sauce. Remove from heat and allow to cool slightly. Using a teaspoon, stuff the mushrooms generously with crabmeat mixture and place on a large baking sheet or in individual au gratin style dishes. Top with cheese and sprinkle with paprika for color. Pour sherry around the bottom of the mushrooms and bake uncovered fifteen to twenty minutes. Serve hot.

Changes

SPICY BLACKEYED PEA DIP CONGRE

PREP TIME: 1 Hour
MAKES: 5 Cups
COMMENT:

Blackeyed peas have become a tradition on New Year's Day here in Louisiana. They are wonderful when slowly cooked with smoked ham or even fresh green beans, but I really enjoy them in this less conventional way, as a dip. Try them next January 1st and see if your luck improves.

INGREDIENTS:

2-15 ounce cans blackeyed peas
8 strips of bacon
1 cup finely chopped onions
1/2 cup finely chopped celery
1/2 cup finely chopped red bell pepper
1/4 cup diced garlic
1/2 cup ketchup
3 chicken bouillon cubes
pinch of cinnamon
pinch of nutmeg
1 tsp sugar
2 cups chopped tomatoes
1/4 cup chopped jalapenos
3 tbsps flour
salt and cracked pepper to taste
Louisiana Gold Pepper Sauce to taste

METHOD:

In a heavy bottom dutch oven, cook bacon strips over medium high heat until golden brown and fat is rendered. Remove bacon, chop fine and return to pot. Into the bacon drippings, add onions, celery, bell pepper and garlic. Saute three to five minutes or until vegetables are wilted. Add ketchup, bouillon cubes, cinnamon, nutmeg and sugar. Using a wire whisk, blend until all ingredients are mixed thoroughly. Add tomatoes and jalapenos and continue to cook two to three minutes. Pour in blackeyed peas and continue to simmer for thirty additional minutes. Sprinkle in flour, blend well and cook an additional ten minutes. Season to taste using salt, pepper and Louisiana Gold. Adjust seasonings to your liking, pour into a souffle dish and serve hot with French bread croutons or miniature corn bread muffins.

LAGNIAPPE

Few people realize that the Africans, coming to the New World, gave us not only yams and okra but also their famous congre or blackeyed peas, as we know them today. They arrived in Louisiana from the Virginias and Carolinas around the 1720s and by the Civil War, there were approximately 11,000 Africans in New Orleans. The men tended the fields and the women became cooks and housekeepers, influencing Louisiana cooking like no other nationality.

Changes

Ashland-Belle Helene Plantation

STUFFED CELERY STICKS

PREP TIME: 30 Minutes
SERVES: 6
COMMENT:

Often as a simple hors d'oeuvre, the early planters would cut fresh thistles growing wild in the fields. The thistle would be stripped of its heavy outer skin and thorns, and cut into two inch strips. The strips were then filled with a variety of stuffings. Today, we substitute celery when thistles are out of season.

INGREDIENTS:

18 – 2″ celery sticks
1 cup grated cheddar cheese
4 grated boiled eggs
1/4 cup minced onions
1 tbsp minced celery
1 tbsp minced red bell pepper
1/2 cup mayonnaise
dash Louisiana Gold Pepper Sauce
salt and cracked black pepper to taste

METHOD:

For a better plate presentation, I always cut the celery sticks from the center of the stalk. This ensures that each stick will not only be two inches in length but also identical in width. Using a sharp paring knife, cut a thin strip from the bottom of each stick so the celery will stand once stuffed. In a large mixing bowl, combine all ingredients except the celery sticks. Blend well to incorporate the mixture. You may wish to add more cheese or mayonnaise depending on your individual taste. Adjust seasonings if necessary. Stuff the celery to the point of overfilling, cover and refrigerate until ready to serve. The stuffing may be made one or two days in advance.

Changes

BARBECUED PECAN HALVES

PREP TIME: 20 Minutes
SERVES: 8-10
COMMENT:

Pecan orchards dot the highways of Louisiana like pirogues dot the bayous. Pecans are found in dishes ranging from rice dressings to desserts. Here is an unusual twist that will be great at your next cocktail party.

INGREDIENTS:

4 cups pecan halves
2 tbsps butter
1/4 cup Worcestershire Sauce
1 tsp Louisiana cane syrup
1 tbsp barbecue sauce
salt to taste
Louisiana Gold Pepper Sauce to taste

METHOD:

Preheat oven to 325 degrees F. In a black iron skillet, melt butter over medium high heat. Add Worcestershire Sauce, cane syrup, barbecue sauce and Louisiana Gold. Stir until all ingredients are well blended. Pour in pecan halves and stir gently until well coated with the barbecue mixture. Pour the pecans onto a large cookie sheet, spread evenly across bottom, and bake for fifteen minutes, stirring occasionally. Place the pecans on a paper towel to drain and sprinkle with salt. Cool thoroughly and serve as an interesting hors d'oeuvre.

The Entrance Way to Catalpa

Changes

BAKED SPARERIBS PIERRE LAFITTE

PREP TIME: 1 1/2 Hours
SERVES: 6-8
COMMENT:

Pierre Lafitte, brother of the pirate, Jean Lafitte, was rumored to be quite a cook. Some say he invented Cafe Brulot. Others say he was great with candies and jellies. This spareribs dish is credited to Pierre and I have to agree, it is quite an accomplishment!

INGREDIENTS:

2 pounds spareribs
1/4 cup butter
1/4 cup minced onions
1 tbsp minced garlic
1 1/2 cups mayhaw or muscadine jelly
1/4 cup Louisiana cane syrup
1/4 cup soy sauce
pinch of ground ginger
salt and cracked pepper to taste
Louisiana Gold Pepper Sauce to taste

METHOD:

Have your butcher cut spareribs into individual pieces then again across the center to form two to three inch pieces. Rinse ribs in cold water, drain well, place in a large bowl and season lightly with salt and pepper. Set aside. In a heavy bottom black iron skillet, melt butter over medium high heat. Add onions and garlic. Saute three to five minutes or until vegetables are wilted. Add jelly, cane syrup and soy sauce. Using a wire whisk, blend well into the vegetable mixture and reduce heat to low. Season to taste using ginger, salt, pepper and Louisiana Gold. Remove from heat and pour over the ribs. Blend well, cover and place in the refrigerator three to four hours. While ribs are marinating, preheat oven to 350 degrees F. Pour the ribs onto an oiled 11" x 14" baking sheet with one inch lip, separate and cook uncovered for approximately one hour.

Changes

SPICY MEATBALL SANS FRUSCINS

PREP TIME: 1 Hour

MAKES: 3 dozen

COMMENT:

When asked how much his beautiful mansion cost to build, Edmond Marmillion replied, "it was quite a bit and I am now sans fruscins". Loosely translated, he meant he was without a penny or busted. The home continued to be called by this name for many years until eventually sans fruscins was changed to San Francisco. Obviously, this was much easier to pronounce and the home is still known by this name today.

INGREDIENTS:

1/2 pound ground beef
1/2 pound ground pork
1/4 cup minced onions
1/4 cup minced celery
1/4 cup minced red bell pepper
1 tbsp minced garlic
2 eggs
salt and cracked pepper to taste
pinch of thyme
pinch of basil
Louisiana Gold Pepper Sauce to taste
3/4 cup seasoned Italian bread crumbs

1/4 cup butter
1/2 cup ketchup
1/2 cup barbecue sauce
1 tbsp minced jalapenos
2 tbsps brown sugar
1 tbsp Louisiana cane syrup
1 tbsp red wine vinegar
1 tsp Creole mustard
dash of Worcestershire Sauce
salt to taste
Louisiana Gold Pepper Sauce to taste
1/4 cup chopped parsley

METHOD:

In a large mixing bowl, combine meats, onions, celery, bell pepper, garlic and eggs. Using your hands, blend all ingredients well. Season to taste using salt, pepper, thyme, basil and Louisiana Gold. Continue to mix until seasonings are well blended. Sprinkle in bread crumbs and mix well. Shape into one inch meatballs. In a fourteen inch saute pan, melt butter over medium high heat. Add meatballs and brown on all sides. Remove and set aside. Into the same pan, add ketchup, barbecue sauce, jalapenos, brown sugar, cane syrup and vinegar. Using a wire whisk, stir until well blended. Add mustard, Worcestershire, salt and Louisiana Gold. Continue to whisk until ingredients begin to simmer. Add cooked meatballs, reduce heat to simmer and cook fifteen to twenty minutes. Sprinkle in fresh parsley. Transfer meatballs and sauce to a chafing dish and serve hot.

Changes

JALAPEÑO CHEESE & SAUSAGE DIP

PREP TIME: 45 Minutes
SERVES: 15-20
COMMENT:

The Spanish brought peppers to North America after developing a taste for them during their contact with the Mayans and Incas. A variety of these peppers thrived in Mexico and eventually came through Texas into plantation country. Thank God for the Spanish or should I say, the Mayans and Incas!

INGREDIENTS:

1 pound heavy smoked andouille sausage
2 pounds Velveeta cheese, diced
1-12 ounce can jalapeños, seeded
1/4 cup butter
1 cup chopped onions
1/4 cup chopped celery
1/4 cup chopped red bell pepper
2 tbsps diced garlic
4 cups mayonnaise
salt and cracked pepper to taste
Louisiana Gold Pepper Sauce to taste
1/4 cup chopped parsley

METHOD:

Dice the andouille or other heavy smoked sausage. Allow cheese to set at room temperature for thirty minutes. Remove seeds from jalapeño peppers and if you are a bit squeamish, you may rinse the jalapeños under cold running water. This will remove some of the heat. In a heavy bottom saute pan, melt butter over medium high heat. Add onions, celery, bell pepper, garlic and andouille. Saute three to five minutes or until vegetables are wilted. Add jalapeños and continue to saute two to three minutes more. Remove from heat and allow to cool. Pour the ingredients from saute pan into the bowl of a food processor fitted with a metal blade. Blend well until smooth. Place the blended ingredients in a large mixing bowl and add cheese and mayonnaise. Using a wire whisk, whip until smooth and of a dipping sauce consistency. Season to taste using salt, pepper and Louisiana Gold. Sprinkle in parsley. Pour ingredients into a decorative serving bowl and heat to serving temperature in the microwave. Place in the center of a large serving platter surrounded by garlic croutons, toast points or tortilla chips. This dip may also be served cold and will hold well in the refrigerator for a couple of days.

Changes

STUFFED EGGS ITALIAN STYLE

PREP TIME: 1 Hour

MAKES: 24

COMMENT:

One of the greatest flavors associated with the Italians is pesto. Although normally thought of as a basil-based sauce, pesto may be made with parsley, sage or any other fresh herb. The best thing about it, though, is that it holds well in the refrigerator and has multiple uses.

INGREDIENTS:

12 eggs
4 1/2 cups fresh basil, loosely packed
1 cup extra virgin olive oil
1/2 cup pine nuts or pecans
5 cloves garlic
salt to taste
1/2 cup grated Parmesan cheese
1/2 cup mayonnaise
1/4 cup minced celery
1/4 cup red bell pepper
1/4 cup minced sweet pickles
salt and cracked pepper to taste
Louisiana Gold Pepper Sauce to taste

METHOD:

Boil eggs in a sauce pan covered with approximately two inches of water. Bring to a rolling boil and cook ten minutes. Remove from heat, drain and plunge in cold water until cool. Peel and set aside. In the bowl of a food processor fitted with metal blade, place basil leaves, olive oil, pine nuts, garlic, salt and Parmesan cheese. Blend on high until pureed. Adjust seasonings if necessary. Remove pesto from processor, place in bowl with lid and set aside. Slice eggs in half lengthwise and place yolks in a mixing bowl. Mash yolks with fork and add mayonnaise, celery, bell pepper and pickles. Blend well to incorporate all flavors. Season to taste using salt, pepper and Louisiana Gold. Blend two tablespoons of pesto into the egg mixture. When thoroughly blended, fill the egg whites with egg/pesto mixture, cover with clear wrap and refrigerate. These eggs may be stuffed one day prior to use and will actually get better as flavor develops. Refrigerate the remaining pesto as you may wish to use it as a pasta sauce, a flavoring for grilled fish or chicken, or brushed on hot French bread in the place of butter.

The Garden Blooms at Layton

Changes

GRILLED TENDERLOIN OF VENISON WITH CREOLE MUSTARD GLAZE

PREP TIME: 2 Hours
SERVES: 6
COMMENT:

The Randolph family of Nottoway was known for expertise in hunting. In fact, lavish game dinners were often held in the magnificent dining room of the plantation. This grilled tenderloin recipe was a Randolph favorite.

INGREDIENTS:

1 venison tenderloin, trimmed
1/4 cup olive oil
1/2 cup port wine
dash of Worcestershire Sauce
1 tbsp Louisiana cane syrup
Louisiana Gold Pepper Sauce to taste
1 tbsp cracked black pepper
1 tbsp chopped tarragon
1 tbsp chopped rosemary
1 tbsp chopped thyme
1 tbsp minced garlic
salt to taste
1/2 cup mayonnaise
1/2 cup sour cream
1/4 cup Creole style mustard
1 tsp chopped parsley

METHOD:

Trim tenderloin of silver skin and grizzle and place on a large baking sheet. Top with olive oil, port, Worcestershire, cane syrup and Louisiana Gold. Rub the venison well with the liquid seasonings three to five minutes to insure that the flavors are well incorporated and venison is well coated. Season well with pepper, tarragon, rosemary, thyme and garlic. Once again, using your hands, massage the seasonings well into the meat. Season to taste using salt. Cover with clear wrap and allow the venison to sit at room temperature a minimum of two hours. While meat is marinating, prepare barbecue grill according to manufacturer's directions. Soak a small amount of pecan wood chips for added flavor. When coals are ready, sear tenderloin on all sides and add pecan wood. Close lid and smoke ten to fifteen minutes for medium rare, turning occasionally. Internal temperature of venison should not exceed 135 degrees F. Remove from grill and allow meat to rest ten to fifteen minutes before slicing. While meat is resting, combine mayonnaise, sour cream, Creole mustard and parsley. Season to taste using salt and Louisiana Gold. Blend thoroughly and serve as a dipping sauce for the tenderloin.

LAGNIAPPE

I can only imagine the abundance of seafood, vegetables, fruits and game in and around South Louisiana when the white man arrived. We know there was no need for agriculture because harvesting foodstuffs was so simple. But venison and buffalo were considered the true trophies of the hunt back then. So much so in fact, that when beef arrived for the colonists, the Native Americans turned up their noses at this so called delicacy. Today buffalo is making a come back, but roast of venison has always been considered a premier delicacy on our Louisiana tables.

Changes

PEPPERED BEEF BRISKET

PREP TIME: 3 Hours
SERVES: 15-20
COMMENT:

It has been said that though only one hundred fifty German families arrived here in early Louisiana, they were responsible for feeding the City of New Orleans. They were not only master gardeners, but also ranchers of beef cattle and pork. This recipe is one of the results of their labor.

INGREDIENTS:

5 pounds beef brisket
1/2 cup coarsely ground black pepper
2/3 cup Worcestershire Sauce
1/4 cup cider vinegar
1/4 cup ketchup
2 tbsps diced garlic
2 tbsps chopped thyme
2 tbsps chopped basil
2 tbsps chopped sage
2 tbsps chopped tarragon
1/2 cup red wine
salt to taste
Louisiana Gold Pepper Sauce to taste
1/2 cup vegetable oil
1/2 cup Louisiana cane syrup

METHOD:

In a large mixing bowl, combine pepper, Worcestershire, vinegar, ketchup, garlic, thyme, basil, sage and tarragon. Using a wire whisk, blend the ingredients to incorporate the flavors. Add red wine and continue to blend one additional minute. Using a large kitchen fork, pierce the beef brisket ten to fifteen times on both sides and place in a large plastic browning bag. Pour the marinade into the bag with brisket, squeeze out all air and then seal tightly with a twist tie. Turn the bag three to four times to coat the brisket with marinade ingredients, then place in the refrigerator overnight. Before retiring for the evening, you should attempt to turn the bag every half hour to continue coating the brisket with the marinade. When ready to cook, preheat oven to 325 degrees F. Remove beef from marinade, reserving one cup of the liquid. In a large roasting pan big enough to hold the brisket, heat oil over medium high heat. Season brisket with salt and Louisiana Gold. Brown the brisket well on all sides and add marinade. Cover tightly and bake in oven for approximately three hours. During the last half hour of cooking, baste the roast occasionally with cane syrup and drippings in roasting pan. When done, remove and allow to rest for thirty minutes. Slice against the grain and serve with small French rolls and Creole style mustard as an appetizer. This roast may also be cooked on a barbecue grill or smoker and served as an entree.

Changes

Chapter Three

Soups

Boscobel Cottage

Boscobel Cottage

"Famous Names"

Did you ever wonder where the famous homes of America got their names? In Washington, the White House was named for its color. In Memphis, Elvis named Graceland for his mother. Out past the West Coast on Catalina Island, the Wrigley Mansion was named not only for the chewing gum but also for the family who founded the company. Here in North Louisiana we have a wonderful little cottage called Boscobel. The name literally means "beautiful woods". Obviously this name honors the gorgeous Louisiana landscape that surrounds the home.

Munchkin Cats, a New Breed (above)
A Decorative Patio Window (left)

Built in 1820 by Judge Henry Bry, the building served as a residence while he was constructing the "Big House". The cottage was subsequently used as an overseer's home. Hewn timbers, approximately 9" x 12", with mortise and tenon joinings were used in the foundation. Cypress and blue poplar were mainly used in the framing. While renovating the home, it was discovered that sassafras wood was used in the walls and ceilings of the drawing room and main hall. This is one of the few homes in Louisiana to make use of sassafras in this way. Originally Federal-West Indies in style, the house was enlarged in 1840 to take on its present simple Greek revival style. The two original federal mantles still remain as do the third and fourth which were added in the 1840s. Most of the hardware and glass on the windows and doors is original.

Boscobel is one of the very few upland plantation cottages in existence. Extraordinarily fine materials and details made it comparable to its "Big House", which was one of the few grand plantations built in Northeast Louisiana. The "Big House" fell victim to neglect and is no longer standing today. The cottage is now the private residence of the LaFrance family and is open to the public as a bed and breakfast.

To reach the home, take US Highway 165 North from Alexandria to Columbia, Louisiana. The home is located in Bosco, approximately fourteen miles south of Monroe. 318-325-1550.

At left, clockwise from bottom left, Chilled Peach Soup (page 68), Shoepeg Corn Salad (page 118), Mint Julep (page 32), and Sweet Potato Pecan Balls (page 153)

CHILLED PEACH SOUP

PREP TIME: 1 Hour
SERVES: 10-12
COMMENT:

Fruit is often used to create a wonderful sauce or soup. Of all the chilled soups using fruit as a main ingredient, this peach soup is my favorite. You may wish to ask your market supplier to give you a call when peaches are plentiful and the price a bit cheaper.

INGREDIENTS:

6 cups peeled and diced peaches or 2-14 ounce cans sliced peaches, reserve half of the syrup
2 tbsps triple sec
2 tbsps lemon juice
2 tbsps almond extract or Frangelico
1/2 tsp salt
2 cups sour cream or yogurt

METHOD:

In the bowl of a food processor, combine peaches, triple sec, lemon juice, almond extract and salt. Blend on high speed until pureed and very smooth. Add sour cream or yogurt and continue to puree until well blended. Taste the soup and if a slightly sweeter taste is desired, you may wish to add a bit of Louisiana cane syrup, honey or sugar. Remove from processor and place in a bowl or crock pitcher, cover and refrigerate. Allow to chill completely and serve in punch cups, demitasse or small soup bowls. For added texture, you may wish to garnish each cup with a teaspoon of finely chopped fresh peaches.

LAGNIAPPE

Often people have questions about serving soup. When asked how much soup should be served in a bowl or cup, I say it depends on whether it's a starter or an entree. As a starter, the soup should never exceed two thirds volume of the cup. As an entree, a terrine or pot of soup should be placed in the center of the table, welcoming guests to have more. The more complex the soup, the simpler the garnish. A sprig of mint will often do the job, while at other times a seafood or vegetable garnish will be needed. You decide!

Changes

CREAMED STRAWBERRY SOUP

PREP TIME: 1 Hour
SERVES: 6-8
COMMENT:

Blythewood is located in the heart of strawberry country. Since strawberries are in season in the warm spring and early summer days in South Louisiana, this soup is a natural.

INGREDIENTS:

4 cups stemmed and sliced fresh strawberries
1 1/2 cups water
1 1/2 cups white wine
1/2 cup sugar
2 tbsps fresh lemon juice
1/4 cup strawberry liqueur or Grenadine
1 1/2 tbsps corn starch
(mixed in 1 1/2 tbsps cold water)
1/2 cup heavy whipping cream
3 tsps grated orange zest

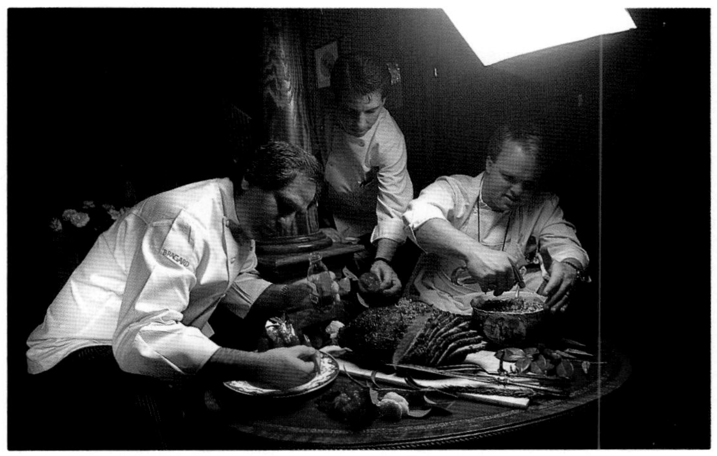

The Stylists at Work: Donnie Bergeron and Frank Harris with Chef Folse at left

METHOD:

In a one quart sauce pan over medium high heat, combine strawberries, water, wine, sugar and lemon juice. Simmer, covered, for approximately five to seven minutes or until sugar is dissolved in the liquid. Add the strawberry liqueur, return to a low simmer and add corn starch. Stir until sauce is slightly thickened and smooth. Transfer the ingredients of the sauce pan into the bowl of a food processor. Add heavy whipping cream and orange zest and blend until smooth. Pour the mixture into a bowl and cool in the refrigerator until well chilled. You may wish to adjust the sweetness of the soup with a touch of Louisiana cane syrup, honey or sugar. Serve the soup in large crystal wine glasses or soup cups.

Changes

BLACKEYED PEA AND OKRA SOUP

PREP TIME: 1 1/2 Hours
SERVES: 8-10
COMMENT:

In the early days, this soup was referred to around the plantations as "good luck" soup. The name originated from the fact that many think that eating blackeyed peas on New Year's Day will give you good luck throughout the year. I often wonder if gumbo didn't originally influence the creation of this soup.

INGREDIENTS:

1 pound dried blackeyed peas
1-10 ounce package cut okra
1 pound cubed ham
1/4 cup butter
2 cups chopped onions
1 cup chopped celery
1/2 cup chopped red bell pepper
1/4 cup diced garlic
1 bay leaf
1 sprig of thyme
2 1/2 quarts chicken stock (see recipe)
1 cup chopped tomatoes, seeded
1/4 cup sliced green onions
1/4 cup chopped parsley
salt and cracked pepper to taste
Louisiana Gold Pepper Sauce to taste

METHOD:

In a heavy bottom dutch oven, melt butter over medium high heat. Add onions, celery, bell pepper and garlic. Saute three to five minutes or until vegetables are wilted. Add ham, bay leaf and thyme and cook an additional three to five minutes. Pour in chicken stock and add blackeyed peas. Bring to a rolling boil and reduce to simmer. Cover and cook for approximately one hour. While stirring, mash peas on side of pot with a cooking spoon. This will help thicken the finished soup. Add okra and tomatoes and season to taste using salt, pepper and Louisiana Gold. Add green onions and parsley, blend well into the soup and allow to cook twenty to thirty minutes longer or until peas are tender and soup is creamy. I recommend serving cornbread muffins (see recipe) with this soup.

Changes

VIDALIA ONION SOUP AU GRATIN

PREP TIME: 1 1/2 Hours
SERVES: 8-10
COMMENT:

Remember that old standby, French Onion Soup? Well, somehow along the way, it lost respect. This version, using sweet Vidalia onions, is by far one of the best I've ever tasted.

INGREDIENTS:

3 large Vidalia onions, thinly sliced
1/2 cup butter
1/2 cup finely diced smoked sausage
1/4 cup diced garlic
3 tbsps flour
2 quarts beef stock (see recipe)
1/2 cup Madeira wine
salt and cracked pepper to taste
Louisiana Gold Pepper Sauce to taste
1/2 cup sliced green onions
1/2 cup chopped parsley
10 slices French bread, cut 3/4 inch thick
1 cup shredded smoked Mozzarella cheese
1 cup shredded Mozzarella cheese
grated Parmesan cheese
paprika for color

METHOD:

Butter the French bread slices and toast until golden brown. In a heavy bottom dutch oven, melt butter over medium high heat. Add onions and saute until translucent and caramelized, stirring occasionally, approximately thirty minutes. Add sausage and garlic and continue to saute an additional five minutes. Sprinkle in flour and blend well into the onion mixture. Add beef stock, one ladle at a time, until all is incorporated. You may wish to use six ten-ounce cans of undiluted beef broth which may be found at your local store. Bring to a rolling boil, reduce heat to simmer and allow to cook forty-five minutes. Add wine and season to taste using salt, pepper and Louisiana Gold. Add green onions and parsley and cook five to ten additional minutes. Preheat oven broiler. Place one toasted bread slice in each bowl and ladle soup over bread. Top with generous amounts of cheeses and paprika. Broil six inches from the heat for one minute or until cheese melts and bubbles.

Changes

SPICY CREOLE GAZPACHO

PREP TIME: 1 Hour
SERVES: 8-10
COMMENT:

It is easy to see why a chilled tomato soup would be revered as a delicacy in this hot Louisiana climate. I like this soup because it can be served in a punch or coffee cup before the guest is seated at the dinner table.

INGREDIENTS:

1/4 cup butter
1/4 cup olive oil
1 tsp chopped oregano
1/2 tsp chopped rosemary
1 tsp chopped basil
1 tsp minced garlic
4 French bread slices, cut 3/4 inch thick
6-6 ounce cans V-8 juice
2 cups tomato juice
1 cup diced tomatoes, seeded
1 cup diced cucumber
1/2 cup diced green bell pepper
1/2 cup diced yellow bell pepper
1/2 cup diced zucchini
1/2 cup diced summer squash
1/4 cup minced onion
1/4 cup minced garlic
3 tbsps white wine vinegar
juice of 1/2 lemon
salt and cracked pepper to taste
Louisiana Gold Pepper Sauce to taste
1/4 cup chopped cilantro or parsley

METHOD:

Preheat oven to 300 degrees F. Cut French bread into three quarter inch cubes with crust on. In a heavy bottom black iron skillet, melt butter and olive oil over medium high heat. Add oregano, basil, rosemary and garlic. Saute one to two minutes, taking care not to scorch the garlic. Add French bread and saute until croutons are thoroughly coated. Season lightly with salt. Remove from skillet, spread evenly on a large cookie sheet and bake for thirty minutes or until crisp. Set aside. In a large mixing bowl, combine juices and remaining vegetables, including onions and garlic. Blend well into the juice mixture and add vinegar and lemon juice. Season to taste using salt, pepper and Louisiana Gold. Add cilantro, cover tightly with clear wrap and chill a minimum of four to six hours. To serve, pour gazpacho into chilled cups or bowls and top with croutons and an additional sprinkle of parsley or cilantro.

Changes

SPINACH AND SWEET POTATO SOUP

PREP TIME: 1 Hour

SERVES: 8-10

COMMENT:

While visiting Japan recently, I worked with a Japanese chef who taught me a simple truth about cooking. If food looks good, it will certainly taste good. This recipe incorporates that very basic principle. The bright orange sweet potato and the vivid green spinach give the soup visual appeal and the flavor is out of this world.

INGREDIENTS:

2 cups sweet potatoes, diced
4 cups spinach leaves
1 cup julienned smoked sausage
3/4 cup butter
1 cup chopped onions
1/2 cup chopped celery
1/4 cup chopped red bell pepper
1/4 cup diced garlic
1 cup flour
3 quarts chicken stock (see recipe)
1 quart heavy whipping cream
1/2 cup sliced chives
1/2 cup chopped parsley
salt and cracked pepper to taste
Louisiana Gold Pepper Sauce to taste

METHOD:

The sweet potatoes should be cubed into one quarter inch squares. Wash spinach leaves to remove any sand or grit and finely chop into one quarter inch squares. In a heavy bottom dutch oven, melt butter over medium high heat. Add smoked sausage, onions, celery, bell pepper and garlic. Saute three to five minutes or until vegetables are wilted. Add spinach and continue to saute an additional three to five minutes, stirring constantly. Sprinkle in flour and using a wire whisk, whip into vegetable mixture to form a blonde roux (see roux techniques). Add chicken stock, one ladle at a time, whisking constantly until soup consistency is achieved. Add sweet potatoes, bring to a rolling boil, reduce to simmer and cook approximately thirty minutes. Additional stock may be added to retain proper consistency. Add cream, chives and parsley and season to taste using salt, pepper and Louisiana Gold. Once potatoes are tender, serve in individual soup bowls and garnish with finely chopped spinach.

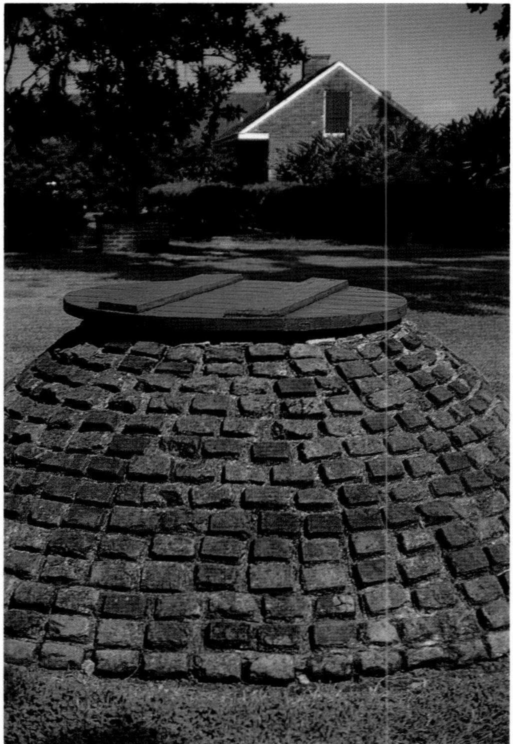

The Cistern at Shadows

Changes

BACON, LETTUCE AND TOMATO SANDWICH SOUP

PREP TIME: 1 Hour
SERVES: 8-10
COMMENT:

Imagination and creativity have always been the hallmarks of the Louisiana cook. Just to prove that fact, the wonderful flavor of a bacon, lettuce and tomato sandwich has been combined with a chicken veloute to create a soup that is sure to excite your dinner guest.

INGREDIENTS:

1/2 pound cooked bacon, drained
1 head romaine lettuce, sliced
1 head red leaf lettuce, sliced
3 tomatoes, seeded and diced
1/2 cup butter
1 cup chopped onions
1/2 cup chopped celery
1/2 cup chopped red bell pepper
1/2 cup chopped yellow bell pepper
1/4 cup diced garlic
1 cup flour
3 quarts chicken stock (see recipe)
1 pint heavy whipping cream
pinch of thyme
pinch of basil
salt and cracked pepper to taste
Louisiana Gold Pepper Sauce to taste
16 garlic croutons

METHOD:

It is important to wash the lettuce leaves well to remove any sand or grit that may exist. Remove the heavy spine from the leaf, slice in the fashion of coleslaw and set aside. In a two gallon stock pot, melt butter over medium high heat. Add chopped bacon and saute one to two minutes. Add onions, celery, bell peppers and garlic. Saute three to five minutes or until vegetables are wilted. Add half of the mixed lettuces and blend well into the bacon/ vegetable mixture. Cook three to five additional minutes. Sprinkle in flour and using a wire whisk, whip until blonde roux is achieved (see roux techniques). Add chicken stock, stirring constantly, until all is incorporated. Add remaining lettuces, tomatoes, whipping cream, thyme and basil. Blend well into the soup mixture. Season to taste using salt, pepper and Louisiana Gold. Bring soup to rolling boil, reduce to simmer and cook thirty to forty-five minutes, stirring occasionally. Adjust seasonings if necessary. Serve in individual bowls and garnish with croutons.

Changes

SEVEN BEAN SOUP WITH HOCKS

PREP TIME: 1 Hour
SERVES: 8-10
COMMENT:

Vegetables were always canned or jarred during the spring months, to ensure a good supply over the winter. Often, in the cold of January and February, I remember a huge pot of this vegetable soup on the stove, available for tasting all day long.

INGREDIENTS:

1/2 cup white beans
1/2 cup red kidney beans
1/2 cup black beans
1/2 cup lima beans
1/2 cup split peas
1/2 cup black-eyed peas
1/2 cup whole kernel corn
2 smoked ham hocks
1/4 cup butter
1 cup chopped onions
1 cup chopped celery
1/2 cup chopped bell pepper
1/4 cup diced garlic
1 bay leaf
4 quarts chicken stock (see recipe)
2 diced tomatoes
1 cup sliced green onions
salt and cracked pepper to taste
Louisiana Gold Pepper Sauce to taste

METHOD:

It is always preferable to rinse the beans once or twice, discarding any discolored or deformed beans. You should always soak the beans a minimum of eight hours prior to cooking. This will cut the cooking time by one third. However, when soaking, always remember to discard the water and rinse the beans once again before cooking. NOTE: Since black beans will discolor the liquid, they should not only soak separately, but they should also cook in lightly salted water separate from the rest of the soup. When tender, rinse again, and set aside to be added later. In a two gallon stock pot, melt butter over medium high heat. Add onions, celery, bell pepper and garlic. Saute three to five minutes or until vegetables are wilted. Add smoked hocks or heavy smoked sausage and ham, if preferred, and continue to saute three to five minutes. Add beans (except black beans), peas, corn and bay leaf, stirring into vegetable mixture. Pour in chicken stock, bring to a rolling boil and reduce to simmer. Cook approximately one hour, stirring occasionally to keep beans from sticking. Additional chicken stock or water may be needed to retain proper consistency, as beans absorb the liquid. While stirring, always mash the beans against the side of the pot with a cooking spoon. This will thicken the soup and create a creamy finished consistency. Add tomatoes and green onions and season to taste using salt, pepper and Louisiana Gold. When beans are tender and soup is ready to serve, add black beans and allow to heat thoroughly before serving. For added flavor, remove the ham hocks from the pot, cut away the skin and bones and finely chop the meat. Return the chopped hock meat to the pot, blending it well into the beans.

LAGNIAPPE

Beans of every type have been known and used for generations. When the New World was discovered, beans of every shape, color and size were found but they received little notoriety in the Old World. Beans and corn were normally considered animal food and were sometimes referred to as "poor man's meat" because they were filling and high in protein. The beans associated with the discovery of America include black, pinto, kidney, lima, navy, string beans and dozens more. It is interesting to note that the Native Americans were bean eaters long before Columbus came. In fact, they flavored their beans with honey, maple syrup and a touch of bear fat, giving us the first rendition of "Boston Baked Beans".

CREAMY POTATO, GREEN ONION AND SAUSAGE SOUP

PREP TIME: 1 Hour
SERVES: 10-12
COMMENT:

The Germans, settling the river parishes of Louisiana, brought not only smoked sausage but also the love of potatoes to our state. Potato and sausage recipes were often on their tables and eventually made their way into the plantation kitchens.

INGREDIENTS:

6 cups peeled and diced potatoes
4 cups each sliced white and green scallion sections
1 pound sliced smoked sausage
3 quarts chicken stock
1/4 cup melted butter
1 cup chopped celery
1 cup chopped red bell pepper
1/4 cup diced garlic
2 cups heavy whipping cream
1/2 cup chopped parsley
salt and cracked pepper to taste
Louisiana Gold Pepper Sauce to taste

METHOD:

In a two gallon stock pot, place four cups of potatoes and three quarts of chicken stock. Bring to a rolling boil and cook until potatoes are tender for mashing. Strain the chicken stock from the potatoes and set aside. Mash the potatoes with a fork and reserve for later. In the same stock pot, melt butter over medium high heat. Add sausage and saute until oil is rendered. Using a slotted spoon, remove sausage and set aside. Add the white portion of the scallions, celery, bell pepper and garlic. Saute three to five minutes or until vegetables are wilted. Add half of the mashed potatoes and stir well into vegetable mixture. Pour in chicken stock and heavy whipping cream, bring to a rolling boil and reduce to simmer. Cook for thirty minutes. Add the remaining potatoes, sausage and scallion greens. Continue to simmer until potatoes are tender. Add parsley and season to taste using salt, pepper and Louisiana Gold.

Changes

ROASTED RED, YELLOW AND GREEN SWEET PEPPER SOUP

PREP TIME: 1 Hour
SERVES: 10-12
COMMENT:

The roasting of sweet peppers has been a tradition here in Louisiana ever since the Italians arrived to work in the cane fields and markets of this state. When served with virgin olive oil, basil and cracked pepper, these roasted peppers are magnificent. But their addition to a cream soup make it not only tasty but also beautiful.

INGREDIENTS:

4 each red, yellow and green peppers
1/2 cup diced tasso ham
1 cup melted butter
1 cup chopped onions
1 cup chopped celery
1/4 cup diced garlic
1 cup diced tomatoes, seeded
1 cup flour
3 quarts chicken stock (see recipe)
1 cup heavy whipping cream
2 tbsps chopped basil
salt and white pepper to taste
Louisiana Gold Pepper Sauce to taste

METHOD:

Roast bell peppers over an open gas flame or under the broiler until blackened on all sides. Remove from broiler and place in paper bag, seal tightly and let stand fifteen to twenty minutes. Remove and peel or rinse under cold water until all of the charred peel is removed. Dice tasso ham and set aside. In a two gallon stock pot, melt butter over medium high heat. Add tasso ham, onions, celery and garlic. Saute three to five minutes or until vegetables are wilted. Add seeded tomatoes and half of the peppers, blending well into sauteed vegetables. Sprinkle in flour and using a wire whisk, whip constantly until white roux is achieved. (see roux techniques) Add chicken stock, one ladle at a time, until all is incorporated. Add cream, bring to a low boil and reduce to simmer. Cook for thirty minutes. Add basil and remaining peppers. Season to taste using salt, pepper and Louisiana Gold. This soup, when reduced to one half volume, makes a wonderful sauce for pasta, fish and chicken.

Rare 1820s Staffordshire Doll Painted to Match a Bridesmaid and Given as Wedding Favor

Changes

WHITE BEAN, GARLIC AND ROSEMARY SOUP

PREP TIME: 2 Hours
SERVES: 10-12
COMMENT:

White beans and garlic are two ingredients commonly associated with the Louisiana table. White beans came to Louisiana with the Acadians from Nova Scotia. However, we know today that white beans were brought to Nova Scotia by these same French settlers from their original homeland on the coast of France, near Brittany.

INGREDIENTS:

4 cups Great Northern beans
12 cloves garlic
1 sprig rosemary
1/4 cup olive oil
1 cup chopped onions
1 cup chopped celery
1/2 cup chopped red bell pepper
1/2 cup chopped green bell pepper
1 cup julienned andouille sausage
3 quarts chicken stock (see recipe)
1 cup sliced green onions
1/2 cup chopped parsley
salt and cracked pepper to taste
Louisiana Gold Pepper Sauce to taste

METHOD:

You may wish to buy the Great Northern beans pre-cooked in the can. This will cut the cooking time considerably. If using uncooked beans, soak in cold water overnight in the refrigerator. This will soften the beans and reduce the cooking time by about thirty minutes. Once soaked, rinse beans under cold running water in a colander and set aside. In a two gallon stock pot, heat olive oil over medium high heat. Saute garlic cloves until slightly browned. Using a slotted spoon, remove and set aside. Add onions, celery, bell peppers and andouille. Saute three to five minutes or until vegetables are wilted. Add the beans and blend well into vegetable mixture. Pour in the chicken stock, bring to a rolling boil and reduce to simmer. Cook approximately one hour, stirring occasionally to keep the beans from settling at the bottom and scorching. Add rosemary sprig and allow to cook with the mixture about thirty minutes before removing. The rosemary will tend to overpower the dish if you fail to remove it from the soup. After the soup has cooked for one hour, mash the beans on the inside of the pot using a cooking spoon. This will cream the soup and thicken it at the same time. Add green onions and parsley and season to taste using salt, pepper and Louisiana Gold.

Changes

WINTER SQUASH AND WILD PEAR SOUP

PREP TIME: 1 1/2 Hours
SERVES: 10-12
COMMENT:

The hard or wild pear is plentiful here in Louisiana. Most people prefer to can or jar this delicacy and serve it as a breakfast condiment or in a freshly baked pie. This fruit and vegetable combination is a new and interesting way to create a fabulously flavored soup.

INGREDIENTS:

2 pounds peeled and cubed white or other squash
4 cups peeled and cubed wild pears
2 1/2 quarts chicken stock
2 cups unsweetened apple juice
1 cup melted butter
1 large peeled and diced sweet potato
1 cup diced onions
1 cup diced celery
1/2 cup diced red bell pepper
1 cup flour
2 cups heavy whipping cream
nutmeg to taste
salt and white pepper to taste
Louisiana Gold Pepper Sauce to taste

METHOD:

In a two gallon stock pot, place squash, pears, chicken stock and apple juice. Bring to a rolling boil, reduce to simmer and cook until squash and pears are tender. Strain the stock through a fine chinois and set aside. Place the poached ingredients in the bowl of a food processor fitted with a metal blade. Add two cups of stock and puree until blended. In the same stock pot, melt butter over medium high heat. Add sweet potatoes, onions, celery and bell pepper. Saute three to five minutes or until vegetables are wilted. Sprinkle in flour and using a wire whisk, whip constantly until white roux is achieved (see roux technique). Add stock, one ladle at a time, stirring constantly until all is incorporated. Pour in contents of the blender bowl and heavy whipping cream, stirring into the soup mixture. Bring to a low boil and cook approximately thirty minutes or until sweet potatoes are tender. Season to taste using nutmeg, salt, pepper and Louisiana Gold.

Changes

TURNIP & POTATO SOUP

PREP TIME: 1 Hour
SERVES: 12-15
COMMENT:

When growing up in Louisiana, turnips were the only vegetables I refused to eat. Mama would cook them every way imaginable, but I never quite developed a taste for them. However, at some point in time, I grew to love turnips, both raw and cooked, and I think about how many great dishes I passed up in my youth.

INGREDIENTS:

12 diced turnips
2 cups diced potatoes
6 cups chicken stock (see recipe)
1/4 pound butter
1 cup chopped onions
1 cup chopped celery
1/2 cup chopped red bell pepper
1/4 cup diced garlic
2 cups sliced green onions
2 cups milk
2-13 ounce cans evaporated milk
salt and cracked pepper to taste
soy sauce to taste
Louisiana Gold Pepper Sauce to taste

METHOD:

In a one gallon stock pot, simmer turnips and potatoes in the chicken stock until tender. In a large saute pan, melt butter over medium high heat. Add onions, celery, bell pepper, garlic and green onions. Saute three to five minutes or until vegetables are wilted. Add milk and evaporated milk, bring to a low boil and reduce heat to simmer. Season to taste using salt and cracked pepper. Place the tender turnips and potatoes in a blender, along with two cups of chicken stock, and puree until smooth. Return to pot with the remaining stock and add the vegetable/milk mixture. Bring to a low boil and adjust seasonings using soy sauce and Louisiana Gold. Remove from heat and serve hot or cold. This soup also freezes well.

The Overseer's Cabin at Ashland

Changes

SWEET CORN AND SHRIMP SOUP

PREP TIME: 1 Hour
SERVES: 12
COMMENT:

Long before lake and gulf shrimp were available to Louisianians, river shrimp were in great supply. Many dishes featured this unique ingredient, but none is more famous than the Creole Style Sweet Corn and Shrimp Soup. The marriage of these items came about because of our friendship with the native American Indians and their gift of corn.

INGREDIENTS:

3 cups whole kernel corn
2 pounds freshwater or other shrimp
1 cup butter
1 cup chopped onions
1 cup chopped celery
1/2 cup chopped red bell pepper
1/2 cup chopped green bell pepper
1/4 cup diced garlic
1 cup diced tomatoes, seeded
1 cup flour
1 cup tomato sauce
2 1/2 quarts shellfish stock (see recipe)
1 cup heavy whipping cream
1/2 cup sliced green onions
1/2 cup chopped parsley
salt and cracked pepper to taste
Louisiana Gold Pepper Sauce to taste

METHOD:

In a two gallon stock pot, melt butter over medium high heat. Add corn, onions, celery, bell peppers and garlic. Saute three to five minutes or until vegetables are wilted. Add tomatoes, blend well into the vegetable mixture and add flour. Using a wire whisk, whip constantly until white roux is achieved (see roux technique). Do not brown. Add tomato sauce and stock, one ladle at a time, stirring constantly until all is incorporated. Bring to a low boil and reduce to simmer. Add half of the shrimp and cook for thirty minutes. Add remaining shrimp, cream, green onions and parsley. Allow the shrimp to cook approximately ten minutes. Season to taste using salt, pepper and Louisiana Gold.

Changes

____

____

____

____

____

____

LAGNIAPPE

Mamere (grandmother) made the best corn and shrimp soup, period! Many days my brothers and I would sit around her large kitchen table peeling river shrimp and pulling the silk from the freshly picked corn. Using an "Old Hickory" knife, she would remove the kernels from the cobs and then the secret to her tasty recipe was revealed. She would boil the corn cobs with the shells of the river shrimp in a large pot, seasoned with yellow onions, celery, garlic and one hot pepper. The aroma was incredible. This secret stock was then strained through her old bent colander. The results of her labor still linger on in my memory, so many years later.

BROILED CREOLE TOMATO AND SHRIMP SOUP

PREP TIME: 1 Hour
SERVES: 10-12
COMMENT:

The Creole tomato is a variety receiving many accolades in and around the French Market of New Orleans. The first of this crop each season draws many bidders to the market and it is not uncommon for thousands of dollars to be paid for that first case. If you do not have Creole tomatoes, use any other variety for this soup.

INGREDIENTS:

5 pounds sliced Creole tomatoes
2 pounds peeled and deveined (21-25 count) shrimp
1 cup olive oil
2 tbsps chopped fresh thyme
2 tbsps chopped fresh basil
2 tbsps cracked black pepper
1 cup melted butter
1 cup chopped onions
1 cup chopped celery
1/2 cup chopped green bell pepper
1/4 cup diced garlic
1 cup flour
3 quarts chicken stock (see recipe)
salt and cracked black pepper to taste
Louisiana Gold Pepper Sauce to taste

METHOD:

Set oven thermostat on broil or 500 degrees F. Place tomatoes and shrimp in a large mixing bowl and top with olive oil, thyme, basil and cracked pepper. Using your hands, blend well to coat with all of the flavorings. Remove tomatoes and shrimp to a large baking pan and place in oven. Broil until shrimp are pink and curled and tomatoes are tender and rendering their juices. When done, remove and set twenty-four shrimp aside. Place the remaining shrimp and tomatoes in the bowl of a food processor equipped with a metal blade. In a two gallon stock pot, melt butter over medium high heat. Add onions, celery, bell pepper and garlic. Saute three to five minutes or until vegetables are wilted. Place vegetables in food processor along with the tomatoes and blend until mixture is pureed. Return to the stock pot and sprinkle in the flour. Using a wire whisk, blend flour into the pureed vegetable mixture. Return mixture to a slow boil and add the chicken stock, one ladle at a time, until all is incorporated. Bring mixture to a boil, reduce to simmer and cook thirty minutes. Season to taste using salt, pepper and Louisiana Gold. When seasoning, you may wish to add a dash of sugar depending on the acidity of the tomatoes. To serve, place two shrimp in the bottom of a soup bowl and top with the hot soup.

Changes

San Francisco Plantation

San Francisco Plantation

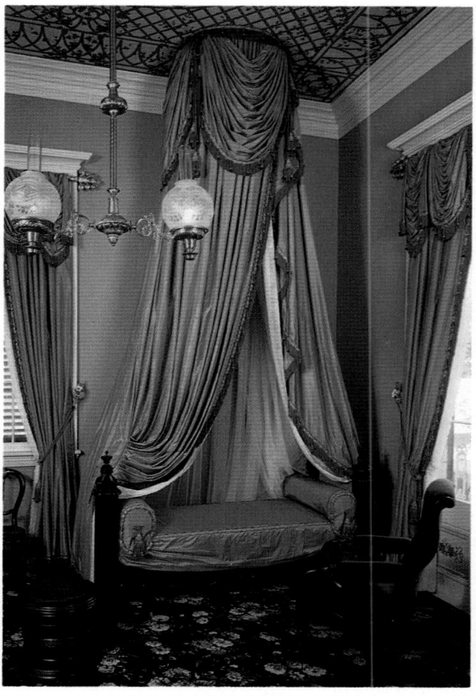

The Blue Boudoir at San Francisco

"Without A Penny"

When Edmund Marmillion began building his mansion in the 1850s, he planned a riverside landmark to excite and interest the passing river traffic and he named the house Marmillion. Years later, Edmund's son, Antoine Valsin, married Louise von Seybold, and they decided to redecorate the mansion. Velvet drapes and ornate chandeliers were manufactured and sent upriver from New Orleans. Wallpaper was designed and purchased in Europe to cover the vast wall space. Most plantation walls at this time were painted white or pale pastel colors, but Louise chose brilliant purples, vibrant blues and fluorescent greens, which shocked the inhabitants of this small river parish. She went one step further by hand-painting every wall and ceiling with designs and murals. It was definitely the most decorated and colorful home in Louisiana. These costly repairs prompted Valsin to comment that he was "sans fruscins" or without a penny. The name, Sans Fruscins, stuck for a while until a subsequent owner changed it to San Francisco.

The exterior of San Francisco is Victorian with Italianate brackets, Corinthian columns and Gothic revival dormer windows. In contrast, the interior floor plan is Louisiana-Creole. There are no hallways, but large doors and windows are arranged to provide passage and ventilation. The main living areas are located on the second floor instead of the ground level. The walls are of brick-entre-poteaux or brick between post. There are seventeen rooms in the home but only four fireplaces. Huge wooden cisterns on each side of the home were used to supply running water to pipes throughout the house. This was well ahead of its time. These cisterns each held approximately 9,000 gallons of water and are still in place today.

The interior was designed to be elegant and colorful, similar to the riverboats Mrs. Marmillion admired. The house is noted for its false marbling and woodgraining throughout. Even the cypress fireplaces are painted to resemble marble. Five magnificent hand-painted ceiling murals are visible. Though three have been restored, two are original and untouched since the 1860s. This plantation home is indisputably the most unique of the Mississippi River's plantation parade.

To reach San Francisco, take I-10 west from New Orleans to the Laplace exit. Follow US 61 to Highway 637 and the River Road. 504-535-2341.

At left, clockwise from bottom left, Poached Seafood in Tomato Essence (page 86), Pan Fried Quail von Seybold (page 255), and Asparagus with Lemon Sauce (page 149)

POACHED SEAFOOD IN TOMATO ESSENCE

PREP TIME: 1 Hour
SERVES: 10-12
COMMENT:

The poaching of seafoods, which led to the creation of our famous Creole Bouillabaisse, was common at San Francisco Plantation. Although most cultures poach fish to capture its wonderful fresh flavor, today we enjoy it because it is healthy and low in fat.

INGREDIENTS:

6 6-8 ounce trout or flounder fillets
24 (21-25 count) shrimp, peeled and deveined
1 pound cooked crawfish tails
12 fresh oysters
1 pound jumbo lump crabmeat
1/2 cup olive oil
1 cup chopped onions
1 cup chopped celery
1/2 cup chopped yellow bell pepper
1/4 cup diced garlic
1 cup fresh tomatoes, diced
2 quarts shellfish stock (see recipe)
1 cup dry white Vermouth
2- 8 ounce cans V-8 juice
1 bay leaf
2 sprigs fresh thyme
2 tbsps chopped basil
1/2 cup sliced green onions
1/4 cup chopped parsley
salt and cracked pepper to taste
Louisiana Gold Pepper Sauce to taste

METHOD:

In a two gallon stock pot, heat olive oil over medium high heat. Add onions, celery, bell pepper, garlic and tomatoes. Saute three to five minutes or until vegetables are wilted. Add shellfish stock, Vermouth and V-8 juice. Bring to a rolling boil, reduce to simmer, and add bay leaf, thyme and basil. Cook approximately thirty minutes, adding additional stock or water to retain volume. Season to taste using salt, pepper and Louisiana Gold. Add shrimp, crawfish, oysters and lump crabmeat. Gently stir the ingredients in the poaching liquid. Add green onions and parsley and place the fish fillets in the stock. Poach three to five minutes or until fish is done to your liking. Adjust seasonings if necessary. Ladle the seafoods into a soup bowl and top with the poaching liquid.

Changes

SMOKED CORN AND CRAWFISH CHOWDER

PREP TIME: 1 1/2 Hours
SERVES: 10-12
COMMENT:

The smoking of meats, fish and vegetables is common place today in Louisiana. This technique was in use by the Native Americans when the colonists arrived in the late 1600's. It was the Germans, however, who made the smoking of meats and vegetables a regular part of our culinary heritage.

INGREDIENTS:

6 ears sweet corn
2 pounds cooked crawfish tails
1 cup cubed smoked ham
1/4 cup melted butter
4 cups diced potatoes
1 cup chopped onions
1 cup chopped celery
1 cup chopped red bell pepper
1/4 cup diced garlic
6 cups chicken stock (see recipe)
2-16 ounce cans cream style corn
2 cups heavy whipping cream
1 tsp dried marjoram
1/4 cup chopped chives
1/4 cup chopped parsley
salt and cracked pepper to taste
Louisiana Gold Pepper Sauce to taste

METHOD:

Preheat homestyle smoker according to manufacturer's directions. Place corn and crawfish in baking pan with one inch lip. Smoke the crawfish and corn thirty-five to forty-five minutes, or until crawfish have a prominent smoked flavor. Remove and using a sharp knife, pare the kernels from the cob and set aside. You may wish to boil the smoked cobs along with the four cups of chicken stock and one additional cup of water for fifteen to twenty minutes to impart the smoked flavor into the stock. In a two gallon stock pot, melt butter over medium high heat. Add ham, potatoes, onions, celery, bell pepper and garlic. Saute three to five minutes or until vegetables are wilted. Add smoked corn and half of the crawfish along with the stock. Bring to a rolling boil, reduce to simmer and cook until potatoes are tender, approximately thirty minutes. Add cream style corn, heavy whipping cream, marjoram, chives and parsley. Continue to simmer an additional twenty minutes. Add remaining crawfish tails and season to taste using salt, pepper and Louisiana Gold.

Changes

WORLD'S FAIR OYSTER SOUP

PREP TIME: 15 Minutes
SERVES: 8-10
COMMENT:

Poplar Grove Plantation originated as the Bankers' Pavilion at the 1884 World's Fair in New Orleans. Once the house was moved to West Baton Rouge, a specialty of the home was its oyster stew, or soup, as it is called today.

INGREDIENTS:

4 dozen freshly shucked oysters, reserve liquid
1/4 cup butter
1/2 cup minced onions
1/4 cup minced celery
1/2 cup sliced green onions
1/4 cup minced garlic
2 quarts heavy whipping cream
1 tsp chopped thyme
1/2 tsp chopped dill
nutmeg to taste
salt and cracked pepper to taste
Louisiana Gold Pepper Sauce to taste
10 pats cold butter
parsley for garnish
paprika for garnish

METHOD:

In a heavy bottom dutch oven, melt butter over medium high heat. Add onions, celery, green onions and garlic. Saute three to five minutes or until vegetables are wilted. Add oyster liquor and oysters. Saute until oysters are curled and juices are rendered. Add heavy whipping cream, thyme, dill and nutmeg. Bring to a rolling boil, reduce to simmer and cook until cream is thickened and has a full oyster flavor. Season to taste using salt, pepper and Louisiana Gold. Serve in heated soup bowls and garnish with one pat of cold butter, parsley and paprika.

LAGNIAPPE

The Roman rich had access to an astonishing variety of foods. One of them was oysters. They were imported from Britain and were considered by the Romans not only a delicacy but also an aphrodisiac. In 1100, the Chinese sold oysters in one of the ten markets of Hangzhou and prepared them for nourishment of the poorer classes. Even 30,000 years ago, oysters were being consumed in Australia in great quantities. In Louisiana, the Native Americans have been eating oysters for at least 4,000 years. Evidence shows that the oysters were tossed into a fire and when the shells popped open, the steamed oysters were revealed. Who said things were so bad back then?

Changes

SHRIMP, CRAB AND OKRA GUMBO

PREP TIME: 1 Hour
SERVES: 12
COMMENT:

Cooks tend to argue whether okra should be sauteed first or put fresh into gumbo stock. I have tried both techniques and have had great results. I do find, however, that most of the "seasoned" gumbo cooks in Louisiana, those who pride themselves in the art of this dish, saute the okra first.

INGREDIENTS:

2 pounds (35 count) shrimp, peeled and deveined
1 pound jumbo lump crabmeat
2 pounds fresh okra
1/2 cup vegetable oil
1 cup chopped onions
1 cup chopped celery
1/2 cup chopped bell pepper
2 tbsps diced garlic
1 cup vegetable oil
1 cup flour
1 cup diced tomatoes
1-8 ounce can tomato sauce
3 quarts shellfish stock (see recipe)
1 cup sliced green onions
1/2 cup chopped parsley
salt and cracked pepper to taste
Louisiana Gold Pepper Sauce to taste

METHOD:

In a large black skillet, heat vegetable oil over medium high heat. Add okra, onions, celery, bell pepper and garlic. Slowly saute the mixed vegetables until the okra is well cooked and slightly browned. You must stir this mixture constantly as the okra will tend to stick and scorch. Once cooked, remove from heat and set aside. In a heavy bottom dutch oven, heat remaining vegetable oil over medium high heat. Add flour and using a wire whisk, whip until dark brown roux is achieved (see roux techniques). Add tomatoes and tomato sauce and stir to incorporate well. Pour off the excess oil from the okra mixture and add the contents of the skillet to the roux. Blend well and slowly add the hot shellfish stock, one ladle at a time, until all is incorporated. Bring to a rolling boil and reduce to simmer. More stock may be needed to maintain a soup-like consistency. Add green onions and parsley. Season to taste using salt, pepper and Louisiana Gold and allow to cook for fifteen minutes. Add shrimp and cook ten to fifteen minutes longer. Add lump crabmeat and adjust seasonings if necessary. Serve over steamed white rice.

Creamware from Leeds Foundry, England

Changes

VELOUTE OF BOILED CRAWFISH, CORN AND POTATOES

PREP TIME: 1 Hour
SERVES: 12
COMMENT:

One Saturday afternoon, immediately following a crawfish boil, I noticed a table still piled with boiled crawfish, corn and potatoes. With the help of a few friends, I peeled the crawfish and using the shells, made a boiled crawfish stock. I guess the rest of the story is obvious. This wonderful soup was created!

INGREDIENTS:

2 lbs boiled crawfish tails
1 cup whole kernel corn
6 small potatoes, cubed
1 cup melted butter
1 cup chopped onions
1 cup chopped celery
1/2 cup chopped red bell pepper
1/4 cup diced garlic
1 cup flour
2 1/2 quarts crawfish stock (see recipe)
1 pint heavy whipping cream
1 cup sliced green onions
1 cup chopped parsley
salt and white pepper to taste
Louisiana Gold Pepper Sauce to taste

METHOD:

Into a one gallon stock pot, place the shells of the boiled crawfish along with any remaining onions, lemons, etc. Add three quarts of cold water, bring to a low boil and cook for thirty minutes. This will impart a concentrated boiled crawfish flavor into the water. If you do not have boiled crawfish, simply boil the corn and potatoes in water lightly seasoned with crab boil for the same effect or use chicken stock. Once stock is flavorful, strain and reserve three quarts of liquid. In the cleaned stock pot, melt butter over medium high heat. Add onions, celery, bell pepper and garlic. Saute three to five minutes or until vegetables are wilted. Add corn and continue to cook another three to five minutes. Sprinkle in flour and stir until well blended. Slowly pour in the crawfish stock, stirring constantly until the consistency of a cream soup is achieved. Bring to a low boil and add half of the crawfish and all of the cubed potatoes. Cook until potatoes are tender, but not mushy. Add the remaining crawfish, heavy whipping cream, green onions and parsley. Season to taste using salt, pepper and Louisiana Gold. You may wish to add a bit more of the crawfish stock to retain the consistency of the soup.

Changes

BRIE CHEESE, CRAB AND BERMUDA ONION SOUP

PREP TIME: 1 Hour
SERVES: 10-12
COMMENT:

The French have always been lovers of brie cheese and hence, this ingredient has found its way into many Louisiana dishes. This combination of cheese, crab and spicy bermuda onions tastes great to our bayou state palates.

INGREDIENTS:

1/2 pound brie cheese, rind removed
1 pound jumbo lump crabmeat
4 sliced Bermuda onions, halved
1 cup melted butter
1 cup chopped celery
1 cup sliced green onion tops
1/2 cup chopped red bell pepper
1/4 cup diced garlic
1 cup flour
3 quarts chicken stock (see recipe)
1 cup heavy whipping cream
1 bay leaf
2 whole cloves
1 sprig fresh thyme
salt and cracked pepper to taste
Louisiana Gold Pepper Sauce to taste

METHOD:

Allow the brie cheese to soften at room temperature. Remove any shells from the crabmeat and set aside. In a two gallon stock pot, melt butter over medium high heat. Add celery, green onions, bell pepper and garlic. Saute three to five minutes or until vegetables are wilted. Sprinkle in flour and using a wire whisk, whip constantly until white roux is achieved (see roux techniques). Add chicken stock, one ladle at a time, until all is incorporated. Using the same wire whisk, blend in the brie cheese until thoroughly melted into the stock. Add Bermuda onions, heavy whipping cream, bay leaf, cloves and thyme. Bring mixture to a rolling boil, reduce to simmer and cook approximately thirty minutes. Remove the bay leaf and thyme sprig. Add lump crabmeat being careful not to break the lumps while stirring. Season to taste using salt, pepper and Louisiana Gold.

Changes

TURTLE SOUP TERREBONNE

PREP TIME: 2 Hours
SERVES: 12
COMMENT:

Terrebonne Parish is located in the center of the Cajun triangle of South Louisiana. It is also in the heart of the swamplands and turtle is considered a delicacy by the people living in this area. This particular recipe was discovered in a centuries-old collection from that area.

The Entrance to Ardoyne

INGREDIENTS:

3 pounds cleaned snapping turtle
1/2 pound diced andouille or ham
1 cup vegetable oil
1 cup flour
2 cups chopped onions
2 cups chopped celery
1 cup chopped bell pepper
1/4 cup diced garlic
1 cup chopped tomatoes
1 cup tomato sauce
3 quarts turtle stock (see stock technique)
2 whole bay leaves
1 tsp thyme
1 tsp basil
pinch of allspice
pinch of nutmeg
pinch of clove
1 tbsp lemon juice
1/2 cup sherry
3 hard boiled eggs, grated
salt and cracked pepper to taste
Louisiana Gold Pepper Sauce to taste

METHOD:

In a two gallon stock pot, place the turtle and four quarts of cold water. You may add one onion, quartered, one head of garlic, split, and six whole cloves. Bring to a rolling boil, reduce to simmer and cook until the turtle is tender and falling from the bones, approximately one hour. During the simmering process, you should skim the foam that rises to the top of the pot. Do not allow the water to fall below the one gallon mark. Once tender, remove the turtle and strain the stock through a fine chinois or cheesecloth. Debone the turtle and set aside. Measure three quarts of the turtle stock for the soup. In the same two gallon stock pot, heat oil over medium high heat. Sprinkle in flour and using a wire whisk, whip constantly until golden brown roux is achieved (see roux technique). Do not scorch. Should black specks appear, discard and begin again. Add onions, celery, bell pepper, garlic and tomatoes. Saute three to five minutes or until vegetables are wilted. Add tomato sauce, turtle meat and andouille, blending well into roux mixture. Add turtle stock, one ladle at a time, stirring constantly until all is incorporated. Add bay leaves, thyme, basil, allspice, nutmeg, clove and lemon juice. Bring to a low boil, reduce to simmer and cook approximately one hour, adding additional stock or water to retain volume. Add sherry and grated eggs. Season to taste using salt, pepper and Louisiana Gold. Serve hot with a tablespoon of sherry for added flavor.

Changes

CHICKEN AND SAUSAGE GUMBO

PREP TIME: 2 Hours
SERVES: 8-10
COMMENT:

Almost every species of wild game in Louisiana has been used in the creation of gumbo. Since most Cajun men were hunters and trappers, it is not surprising that they preferred Mallard duck and smoked andouille gumbo. However, chicken and sausage is still the most popular gumbo choice in Louisiana.

INGREDIENTS:

1-5 pound stewing hen
1 pound smoked sausage or andouille
1 cup oil
1 1/2 cups flour
2 cups chopped onions
2 cups chopped celery
1 cup chopped bell pepper
1/4 cup diced garlic
3 quarts chicken stock (see recipe)
24 button mushrooms
2 cups sliced green onions
1 bay leaf
sprig of thyme
1 tbsp chopped basil
salt and cracked pepper to taste
Louisiana Gold Pepper Sauce to taste
1/2 cup chopped parsley
4 cups cooked white rice

METHOD:

Using a sharp boning knife, cut the stewing hen into eight to ten serving pieces. Remove as much of the fat from the chicken as possible. Cut smoked sausage or andouille into half inch slices and set aside. In a two gallon stock pot, heat oil over medium high heat. Sprinkle in flour and using a wire whisk, whip constantly until golden brown roux is achieved (see roux technique). Do not scorch. Should black specks appear, discard and begin again. Add onions, celery, bell pepper and garlic. Saute three to five minutes or until vegetables are wilted. Add chicken and sausage, blending well into vegetable mixture. Saute approximately fifteen minutes. Add chicken stock, one ladle at a time, stirring constantly until all is incorporated. Bring to a rolling boil, reduce to simmer and cook approximately one hour. Skim any fat or oil that rises to the top of the pot. Add mushrooms, green onions, bay leaf, thyme and basil. Season to taste using salt, pepper and Louisiana Gold. Cook an additional one to two hours if necessary, until chicken is tender and falling apart. Add parsley, adjust seasonings and serve over hot, steamed white rice. You may wish to boil the chicken one to two hours prior to beginning the gumbo. This will tenderize the meat and you may reserve the stock, debone the chicken and use the meat and stock in the gumbo.

Changes

CREAM OF CHICKEN AND ARTICHOKE SOUP

PREP TIME: 1 Hour
SERVES: 10-12
COMMENT:

I had no idea artichokes grew here in Louisiana. It was not until I toured the many plantations along the Mississippi River and researched the foods, that I came to notice many references to artichokes. Today, I grow them in my own garden.

INGREDIENTS:

1 whole young fryer
8 artichoke bottoms, sliced and uncooked
1 cup butter
1 cup chopped onions
1 cup chopped celery
1/2 cup chopped red bell pepper
1/4 cup diced garlic
1 cup flour
3 quarts chicken stock (see recipe)
1 pint heavy whipping cream
1 cup sliced green onions
1 cup chopped parsley
1 tbsp thyme
1 tbsp basil
salt and white pepper to taste
Louisiana Gold Pepper Sauce to taste

METHOD:

In a two gallon stock pot, place fryer with three and a half quarts cold water. You may wish to add one onion, quartered, one head of garlic, split, and one celery stick. Bring to a rolling boil and allow to cook until chicken is tender and falling off the bones. When tender, remove chicken and strain stock through a fine chinois or cheesecloth. Debone chicken and measure three quarts of chicken stock and set aside. In the same pot, melt butter over medium high heat. Add onions, celery, bell pepper, garlic and artichokes. Saute five to ten minutes or until vegetables are wilted and artichokes are tender. Sprinkle in flour and using a wire whisk, whip constantly until white roux is achieved (see roux technique). Add chicken stock, one ladle at a time, stirring constantly until all is incorporated. Bring to a low boil, reduce to simmer and cook thirty minutes. Add chicken and heavy whipping cream, return to simmer and add all remaining ingredients. Season to taste using salt, pepper and Louisiana Gold.

Changes

Chapter Four
Salads

Magnolia Ridge Plantation

Magnolia Ridge Plantation

"A Garden Restored"

When Evalina Prescott's father decided to build his plantation home in the early 1800s, he knew he had selected the perfect location. It was high up on a bluff, complete with cypress swamps and ponds and surrounded by a variety of Louisiana trees and flowers. Evalina even wrote in her diary about the briar roses, oleander and hydrangeas that grew everywhere. When the present owners purchased the home in 1985 and renovated it, they knew they had to reconstruct Evalina's beautiful gardens and give them back to the State of Louisiana and the world free of charge.

Magnolia Ridge Plantation was completed in 1830 under the direction of John Moore. After the death of his wife, Judge Moore married the widow of David Weeks, owner of Shadows on the Teche Plantation. The original site consisted of 3,000 acres and was named Oakland. Later the name was changed to Prescott House after Moore's daughter married Captain Prescott. The captain achieved local fame as commander of the Confederate Second Cavalry, the last military group to surrender to the Union, June 5, 1865. During the Civil War, Magnolia Ridge was headquarters for the Confederate Army, but was later occupied by Union forces. It was in the main dining room downstairs that Evalina, during the war, had her dinner interrupted by General Banks. He walked into the home and demanded food for his officers. Evalina spoke to him with her back turned, as she refused to look him in the face. She told him to take what was left on the stove, a large pot of gumbo. When the general looked into the pot, he refused to eat it, and went out instead to hunt rabbits for dinner. Evalina was quoted as saying, "The North will never win this war with men too stupid to dine on gumbo!" In addition to the dining room, this floor contains a large parlor, warming room and pantry.

Ann and Tipton Golias restored the property and grounds in the late 1980s. In addition to the beautiful antiques and art, the home features sixty acres of manicured grounds and gardens.

The Birdhouse Matches the Plantation Home at Magnolia Ridge

With over five miles of paved walking paths, the grounds are open to the public and accessible to the handicapped. One of the most unique features of the grounds is the natural cypress swamp to the rear of the home.

To reach Magnolia Ridge, take I-49 North from Lafayette to the Washington exit. Proceed to 103 Prescott Street. 318-826-3027.

At left, Layered Fruit and Shrimp Salad (page 98)

LAYERED FRUIT AND SHRIMP SALAD

PREP TIME: 1 Hour
SERVES: 6
COMMENT:

Fruit is not just for dessert anymore! With its wide range of color and texture, nothing makes a more beautiful entree salad than layers of fresh or canned fruit. Why not create an interesting and unique summer salad by combining colorful, healthy fruit with fresh shrimp or other seafoods.

INGREDIENTS:

2 dozen (21-25 count) shrimp, boiled
2 cups crawfish tails
1 cup jumbo lump crabmeat
2 cups watermelon balls
2 cups cantaloupe balls
2 cups honeydew balls
2 cups sliced peaches
2 cups sliced pears
2 cups quartered orange sections
2 cups sliced plums
1 cup fresh blueberries
1 cup fresh strawberries
1 cup cubed pineapple
6 chopped apple mint leaves
6 chopped lemon balm leaves
1 cup orange juice
1/2 cup chopped pecans
8 ounces strawberry yogurt

METHOD:

In a large glass serving bowl, layer fruit by alternating stratas of color. Once all the fruit has been layered, line shrimp, crawfish and crabmeat in a decorative pattern around the edge of the bowl. In a separate bowl, combine apple mint, lemon balm, orange juice and yogurt. Using a wire whisk, whip until ingredients are well blended. When ready to serve, sprinkle in pecans and pour the yogurt dressing over the salad ingredients. Toss the mixture to blend the dressing into the fruit and serve immediately.

Changes

SHRIMP AND LUMP CRAB SALAD IN TOMATO ASPIC

PREP TIME: 1 Hour
SERVES: 6-8
COMMENT:

It is no wonder, with the Creole influence in and around the city of Natchitoches, that a tomato aspic salad would emerge. This simple salad has an added twist with the addition of shrimp and crabmeat. You may try adding a bit of leftover grilled chicken or roast beef to this recipe in place of the seafood.

INGREDIENTS:

1 cup (150-200 count) shrimp, cooked and peeled
1 cup jumbo lump crabmeat
2-8 ounce cans V-8 juice
2-8 ounce cans tomato juice
2 pkgs unflavored gelatin, (dissolved in 1/2 cup cold water)
1/4 cup chopped parsley
1/4 cup sliced green onions
1/4 cup finely diced onions
1/4 cup finely diced celery
1/2 cup finely diced stuffed olives
1 peeled avocado, finely diced
2 tbsps lemon juice
2 tsps Worcestershire Sauce
salt and cracked pepper to taste
Louisiana Gold Pepper Sauce to taste
1 tsp sugar

METHOD:

In a two quart sauce pot, heat V-8 juice and tomato juice over medium high heat. Add dissolved gelatin and blend well into the juice. Remove from heat and add parsley, green onions, onions, celery and olives. Allow mixture to cool slightly before adding avocadoes, lemon juice and Worcestershire. Season to taste using salt, pepper, Louisiana Gold and sugar. Fold in shrimp and crabmeat, adjust seasonings if necessary, and pour into your favorite seafood mold. This full-flavored aspic salad is wonderful as an accompaniment to roasted leg of lamb or any wild game dish. However, you may wish to use it as a main luncheon entree by serving it over a mixture of salad greens.

Changes

GRILLED FISH SALAD

PREP TIME: 2 Hours
SERVES: 6-8
COMMENT:

Poached fish salads were often presented at Louisiana plantation events. Most of these homes were located on rivers and bayous, so seafoods were plentiful and had to be used. This is one of those dishes that survived over the years and today, has many variations.

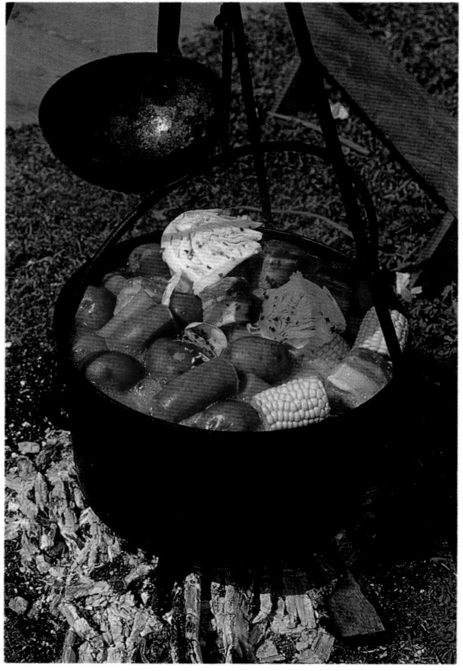

The Stew Simmers at Rene Beauregard

INGREDIENTS:

2 pounds white fish fillets
1/2 cup vegetable oil
1 tbsp chopped dill
1 tsp ground sassafras
pinch of dried thyme
juice of 1 lemon
1 1/2 cups mayonnaise
1/2 cup sour cream
1/2 cup minced onions
1/4 cup minced celery
1/4 cup minced red bell pepper
1/4 cup minced yellow bell pepper
1 tsp chopped dill
1 tsp chopped basil
1 tsp chopped tarragon
juice of 1/2 lemon
salt and cracked pepper to taste
Louisiana Gold Pepper Sauce to taste
Worcestershire Sauce to taste

METHOD:

Whenever possible, I prefer to use striped bass or flounder for this dish. However, catfish also works well. Preheat barbecue grill according to manufacturer's directions. You may wish to pre-soak some pecan wood chips to give the fish an added Louisiana flavor. In a large mixing bowl, combine fillets with oil, dill, sassafras, thyme and lemon. Season to taste using salt, pepper and Louisiana Gold. Allow fish to marinate in the seasoning ingredients thirty minutes prior to grilling. If the fish is very delicate, you should line the grill with aluminum foil and pierce fish with a fork to keep it from falling through the grill during cooking. Add the wood chips to the coals and grill fish, covered, for approximately twelve to fifteen minutes or until done. Remove fish, place on cookie sheet and chill in the refrigerator. Once chilled, chop fish including the gelatin that has collected in the pan. Place cubed fish in the bottom of a large mixing bowl and add mayonnaise, sour cream, onions, celery, bell peppers, dill, basil, tarragon and lemon juice. Using a large spoon, blend all ingredients well. Season to taste using salt, pepper, Louisiana Gold and Worcestershire. Form the fish into a decorative loaf or spoon into a fish mold. Chill a minimum of two to three hours allowing flavors to develop. Serve on a mixture of multi-colored lettuces or with croutons and toast points as an appetizer.

Changes

MARDI GRAS CRAWFISH SALAD

PREP TIME: 30 Minutes

SERVES: 6-8

COMMENT:

Though Mardi Gras or Fat Tuesday is celebrated the day before Ash Wednesday, dishes named after the holiday are served all year long. This particular salad can be made with or without the seafood, however, you may wish to substitute smoked chicken or cottage cheese in its place.

INGREDIENTS:

2 cups cooked crawfish tails
1 head red leaf lettuce
1-10 ounce package spinach leaves
1/2 cup crumbled bacon
1/2 cup chopped bermuda onions
2 cups mandarin orange sections
1 cup sliced mushrooms
3/4 cup salad oil
1/2 cup cider vinegar
1/4 cup sugar
1/4 cup orange juice
1 tsp dried mustard
1 tbsp chopped sage
1 tbsp chopped basil
salt and cracked pepper to taste

METHOD:

Wash lettuce and spinach leaves well under cold water. Remove large stems and tear into one inch pieces. Drain and place in a large mixing bowl. Add crawfish, bacon, onions, mandarins and mushrooms. Toss well to blend ingredients. In a separate bowl, combine oil, vinegar, sugar and juice. Using a wire whisk, whip until all ingredients are well blended. Add mustard, sage and basil. Season to taste using salt and pepper. Pour dressing over salad mixture. Toss to coat all ingredients well. Serve equal portions in six cold salad plates.

Changes

____

____

____

LAGNIAPPE

An observer once said that New Orleanians are either planning a party, having a party or recuperating from one. The biggest and most famous party of all is Mardi Gras, "the greatest free show on earth." The term originated on March 4, 1699 when the French explorer, Iberville, arrived at the mouth of the Mississippi River. His ship had just survived a major storm and had tied up on the muddy shores at present day New Orleans. One of his men mentioned that the next day was Fat Tuesday or Mardi Gras, the day before Ash Wednesday. That night they made camp at the first great bend in the river and Iberville recorded that spot as Mardi Gras Point. This was the first official name given to a place in the newly explored territory. They celebrated the success of their exploration and it was on this day that the first Mardi Gras party took place.

CRABMEAT IN ARTICHOKE PIROGUES

PREP TIME: 1 Hour
SERVES: 6
COMMENT:

The French chef, La Varenne, introduced soup as an important starter course and roux as a thickening agent during the 1600's. That alone should have made him famous, but as chef to Marquis'duxelle, he introduced the duxelle stuffing for mushrooms, lemon juice and vinegars as simple sauces and more importantly, the globe artichoke as a main item on the dinner table.

INGREDIENTS:

6 large artichokes
1/2 pound jumbo lump crabmeat
1 lemon sliced
1/4 cup olive oil
1 tbsp chopped garlic
1/2 cup mayonnaise
1/4 cup sour cream
1 tsp Creole mustard
1 tbsp lemon juice
1 tsp grated lemon peel
1 tsp chopped tarragon
1 tsp chopped thyme
1 tsp chopped basil
salt and cracked pepper to taste
Louisiana Gold Pepper Sauce to taste
6 lemon slices
parsley for garnish
paprika for garnish

METHOD:

Trim the pointed ends from the artichoke leaves and rinse under cold water. In a large stock pot, place artichokes, sliced lemon, olive oil, garlic and water to cover. Season to taste with salt and pepper. Bring to a rolling boil, reduce to simmer and cook thirty to forty-five minutes. The large outer leaves at the bottom should pull away easily when cooked. Remove, drain and allow artichokes to cool. In a large mixing bowl, combine mayonnaise, sour cream and mustard. Using a wire whisk, whip until ingredients are well blended. Add lemon juice, peel, tarragon, thyme and basil. Continue to whip until all ingredients are incorporated. Season to taste using salt, pepper and Louisiana Gold. Fold in crabmeat and stir gently being careful not to break lumps. Using a sharp knife, cut artichokes in half and scoop out the center choke with a teaspoon. Season the center with salt and pepper. Stuff artichoke with crabmeat dressing, top with lemon slice and garnish with parsley and paprika. Serve as a lunch or dinner entree salad.

Changes

SEAFOOD GUMBO SALAD

PREP TIME: 1 Hour
SERVES: 6-8
COMMENT:

The ingredients used to create a great seafood gumbo may be incorporated into any dish successfully. Just as in the jambalaya salad, it is natural to create a wonderful starter dish with ingredients that marry so well in the salad bowl.

INGREDIENTS:

1 cup jumbo lump crabmeat
1 cup cooked crawfish tails
1 cup cooked (150-200 count) shrimp
1 head red leaf lettuce
1 bunch watercress
1-10 ounce bag spinach leaves
1/2 pound cooked smoked sausage, sliced
2 small Creole tomatoes, diced
1 cup sliced pickled okra
1/4 cup minced onions
1/4 cup minced celery
1/4 cup minced red bell pepper
1/4 cup minced yellow bell pepper
1 tbsp chopped garlic
1 cup mayonnaise
1 cup sour cream
1/2 cup ketchup
2 tbsps Creole mustard
salt and cracked pepper to taste
Louisiana Gold Pepper Sauce to taste
1/4 cup olive oil

METHOD:

Wash greens well under cold running water. Remove stems and tear into one inch pieces. Drain and place in a large mixing bowl. Add crabmeat, crawfish, shrimp, sausage, tomatoes, okra, onions, celery, bell peppers and garlic. Toss well to blend ingredients. In a separate bowl, mix mayonnaise, sour cream, ketchup and mustard. Using a wire whisk, whip until all ingredients are well blended. Season to taste using salt, pepper and Louisiana Gold. Add olive oil and whip once again. Pour dressing over salad mixture. Toss to coat all ingredients well. Serve in individual salad plates or in a large crystal salad bowl.

Changes

LUMP CRAB & ROASTED PEPPER SALAD

PREP TIME: 1 Hour
SERVES: 6-8
COMMENT:

With the Germans and English both cultivating vegetables in the River Parishes, a wide variety of sweet peppers were available. We quickly saw bell pepper soups, stuffed bell peppers and finally roasted pepper salads begin to emerge from these gardens. It wasn't long before seafoods were added for more interesting flavors.

INGREDIENTS:

1 pound jumbo lump crabmeat
2 large green bell peppers
2 large red bell peppers
2 large yellow bell peppers
1/2 cup olive oil
juice of 1/2 lemon
juice of 1/2 lime
2 tbsps balsamic vinegar
2 tbsps chopped parsley
1 tbsp chopped oregano
1 tbsp chopped purple basil
1 tsp chopped thyme
1 tsp chopped tarragon
1/4 cup chopped green onions
1/4 cup chopped parsley
1/4 cup grated Parmesan cheese
salt and cracked pepper to taste
Louisiana Gold Pepper Sauce to taste

METHOD:

Roast the bell peppers over an open gas flame or under the broiler until blackened on all sides. Place peppers in a brown paper bag, seal tightly and let stand fifteen to twenty minutes. Remove and peel or rinse under cold water until all the charred peel is removed. Seed and julienne each pepper into six equal strips. Place in a large plastic bowl and set aside. In a smaller bowl, combine oil, juices, vinegar, parsley, oregano, basil, thyme and tarragon. Using a wire whisk, whip until all ingredients are well blended. Add green onions, parsley and Parmesan cheese. Season to taste using salt, pepper and Louisiana Gold. Sprinkle crabmeat over peppers and add the dressing. Toss two to three times to coat the peppers and crabmeat well. Cover and refrigerate four to six hours prior to serving.

Brass Middle Eastern Heater at Houmas House

Changes

PECAN POACHED CHICKEN SALAD

PREP TIME: 1 Hour
SERVES: 6
COMMENT:

Although I'm sure this recipe was first designed because of its flavor, it is quite timely in today's nutrition conscious world. Try substituting lite mayonnaise if you want the low fat version.

INGREDIENTS:

6 chicken breasts, deboned
1 cup chopped pecans
4 cups chicken stock (see recipe)
1/2 pound seedless red grapes
1/2 pound seedless green grapes
1/2 cup minced onions
1 cup diced celery
1/2 cup minced red bell pepper
1 cup sour cream
1 cup mayonnaise
1 tsp chopped dill
1 tsp chopped basil
salt and cracked pepper to taste
Louisiana Gold Pepper Sauce to taste

METHOD:

Preheat oven to 350 degrees F. Remove the skin from chicken breasts and place in a single layer in a shallow baking pan. In a small sauce pot, boil chicken stock over medium high heat. Pour stock over chicken and cover with aluminum foil. Bake until thoroughly cooked, approximately thirty minutes. Remove and allow chicken to cool in poaching liquid. Once cool, discard liquid and shred chicken into bite size pieces. In a large mixing bowl, combine chicken, pecans, grapes, onions, celery and bell pepper. Add sour cream, mayonnaise, dill and basil. Toss to incorporate all ingredients. Season to taste using salt, pepper and Louisiana Gold. To serve, place large serving spoon of chicken salad on a nest of decorative lettuces, spinach or watercress.

Changes

LAGNIAPPE

Poaching is normally associated with eggs, but its range is much wider. The technique of poaching never varies. The heat source is hot liquid just under the boiling point. The distinctive flavor achieved in this process is created by the self-basting of the ingredients during cooking. When poaching meat or fish, never cover the dish with a lid. Instead, you may wish to cover with parchment paper, allowing steam to escape. Make sure to season the poaching liquid with your favorite herbs and spices as not to sacrifice flavor. Most importantly, never discard a poaching liquid. Use it as a broth, sauce or save it to use in your next soup or stew.

CHUNKY CHICKEN SALAD PLANTATION STYLE

PREP TIME: 30 Minutes
SERVES: 6
COMMENT:

Do you ever have leftover fried chicken? If not, this salad is so good, you may want to purchase fried chicken from a local fast food outlet to use in this recipe. Try this salad for your next picnic or at home for a lite lunch alternative.

INGREDIENTS:

3 fried chicken breasts, skin on
3/4 cup mayonnaise
1/4 cup orange juice
1/4 cup heavy whipping cream
1/2 cup seedless green grapes, sliced
1/2 cup mandarin sections
1/2 cup toasted pecans, chopped
1/2 cup finely diced celery
1/4 cup chopped parsley
1 tbsp chopped thyme
1 tbsp chopped basil
salt and cracked pepper to taste
Louisiana Gold Pepper Sauce to taste

METHOD:

Remove meat from the breast bone, keeping skin in tact, and cut into three quarter inch cubes. This is very important, since the seasoning on the fried chicken adheres to the skin and will help season the salad. Set aside. In a large mixing bowl, combine mayonnaise, orange juice and heavy whipping cream. Using a wire whisk, whip until the dressing is well blended. Season to taste using salt, cracked pepper and Louisiana Gold. Add all remaining ingredients except chicken, blending well into dressing. Add cubed chicken and gently fold into the mixture. Once coated, adjust seasonings if necessary. Serve on fresh spinach or romaine lettuce leaves.

Changes

GRILLED SIRLOIN AND WILD MUSHROOM SALAD

PREP TIME: 1 Hour
SERVES: 6-8
COMMENT:

It isn't often that we see a quality cut of meat like sirloin used in a salad. With a lack of refrigeration in plantation days, the cooks often used leftovers to prepare interesting dishes. This one was a favorite of the Randolph family at Nottoway Plantation.

INGREDIENTS:

2 pounds boneless beef sirloin steak
1 cup wild oyster or button mushrooms
1 small red bell pepper, halved
3/4 cup salad oil
1/2 cup orange juice
1 tbsp Louisiana cane syrup
1 tbsp Creole mustard
1 tsp chopped thyme
1 tsp chopped basil
1/2 tsp chopped tarragon
1 tsp diced garlic
salt and cracked pepper to taste
Louisiana Gold Pepper Sauce to taste

METHOD:

Have your butcher cut a two pound sirloin approximately two inches thick. Preheat barbecue grill or oven broiler according to manufacturer's directions. Season steak well on both sides using salt, pepper and Louisiana Gold. Allow steak to sit at room temperature while salad dressing is being made. In a large mixing bowl, combine oil, juice, cane syrup, mustard, thyme, basil, tarragon and garlic. Using a wire whisk, whip until all ingredients are well blended. Season to taste using salt, pepper and Louisiana Gold. Remove one fourth cup of the dressing and brush as a marinade over the sirloin, mushrooms and bell pepper. Once grill is ready, cook steak twelve to fifteen minutes on each side, turning occasionally, for medium rare to medium. While steak is cooking, grill the mushrooms and bell pepper to impart a charbroiled flavor. Remove and julienne or slice the vegetables. Remove steak from pit and allow to cool slightly. Using a sharp knife, slice the steak into one quarter inch strips. Place steak, mushrooms and pepper in dressing bowl and toss to coat well. You may serve this salad warm over colorful mixed greens and tiny pear tomatoes or refrigerate and allow the meat to marinate to serve as a cold meat salad.

Changes

JAMBALAYA RICE SALAD

PREP TIME: 1 Hour
SERVES: 6-8
COMMENT:

Though jambalaya is normally a hot rice dish seasoned with ham, chicken and vegetables, it seems obvious that a cold version would have also been served in plantation days. Though different from the entree, this salad course is quite colorful and full-flavored.

INGREDIENTS:

1 1/2 cups long grain converted rice, uncooked
1/4 cup butter
1/2 cup diced ham
1/4 cup diced onions
1/4 cup diced celery
1/4 cup diced red bell pepper
1 tsp chopped garlic
1/2 cup frozen peas
1/4 cup diced carrots
3 cups chicken stock (see recipe)
4 drops yellow food coloring
1 tsp thyme
1 tsp basil
1 tsp chopped parsley
1/4 cup sliced green onions
salt and cracked pepper to taste
Louisiana Gold Pepper Sauce to taste
1/2 cup mayonnaise

METHOD:

In a heavy bottom dutch oven, melt butter over medium high heat. Add ham, onions, celery, bell pepper and garlic. Saute three to five minutes or until vegetables are wilted. Add peas, carrots and chicken stock. Bring to a low boil and reduce to simmer. Add food coloring, thyme, basil, parsley and green onions. Add rice and season to taste using salt, pepper and Louisiana Gold. Blend well into the stock mixture, cover, reduce heat to low and cook for thirty minutes. Do not remove lid or stir during this process. It is important that the rice cooks on the lowest setting possible to prevent scorching. When cooked, remove from heat and allow to cool. Stir in mayonnaise until well blended. Spoon rice mixture into a decorative mold and refrigerate two to three hours. When ready to serve, unmold onto a large serving platter lined with decorative lettuces.

Changes

OLD MAID'S POTATO SALAD

PREP TIME: 1 Hour
SERVES: 6-8
COMMENT:

This simple, hot potato salad gets its name from the ladies who invented the dish. Since "Old Maids" or unmarried women sold their chicken eggs for money, they did not have any left to go into potato salad or other dishes. Instead, these imaginative women substituted vinegar, oil and garden vegetables to enhance this eggless dish.

INGREDIENTS:

20 new potatoes, cubed
3/4 cup olive oil
1/2 cup sliced purple onions
1/4 cup chopped celery
1/4 cup julienned red bell pepper
1/4 cup julienned yellow bell pepper
1/4 cup sliced green onions
1 tbsp diced garlic
1/4 cup red wine vinegar
1 tsp chopped thyme
1 tsp chopped basil
salt and cracked pepper to taste
Louisiana Gold Pepper Sauce to taste
1/4 cup sweet pickle relish

The Upper Bannister Rail Advertises a Wedding in Progress

METHOD:

Wash potatoes and boil in salted water for approximately twenty minutes or until tender. Do not over-cook. When potatoes are just about done, heat olive oil in a black iron skillet over medium high heat. Add onions, celery, bell peppers, green onions and garlic. Saute three to five minutes or until vegetables are wilted. Add vinegar, remove from heat and season to taste using thyme, basil, salt, pepper and Louisiana Gold. Drain potatoes from boiling water, place in a large mixing bowl and top with the hot dressing and pickle relish. Stir to coat potatoes well with the seasoning mixture and serve warm.

Changes

WARM NEW POTATO SALAD WITH BEER DRESSING

PREP TIME: 1 Hour
SERVES: 6
COMMENT:

No two ingredients are more German than potatoes and beer. Both of these staples were in great supply in and around St. James and St. John the Baptist Parishes from the time the Germans arrived in the early 1700s. This dish is exceptional for a patio party or backyard barbecue.

INGREDIENTS:

3 pounds red new potatoes
1/4 cup olive oil
1/4 cup sliced green onions
1/4 cup chopped parsley
1 cup Heineken beer
1/4 cup Louisiana cane syrup
1 tbsp diced garlic
1 tbsp Creole mustard
1/2 tsp sugar
1/4 cup salad oil
2 small bermuda onions, sliced
1/4 cup julienned green bell pepper
1/4 cup julienned yellow bell pepper
salt and cracked pepper to taste
Louisiana Gold Pepper Sauce to taste

METHOD:

In a one gallon stock pot, boil potatoes in lightly salted water until tender, approximately twenty to twenty-five minutes. Do not over-cook. When tender, drain, spread on cutting board and allow to cool slightly. In a saute pan, heat olive oil over medium high heat. Add green onions, parsley, beer, cane syrup and garlic. Bring to a low boil and cook for approximately two to three minutes. Place the hot ingredients in a blender or food processor fitted with a metal blade. Add mustard and sugar and blend ingredients well. While blending, pour in salad oil. Remove from blender and season to taste using salt, pepper and Louisiana Gold. When potatoes are cool enough to handle but still warm, slice one quarter inch thick. Place in a large mixing bowl and add onions and bell peppers. Coat with dressing and serve immediately.

LAGNIAPPE

It's amazing how the first priority of the 17th century colonists was to organize a good supply of fermented drinks. They soon discovered that brews could be made from pumpkins, maple sugar and persimmons. They quickly turned apples from their first orchards into a potent liquor commonly known as applejack, though sometimes referred to as "essence of lockjaw". Some historians argue that it was not the 1773 tea tax that was responsible for the fall out with Britain, but the molasses act forty years earlier that kept sugar away from the brew pots. Alchohol in various forms swept the country not only quenching thirst, but preserving food as well. In fact, by the late 1800s, there were ten German breweries in the city of New Orleans alone. No wonder beer became an important ingredient in our recipes.

Changes

Magnolia Mound
Plantation

FS222
M O-10

Magnolia Mound Plantation

"Acquired Goods"

Sitting on the banks of the Mississippi River in Baton Rouge, one can almost visualize a fleet of English vessels traveling upriver. These ships were carrying the finest of English goods destined for the Port of Baton Rouge and the planters of Louisiana. Bolts of English lace, hand painted wallpapers, exotic foods and spices and, of course, a new supply of English mochaware. These everyday serving dishes of the early colonists were hand-designed and painted in brown, blue, green and yellow. They always featured the wormtrack design, created by running one's finger up and down through the wet paint. Though quite inexpensive in its day, today it is rare and priceless. During excavations around many of the outdoor plantation kitchens, thousands of mochaware fragments were found. Often, large unbroken pieces were located such as pitchers, bowls and platters.

English Mochaware,
The Everyday Dishes of the Planters

Magnolia Mound was built in 1791 as a 1,000 acre tobacco and indigo plantation. John Joyce, a Mobile merchant, bought the plantation and upon his death in 1798, his widow married Armand Duplantier. At this time, the plantation became prominent in the production of cotton. The home is typical Louisiana Colonial/French Creole style architecture. The construction is bousillage - a mixture of mud, moss and deer hair. It is certainly one of the oldest structures in the state. Prince Charles Louis Napoleon Achille Murat, a nephew of Napoleon I, occupied the home as a guest of the Duplantiers. For many years thereafter, the home was referred to as the Prince Murat house. No records exist, however, that show Murat ever leased or purchased any piece of this property. According to local legend, Murat was a man of eccentric habits. He supposedly created delicacies from alligator, owls, rattlesnake and other oddities. He was known as a man who seldom paid his debts and eventually left Baton Rouge, marrying a grandniece of George Washington. He settled down in Florida where he became a town postmaster and wrote several books.

George Hall acquired the plantation in 1849. When Baton Rouge fell to federal troops in 1862, the Union army occupied the home and property. After the war, Helen McCullen bought the plantation and ran it successfully for many years. Today, Magnolia Mound is owned by the East Baton Rouge Parish Recreation and Parks Commission.

To reach Magnolia Mound, take I-10 to Baton Rouge. Exit Government Street to Nicholson Drive. 504-343-4955.

At left, clockwise from bottom left, Sweet Potato Pumpkin Bread (page 308), Beet Marmalade (page 150), Sliced Green Tomato and Onion Salad (page 114), and Open Hearth Grilled Fish (page 223)

SLICED GREEN TOMATO AND ONION SALAD

PREP TIME: 1 Hour
SERVES: 6
COMMENT:

Most of us have eaten fried green tomatoes and the pickled version of this unripened fruit. This marinated salad is excellent. For added eye appeal, try alternating slices of ripe red tomatoes.

INGREDIENTS FOR ORANGE CANE SYRUP VINAIGRETTE:

1/4 cup sugar cane syrup
1/2 cup vegetable oil
1/2 cup olive oil
1/3 cup red wine vinegar
2 tbsps orange juice
1/2 tsp ground allspice
1 tsp grated orange rind
1/2 tsp cracked black pepper
1/2 tsp salt
1/2 tsp dried mustard

Changes

____
____
____
____

METHOD:

Combine all ingredients in a quart jar, cover tightly and shake vigorously. Chill thoroughly and shake well before serving. Use as a marinade over sliced tomatoes or as a dressing on salad greens or fresh fruit.

INGREDIENTS FOR SALAD:

6 sliced green tomatoes
2 thinly sliced bermuda onions
1/4 cup sliced green onions
1/4 cup finely diced red bell pepper
1/4 cup finely diced yellow bell pepper
1/4 cup diced garlic

Changes

____
____
____

METHOD:

In a large mixing bowl, gently place alternating layers of green tomatoes, bermuda onions, green onions and garlic. Pour vinaigrette over the tomatoes to coat generously. Cover with clear wrap and refrigerate two to three hours before using. To serve, place the tomatoes and bermuda onions in a circular pattern around a crystal or glass serving platter. Pour the remainder of dressing over the tomatoes and garnish with red and yellow bell pepper.

MARINATED FRENCH MARKET SALAD

PREP TIME: 1 Hour
SERVES: 6-8
COMMENT:

Every home in South Louisiana, including Chretien Point Plantation, had a vegetable garden. The bayous not only supplied water for the crops but a rich soil bed for planting. The early summer produced varieties of vegetables unseen in other parts of the country. I'm sure it was this abundance that produced the French Market style salad.

INGREDIENTS:

1 cup cooked sliced carrots
1 cup cooked whole kernel corn
1 cup cooked green beans
1 cup diced cucumber
2 cups diced tomatoes
1 cup diced red bell pepper
1 cup diced yellow bell pepper
1/2 cup sliced green onions
1/2 cup diced bermuda onions
1 cup chopped celery
1 1/2 cups olive oil
1 1/2 cups salad oil
3/4 cup red wine vinegar
1 cup Parmesan cheese
1/4 cup chopped ruffled basil
1/4 cup chopped thyme
salt and cracked pepper to taste
Louisiana Gold Pepper Sauce to taste

METHOD:

The hardest thing about making this colorful and fresh salad is chopping the vegetables. You may wish to substitute high quality canned vegetables when possible, such as corn, carrots and green beans. The most important difference is the crunchy texture when using fresh vegetables as opposed to canned. In a large mixing bowl, combine all of the vegetables. Toss well to blend ingredients. In a separate bowl, add oils, vinegar, cheese, basil and thyme. Using a wire whisk, whip until all ingredients are well blended. Season to taste using salt, pepper and Louisiana Gold. Pour dressing over salad mixture. Toss to coat all ingredients well. Cover and chill at least eight hours prior to serving. This salad keeps well in the refrigerator for several days.

LAGNIAPPE

There is no sauce quite as good as homemade mayonnaise. It is much better than those commercial products sold on the grocery store shelves. In today's busy world, we tend to forget how great some of those homemade dishes really are. With that food processor sitting in the corner of your kitchen counter, it is almost as easy to make as to get from the store. When making mayonnaise, always remember, the egg and oil should be at room temperature. The oil must be poured in a steady, slow stream, otherwise the emulsion will not hold. Also, use only the best salad oil and a very mild olive oil as not to overpower the mayonnaise.

Changes

THE PERFECT SALAD WITH MILLIE'S FAMOUS DRESSING

PREP TIME: 1 Hour
SERVES: 10
COMMENT:

There is an art to providing a beautiful bowl of salad to grace a buffet table. One must take into consideration color, texture, flavor and freshness when presenting the perfect salad. Here is my idea of this feat.

INGREDIENTS:

2 cups torn spinach leaves
1 cup torn red oak leaf lettuce
1 cup torn green oak leaf lettuce
2 cups curly endive
2 cups torn romaine
2 cups torn Boston bibb lettuce
1/2 cup mixed edible flower petals (dianthus, marigolds, caladium)
1 cup diced red tomatoes
1 cup diced orange or yellow tomatoes
1 cup diced cucumbers, skin on
2 tbsps chopped purple basil
1 egg
1 tbsp Dijon mustard
1 tsp curry powder
4 tbsps raw cider vinegar
2 cups corn oil
salt and cracked pepper to taste
Louisiana Gold Pepper Sauce to taste

METHOD:

Wash salad greens under cold running water to remove any grit or sand that may exist on the leaves. Drain well in a colander, on paper towels or in a salad spinner. Instead of chopping, tear the leaves for a more attractive, homemade look. Place the greens, flower petals, tomatoes and cucumbers in a large mixing bowl, cover and refrigerate. In a separate bowl, prepare dressing by combining egg, mustard and curry powder. Using a wire whisk, whip until all ingredients are well blended. Add cider vinegar, whipping constantly until well blended. Add the corn oil in a thin steady stream, continuing to whip until a cream vinaigrette is formed. Season to taste using salt, pepper and Louisiana Gold. If a thinner dressing is preferred, you may wish to add an additional cup of vegetable or olive oil. For those who wish a sweeter taste, consider a touch of honey or the juice of one orange. To serve, toss salad greens with dressing and chopped basil immediately before service – no sooner. Transfer into a large crystal salad bowl making sure that the colored ingredients remain on top. Garnish with additional flower petals.

The Baby Stroller at Madewood

Changes

CREOLE TOMATO & WHITE BEAN SALAD

PREP TIME: 1 Hour

SERVES: 6

COMMENT:

Traditionally, white navy beans and red kidney beans are cooked every Monday in Cajun Country. It's said that this is a holdover from the time when Monday was considered wash day and a big pot of beans could be managed easily. I have to assume that our love of beans helped inspire this dish.

INGREDIENTS:

6 small Creole tomatoes
1-19 ounce can white navy beans
1/2 cup finely diced ham
1/2 cup minced bermuda onion
1/2 cup minced celery
1/4 cup minced red bell pepper
1/4 cup chopped parsley
1 tsp diced garlic
1 tsp chopped thyme
1/2 cup extra virgin olive oil
2 tbsps red wine vinegar
salt and cracked pepper to taste
Louisiana Gold Pepper Sauce to taste

METHOD:

Drain and rinse the beans well. In a large mixing bowl, combine beans, ham, onions, celery, bell pepper, parsley, garlic and thyme, blending well. Add olive oil and vinegar. Season to taste using salt, pepper and Louisiana Gold. Cover and refrigerate a minimum of six hours. Two hours prior to serving, remove beans from refrigerator and allow to reach room temperature, stirring occasionally. When ready to serve, cut the top off each tomato. Using a teaspoon, scoop out the pulp removing as many seeds as possible, and chop fine. Add chopped pulp to the bean mixture and blend thoroughly. Adjust seasonings if necessary. Lightly season the inside of the tomato using salt and cracked pepper. Carefully spoon the salad mixture evenly into the tomatoes. Serve on a nest of decorative lettuces.

Changes

SHOEPEG CORN SALAD

PREP TIME: 1 Hour
SERVES: 6
COMMENT:

I'm sure many "old timers" will fondly remember shoepeg corn. Now that we have all of these "designer" varieties, this older, white and tiny corn isn't used very often. You will still see it canned in the grocery store and in those roadside vegetable markets. When you do, pick some up and try this recipe.

INGREDIENTS:

3 cans white shoepeg corn, drained
1 cup chopped celery
1/2 cup chopped red bell pepper
1/2 cup finely sliced green onions
2 diced tomatoes
1 cup mayonnaise
1/4 cup salad oil
2 tbsps red wine vinegar
1 tsp dried mustard
1 tsp sugar
salt and cracked pepper to taste
Louisiana Gold Pepper Sauce to taste

METHOD:

In a large mixing bowl, combine mayonnaise, salad oil, vinegar, mustard and sugar. Using a wire whisk, whip until well blended. Season to taste using salt, cracked pepper and Louisiana Gold. You may wish to slightly over-season with the pepper to enhance the corn. Fold in corn, celery, bell pepper and green onions. Stir well to coat the ingredients thoroughly. Once blended, add tomatoes taking care not to break the tomatoes in the process. Cover with clear wrap and place in refrigerator a minimum of six hours prior to use. You may serve as a buffet type salad or mix with fresh spinach leaves as a starter course.

The Birdbath at Boscobel

Changes

MARINATED SAUERKRAUT SALAD

PREP TIME: 30 Minutes
SERVES: 6-8
COMMENT:

Once again, here we have the influence of those early German immigrants on Creole cuisine. Cabbage and cauliflower are often seen in salads because of this German presence, but nothing exemplifies their cooking better than a sauerkraut.

INGREDIENTS:

1-16 ounce can sauerkraut
1/2 cup white vinegar
3/4 cup sugar
1/4 cup vegetable oil
1/2 cup minced onions
1/2 cup minced celery
1/2 cup minced red bell pepper
1/2 cup minced yellow bell pepper
1 tbsp diced garlic
1/2 cup grated carrots
1 tsp caraway seeds
1 tsp celery seeds
salt and cracked pepper to taste
Louisiana Gold Pepper Sauce to taste

METHOD:

When making sauerkraut salad, it is important to drain and rinse the sauerkraut once or twice. Place sauerkraut in a large mixing bowl and set aside. In a heavy bottom black iron skillet, heat vinegar over medium high heat. Add sugar and oil and using a wire whisk, whip until all ingredients are well blended. Add onions, celery, bell peppers and garlic. Saute three to five minutes or until vegetables are wilted. Add carrots, remove from heat and blend thoroughly into the vegetable mixture. Allow the carrots to wilt then pour over the sauerkraut. Add caraway and celery seeds. Season to taste using salt, pepper and Louisiana Gold. Blend all ingredients well, cover and chill a minimum of six to eight hours, preferably overnight. Serve as a salad over mixed greens or as a topping to sausage, ham or franks.

LAGNIAPPE

Surely no one would consider cabbage a delicacy. If you agree with that statement, take a closer look at early Rome. Cabbage was in such high demand there that it was reserved only for the Roman hierarchy. It became such a popular vegetable, farmers started to give it special attention. They succeeded in growing cabbages weighing 20 pounds and produced most of the variations we see today. In their desire to preserve the vegetable and demand a higher price, experimentation began. The cabbage was thinly sliced and mixed with salt, the formula being one pound of salt for every 40 pounds of cabbage. It was packed firmly in crocks, covered with cheese cloth and weighted down with stones. Sauerkraut, a rare delicacy, was produced sixty days later.

Changes

ROASTED BEET SALAD

PREP TIME: 1 1/2 Hours
SERVES: 6
COMMENT:

Although beets are normally thought of as vegetables, here in Louisiana they are definitely a salad ingredient first. Personally, I think nothing is better than freshly boiled beets with a simple touch of oil, vinegar, salt and pepper. I would probably still feel that way had I not tasted this dish.

INGREDIENTS:

5 pounds medium beets with greens
1/2 cup extra virgin olive oil
1/4 cup balsamic vinegar
1 tbsp minced garlic
1/4 cup chopped chives
6 tbsps mayonnaise
salt and cracked pepper to taste

METHOD:

Preheat oven to 350 degrees F. Separate the beets from tops and reserve greens. Wash beets and wrap tightly in an aluminum foil pouch. Bake for approximately forty-five minutes or until tender when pierced with a fork or knife. Remove, unwrap and allow to cool. While beets are cooling, bring two quarts of lightly salted water to a rolling boil. Clean beet greens by rinsing under cold tap water to remove any sand and grit. Remove the large stem from the center of the greens and poach in boiling water. Cook until tender but not overcooked. Remove, drain and cut into fine strips. Place the greens on plates and set aside. When beets are cool, peel away outer skin which should push away quite easily. Thinly slice beets and equally distribute over the chiffonade of greens. In a mixing bowl, combine olive oil, vinegar, garlic and chives. Using a wire whisk, whip until all ingredients are well blended. Season to taste using salt and pepper. Pour dressing over the beets and greens and top with a dollop of mayonnaise. I enjoy this salad better cold than warm, so I often prepare the beets one day ahead of time.

Changes

SPINACH SALAD WITH SAUTEED PEARS

PREP TIME: 30 Minutes
SERVES: 6
COMMENT:

Obviously spinach greens were combined with other ingredients to create wonderful soups, entrees and salads in early Louisiana. The abundance of wild pears was a good reason for incorporating the fruit with spinach to create this unique salad.

INGREDIENTS:

6 cups torn fresh spinach
2 pears, cored and cubed
1/4 cup olive oil
4 slices chopped bacon
1 cup sliced onions
1/2 cup sliced red bell pepper
1/2 cup sliced yellow bell pepper
1/2 cup white wine vinegar
1/2 cup red wine vinegar
2 tbsps sugar
1 tsp grated orange peel
1 tsp chopped thyme
1/2 tsp chopped basil
salt and cracked pepper to taste
Louisiana Gold Pepper Sauce to taste

METHOD:

It is important to remember that apples and pears oxidize when exposed to air. Once peeled, the fruit will brown and tarnish unless submerged in a lemon/water solution until used. I recommend covering the diced fruit with water and adding about one fourth cup lemon juice. This will hold the fruit to its natural color until cooked. In a large saute pan, heat olive oil over medium high heat. Add bacon and stir until fat is rendered and bacon is crispy. Add onions and bell peppers. Saute three to five minutes or until vegetables are wilted. Add cubed pears and cook until tender but crunchy. It is important to maintain a firm texture with the pears. Add wine vinegars, sugar and orange peel. Bring to a low boil and reduce to simmer. Season to taste with thyme, basil, salt, pepper and Louisiana Gold. Place the spinach in a large salad bowl, pour in the contents of the saute pan and toss quickly. Serve immediately.

Changes

ROASTED GARLIC, GREEN BEAN AND PASTA SALAD

PREP TIME: 1 Hour
SERVES: 6-8
COMMENT:

Garlic is my favorite vegetable seasoning and is perfect with any dish. Though cold green bean salads have been around for many years, this version combining pasta and the flavor of roasted garlic has travelled through time. It is as unique today as it was back then.

INGREDIENTS:

4 elephant toe garlic cloves
1 pound fresh tiny green beans
1 cup cooked tiny sea shell pasta
1 red bell pepper
1 yellow bell pepper
1/2 cup olive oil
3 tbsps balsamic vinegar
2 tbsps lime juice
2 tbsps chopped fresh basil
2 tbsps toasted pecans
salt and cracked pepper to taste
Louisiana Gold Pepper Sauce to taste

METHOD:

Preheat oven to 375 degrees F. Broil bell peppers over an open gas flame or under the broiler until blackened on all sides. Place in a brown paper bag, seal tightly and let stand for ten to fifteen minutes to steam. Remove and peel or rinse under cold water until all the charred peel is removed. Seed and julienne peppers. Set aside. In a one gallon stock pot, cook beans in lightly salted water until tender but firm. When done, drain and cool under tap water to stop the cooking process. Set aside. In a heavy bottom saute pan, heat one fourth cup olive oil over medium high heat. Saute the garlic cloves until golden brown on all sides, approximately five to seven minutes. Do not scorch as garlic will become bitter. Cover skillet and place in oven until garlic cloves are tender, approximately eight to ten minutes. Remove garlic, cool, chop and set aside. If olive oil is not scorched or over-browned, you may reserve and add to the dressing mixture for added flavor. This process along with the peppers may be done one to two days ahead of time. In a large mixing bowl place remaining olive oil, vinegar, lime juice and basil. Using a wire whisk, whip until ingredients are well blended. In a separate bowl, place green beans, garlic, bell peppers, cooked pasta and toasted pecans. Season to taste using salt, pepper and Louisiana Gold. Top with the salad dressing and mix well to coat all ingredients. Serve in a large crystal salad bowl or place the green bean mixture atop a variety of colorful mixed greens.

Changes

LAFITTE'S BLACK, WHITE AND RED BEAN SALAD

PREP TIME: 2 Hours

SERVES: 6

COMMENT:

This beautiful salad is sure to stir up much conversation at the dinner table. Not only is it eye appealing, but the flavor of the beans allows you to change the dressing often. Why not try one of your own favorite dressings for a more personal touch.

INGREDIENTS:

1 cup black beans
1 cup Great Northern white beans
1 cup red kidney beans
1/4 cup chopped parsley
1 tbsp diced garlic
2 tbsps Creole mustard
2 tbsps sour cream
1 small red onion, sliced
1/4 cup diced yellow bell pepper
2 diced tomatoes
3 large radishes, diced
1/4 cup white wine
1/2 cup salad oil
1/2 cup olive oil
salt and cracked pepper to taste
Louisiana Gold Pepper Sauce to taste

Late 17th Century Mahogany Bar at Viala

METHOD:

Soak the beans in individual containers overnight in the refrigerator. Drain and rinse under cold water. Place the beans in three separate sauce pots and boil in lightly salted water until tender, but not mushy, approximately forty-five minutes. Once tender to the bite, rinse under cold water to stop the cooking process. Drain the beans again, transfer to a large bowl and set aside. In a mixing bowl, combine parsley, garlic, mustard and sour cream. Using a wire whisk, whip until all ingredients are well blended. Add wine and oils and continue to whip until all ingredients are well blended. Season to taste using salt, pepper and Louisiana Gold. When ready to serve, place beans, onion, bell pepper, tomatoes and radishes in a mixing bowl and toss with dressing. Allow to sit at room temperature one hour prior to serving. The marinated beans save well in the refrigerator for up to one week.

Changes

CARROT SALAD BON SEJOUR

PREP TIME: 1 Hour
SERVES: 6
COMMENT:

This particular version of carrot salad truly originated in St. James Parish. I've never seen it anywhere else. As a child, I remember eating it at a home in Bon Sejour Lane, next to Oak Alley Plantation.

INGREDIENTS:

12 large carrots, peeled
2 cups (150-200 count) shrimp, peeled and deveined
4 boiled eggs
1 cup mayonnaise
1/4 cup yellow mustard
1 tbsp Creole mustard
3 tbsps salad oil
1/2 cup finely diced celery
1/4 cup diced red bell pepper
1 tbsp diced garlic
1/2 cup sliced green onions
salt and cracked pepper to taste
Louisiana Gold Pepper Sauce to taste

METHOD:

Cut carrots into equal slices approximately one half inch thick. When reaching the larger end of the carrot, you may choose to cut the slice in half for more uniformity in size. In a one quart sauce pot, poach carrots in lightly salted water over medium high heat until tender but not mushy. Quickly chill under cold water to keep from overcooking. Poach shrimp likewise until they are pink and curled but again, not overcooked. Cool and set aside. Separate the egg whites from the yolks and dice whites into one quarter inch cubes. In a large mixing bowl, mash yolks with a fork. Add mayonnaise, mustards and salad oil. Blend well to incorporate yolks into mayonnaise mixture. Add celery, bell pepper, garlic and onions. Season to taste using salt, pepper and Louisiana Gold. Add the cooled carrots, shrimp and egg whites. Fold into dressing mixture and adjust seasonings if necessary. Place in a crystal salad bowl for service or serve one scoop of the salad over a crisp spinach leaf.

Changes

Chapter Five

Vegetables

Chretien Point Plantation

Chretien Point Plantation

"Spared By a Secret Sign"

On the morning of October 15, 1863, twenty thousand Union soldiers and three thousand Confederates met on the lawn of this plantation to fight the Battle of Buzzard's Prairie. The Union forces, led by General Nathaniel Banks, were victorious over the Confederates under the Command of General Thomas Green in a fight that lasted late into the afternoon. Though many plantation homes were destroyed after such battles, this home was spared because its owner walked onto the battlefield and gave the secret Masonic sign to General Banks. The general, also a Mason, witnessed the sign and spared the home.

Built on a 1776 Spanish land grant, the home is located in Sunset, Louisiana, ten miles outside of Opelousas. Stories abound in the area of the friendship between the owner, Hippolyte Chretien, and the famous pirates, Jean and Pierre Lafitte. It seems they used Chretien Point to conceal the movement of their contraband. Hippolyte's son married Felicite Neda, a dynamic strong-willed woman, and together they built the home in 1831. Though Chretien was the first Greek revival plantation home in Louisiana, its French influence makes it different from similar revival structures. Hippolyte and his son died of yellow fever shortly after the mansion was completed. Felicite, being one of Louisiana's first "liberated" women, took over operation of the plantation. She was very active in business management and farming, often smoked cigarettes and was a pro at card playing. Obviously, all of these traits were unbecoming to a lady in the 1830s.

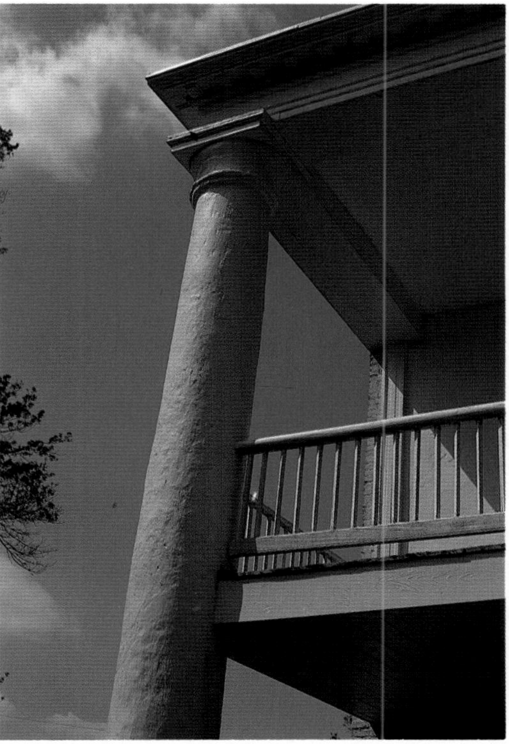

This Column was Removed from the Home by a Union Cannonball but Replaced in the Early 1900s

Felicite was well known for entertaining. Her sophisticated and well educated family often enjoyed gourmet French meals prepared in exquisite fashion. An above ground wine cellar held 460 bottles of the finest wine. It is estimated that approximately two thousand bottles of wine a year were consumed at Chretien Point.

After the war, the plantation fell into disrepair and hay was stored in the rooms where orchestras once played. The home was restored to its original magnificence by the Cornay family in the 1970s.

To reach Chretien Point, take I-49 from Lafayette toward Opelousas. Take Exit #11 at Sunset, Grand Coteau. 318-662-5876.

At left, clockwise from bottom left, Buzzard's Prairie Drop Biscuits (page 306), Strawberry Pecan Muffins (page 307), Planter's Punch (page 32), and Assorted Jellies

BAKED EGGPLANT AND OYSTER CASSEROLE

PREP TIME: 1 Hour
SERVES: 6-8
COMMENT:

One of the interesting things about vegetables in Louisiana cooking is that everyone of them could double as an entree. This vegetable casserole is a perfect example of that theory. Since it freezes well, you may wish to double the portions and freeze half as a mid-week family entree.

INGREDIENTS:

3 large eggplants, peeled and diced
1 pint fresh oysters, reserve liquid
1 pound button mushrooms
1/4 cup butter
2 tbsps olive oil
1/2 cup chopped onions
1/4 cup chopped celery
1/4 cup chopped red bell pepper
1 tbsp diced garlic
2 1/2 tbsps flour
1/2 cup sliced green onions
1/4 cup chopped parsley
1 tbsp chopped oregano
salt and cracked pepper to taste
1 1/2 cups seasoned Italian bread crumbs
6 pats butter

METHOD:

Preheat oven to 400 degrees F. In a one gallon stock pot, boil eggplant in lightly salted water for approximately twenty minutes. Drain and mash with a fork. Remove the stems from mushrooms and dice caps. Boil stems in two cups of water for approximately twenty minutes, reserving one and a half cups of mushroom stock. Discard stems. In a saute pan, melt butter over medium high heat. Saute diced mushrooms three to five minutes or until tender. Into the same saute pan add olive oil. Add onions, celery, bell pepper and garlic. Saute three to five minutes or until vegetables are wilted. Sprinkle in flour and blend well into the vegetable mixture. Add reserved mushroom liquid and liquid from oysters. Using a wire whisk, blend well into the vegetables to create a white sauce. Add mashed eggplants, oysters, green onions, parsley and oregano. Season to taste using salt and pepper. Cook five to ten minutes and pour into a buttered casserole dish. Sprinkle with bread crumbs and top with butter. Bake for thirty minutes or until bubbly.

Changes

CAJUN RATATOUILLE

PREP TIME: 1 1/2 Hours
SERVES: 6-8
COMMENT:

Ratatouille is the most famous vegetable casserole in Italy and the South of France. It is often made with a combination of vegetables and other local seasonings. Here in bayou country, we add a Cajun twist by incorporating smoked sausage into the dish.

INGREDIENTS:

1 cup diced eggplant
1 cup diced zucchini
1 cup diced yellow squash
1 cup diced tomato
1/2 cup sliced black olives
1/2 cup olive oil
1 pound sliced smoked sausage
1 cup chopped onions
1 cup chopped celery
1/4 cup chopped red bell pepper
1/4 cup chopped yellow bell pepper
1/4 cup diced garlic
2 cups tomato sauce
1/4 cup chopped thyme
1/4 cup chopped basil
1/4 cup fresh oregano
salt and cracked pepper to taste
Louisiana Gold Pepper Sauce to taste

METHOD:

Preheat oven to 375 degrees F. In a fourteen inch black iron skillet, heat olive oil over medium high heat. Saute smoked sausage until golden brown. Remove and set aside. Add onions, celery, bell peppers and garlic. Saute three to five minutes or until vegetables are wilted. Add eggplant, zucchini, squash, tomatoes, black olives and sausage. Blend well into the vegetable mixture. Saute thirty minutes, stirring occasionally to keep from scorching. Once eggplant mixture is wilted, add tomato sauce, thyme, basil and oregano. Stir into vegetable mixture. Season to taste using salt, pepper and Louisiana Gold. Continue to cook ten to fifteen minutes. Remove from heat and spoon ratatouille into an oven-proof baking dish. Bake, uncovered, for thirty minutes. Serve as a vegetable casserole or as a stuffing for chicken and game birds.

Changes

ENGLISH PEAS WITH PEARL ONIONS AND ANDOUILLE

PREP TIME: 45 Minutes
SERVES: 6-8
COMMENT:

In early writings about life at Houmas House Plantation, many references were made to the English pea casseroles. Since the Germans lived only a few miles down river, it is understandable that the smoked andouille sausage would have made its way into this pot.

INGREDIENTS:

- 2-17 ounce cans tiny English peas
- 12 pearl onions, peeled
- 1/2 cup julienned andouille
- 3 tbsps butter
- 1/4 cup finely diced celery
- 1/4 cup finely diced red bell pepper
- 1 tbsp finely diced garlic
- 2 tbsps flour
- 1 cup water
- salt and cracked pepper to taste
- sprig of fresh thyme
- pinch of nutmeg

METHOD:

Drain peas and reserve one cup of liquid for later use. In a two quart sauce pot, melt butter over medium high heat. Add celery, bell pepper and garlic. Saute three to five minutes or until vegetables are wilted. Add andouille and saute two to three minutes to give the vegetables a smoked flavor. Add pearl onions and stir into vegetable/meat mixture. Sprinkle in flour, blend well and add liquid from peas and one cup of water. Bring to a rolling boil and reduce to simmer. Add peas and season to taste using salt, pepper, thyme and nutmeg. Allow peas to cook until full flavored, approximately fifteen minutes.

LAGNIAPPE

A Frenchman remarked that America could have peas as good as those of Europe if it were not for our silly delusions. We think that bigger is better and prettier is tastier. These errors do make trouble for cooks because it is true that the best peas are the tiniest ones and the wrinkled uneven peas contain less starch and more sugar than the smooth round ones. Unfortunately for us, we Americans know peas by the large bright green ones eaten in school cafeterias or in T.V. dinners. If we could only remember those sweet green peas grown on the farm and freshly shucked, then we would treat them like the delicacy they really are.

Changes

ITALIAN STYLE OVEN-FRIED SQUASH

PREP TIME: 1 Hour
SERVES: 6-8
COMMENT:

Once the Italians arrived to work in the sugar cane fields of South Louisiana, it wasn't long before they migrated to other parts of the state. With the resettling of these immigrants, we began to see wonderful Italian style dishes present throughout all areas of Louisiana. This is one interesting Italian side dish.

INGREDIENTS:

2 large yellow summer squash
2 large green zucchini squash
4 tbsps olive oil
1 cup seasoned Italian bread crumbs
1/2 cup grated Parmesan cheese
granulated garlic to taste
salt and cracked pepper to taste

METHOD:

Preheat oven to 450 degrees F. Rinse the squash well under cold water and cut each squash into one-inch thick slices. Place in a large plastic bag, add olive oil and season to taste using garlic, salt and pepper. Close the bag tightly and shake vigorously to coat the squash evenly with oil and seasonings. In a separate brown paper bag, combine bread crumbs and cheese. Close the bag tightly and shake to blend the ingredients well. Add the squash into the bag and continue to shake until the vegetable slices are coated with the bread/cheese mixture. Oil the bottom of a shallow non-stick cookie sheet. Arrange the squash slices in a single layer on the cookie sheet. Bake twelve to fifteen minutes, without turning, until slices are lightly browned and tender, yet crisp. This dish is also a wonderful hors d'oeuvre at any cocktail party.

LAGNIAPPE

Squash was grown in the hanging gardens of Babylon and the first post-Roman cookbook featured a recipe for squash soup. This tells us just how long this vegetable has been featured on dinner tables around the world. When European explorers landed in North America, they encountered squash and referred to them as "pompoins" or "big melons". Obviously, this gave origin to the English word "pumpkin". It seems that at one time or another in our history, every type of melon, pumpkin and gourd has been known in the world of cooking as squash. Though many cooks refer to squash as a bland tasteless vegetable, they should realize that this quality allows it to adapt well to all herbs, spices and other seasoning ingredients.

Changes

CREAMED RADISHES

PREP TIME: 1 Hour
SERVES: 6-8
COMMENT:

Creamed radishes didn't have much appeal to this cook, until I had an opportunity to taste them. It seems that this dish was in great favor in the early 1800s and probably dated back to the arrival of the English at Jamestown. Don't shy away from this dish. Try it once and it may become a regular treat on your table.

INGREDIENTS:

4 cups unpeeled radishes, sliced
2 tbsps butter
1/4 cup minced onions
1/4 cup minced celery
1 tsp diced garlic
1/4 cup chopped parsley
2 tbsps flour
1/2 cup heavy whipping cream
1 cup reserved radish liquid
salt and cracked pepper to taste

METHOD:

In a two quart sauce pan, poach radishes in lightly salted water until tender, but not over-cooked. Reserve and strain one cup of the liquid. Cool the radishes under cold running water. Set aside. In a saute pan, melt butter over medium high heat. Add onions, celery, garlic and parsley. Saute three to five minutes or until vegetables are wilted. Sprinkle in the flour and blend well into the vegetable mixture. Pour in heavy whipping cream and poaching liquid to create a pink colored cream sauce. The pink comes from the radish color in the poaching liquid. Season to taste using salt and pepper. Fold the radishes into the cream sauce and cook ten minutes. Place in a serving dish as an interesting and unique vegetable accompaniment to any entree, especially game.

Changes

Melrose Plantation

Melrose Plantation

"A Promise Fulfilled"

There are many unique features that distinguish one plantation from another. In some cases, it's the location, in others, it's the architecture, while in many, it's the elaborate decor and furnishings. A very special plantation home, located six miles below Natchitoches, is known not for these aesthetic features, but rather for the person who built it. Marie Therese Coincoin was born in 1742, a slave in the household of Louis de St. Dennis, first commander of the post of Natchitoches. Upon his death, she was sold to Thomas Metoier who later freed her. She and her eleven children constructed the French Creole style home and ran the plantation successfully for many generations.

Melrose stands in a bend on the Cane River near the oldest settlement in the Louisiana Purchase. Melrose was originally called "Yucca", presumably because of the abundance of the Spanish-like plant in this area. The original residence, built in 1796, now called Yucca House, stands behind the main plantation house. Another building on the property puzzles historians and architects alike. Called "African House", it is a story and a half tall, made from brick with a mushroom-like overhanging roof. The building is similar in appearance to many West African structures. Its precise function has never been explained, but today it is used as a museum housing wall murals by the primitive artist, Clementine Hunter.

In 1884, Melrose was acquired by Joseph Henry. Mrs. Henry became affectionately known as Mrs. Cammie. She was the main force behind the preservation and restoration of this Cane River property. As an authority on Louisiana culture, she kept a grand collection of scrapbooks containing the most complete information on early Louisiana history. Many literary and artistic figures of international repute worked and lived at Melrose. Though not as pretentious as some of its counterparts, Melrose radiates the true feeling of living in a plantation atmosphere.

To reach Melrose, take I-49 North from Lafayette. Take the Highway 119 exit to the plantation. 318-379-0055.

The African House at Melrose

At left, clockwise from bottom left, Shrimp and Crab in Tomato Aspic (page 99), Creamed Red and White Onions (page 136), and Ratatouille Stuffed Chicken (page 170)

CREAMED RED AND WHITE ONION CASSEROLE

PREP TIME: 1 Hour
SERVES: 6
COMMENT:

In South Louisiana we think of onions as a seasoning ingredient only. However, in North and Central Louisiana, the English influence places onions in much higher esteem. It is in this wonderful portion of the state that this casserole was created.

INGREDIENTS:

3 large white onions, sliced
3 large bermuda onions, sliced
1/4 cup butter
1/4 cup diced celery
1/4 cup diced red bell pepper
1 tbsp diced garlic
1/2 cup diced ham
3 tbsps flour
2 cups milk
2 1/2 tbsps sugar
pinch of nutmeg
salt and cracked pepper to taste
Louisiana Gold Pepper Sauce to taste
1 cup seasoned Italian bread crumbs

METHOD:

Preheat oven to 350 degrees F. In a two gallon stock pot, boil onions in lightly salted water until tender and clear. Do not overcook. In a two quart sauce pot, melt butter over medium high heat. Add celery, bell pepper, garlic and ham. Saute three to five minutes or until vegetables are wilted. Sprinkle in flour and blend well into the vegetable mixture. Add milk, sugar and nutmeg. Continue to stir until white sauce achieves a creamy, thickened consistency. Season to taste using salt, pepper and Louisiana Gold. When onions are tender, strain liquid and place onions into white sauce. Coat well and pour into a casserole dish, pressing firmly down into the dish. Sprinkle with bread crumbs and bake twenty to thirty minutes or until casserole is bubbly and slightly browned. This vegetable casserole is excellent with ham, beef or game.

Changes

SPINACH AND ANDOUILLE SOUFFLE

PREP TIME: 1 1/2 Hours

SERVES: 6-8

COMMENT:

The word souffle will often scare the cook! However, this is one souffle recipe that can be accomplished by even the most naive. Since spinach is available all year long, fresh or frozen, there is no excuse not to attempt this recipe. Make it a part of your special occasion table.

INGREDIENTS:

3 pkgs frozen leaf spinach
1 cup minced andouille
1/4 cup butter
1/4 cup minced onions
1/4 cup minced celery
1/4 cup minced red bell pepper
1 tbsp minced garlic
salt and cracked pepper to taste
pinch of nutmeg
1 1/2 cups milk
8 eggs, beaten
1 cup bread crumbs
1 cup grated Swiss cheese

METHOD:

Preheat oven to 350 degrees F. Butter a six cup souffle mold and line the bottom with wax or parchment paper. Set aside. Thaw spinach in refrigerator overnight, drain and squeeze out all excess liquid. This is best done in a colander to make sure all liquid is removed. Place the spinach on a cutting board and using a sharp French knife, chop until almost pureed. You may wish to do this in a food processor. Do not overchop. In a large saute pan, melt butter over medium high heat. Add onions, celery, bell pepper and garlic. Saute three to five minutes or until wilted. Add andouille sausage and continue to cook an additional two to three minutes. Add spinach, blending into the vegetable mixture. Cover and cook five to ten minutes until done, stirring occasionally. Season to taste using salt, pepper and nutmeg. Remove from heat, blend in milk and add eggs slowly, stirring constantly. Once all is well blended, add bread crumbs and cheese. Continue to stir until all is well incorporated. Pour souffle mixture into buttered mold and place in baking pan with three inch lip. Pour one inch of water into pan to form a water bath around the souffle mold. Bake forty-five minutes to an hour or until a knife inserted into the souffle comes out clean. You may make the souffle and freeze it uncooked. Then cook in the same fashion but allow one and a half hours in the oven.

Changes

BAKED PUMPKIN LAFOURCHE

PREP TIME: 1 1/2 Hours
SERVES: 6-8
COMMENT:

Pumpkin is certainly more American than apple pie. One of the first vegetables given to the early colonists by the Native American Indians was pumpkin. In those days, the seeds were as important as the entire pumpkin. These seeds were the snack foods for the children. This candied pumpkin recipe is one of my favorites.

INGREDIENTS:

1 large pumpkin or cushaw
1/4 cup sugar
1/2 cup melted butter
3 large peeled apples, diced
1/2 cup Louisiana cane syrup
1/2 cup honey
cinnamon to taste
nutmeg to taste
allspice to taste
1/2 cup raisins
1/2 cup golden raisins
1 ounce sherry
marshmallows (optional)

METHOD:

Preheat oven to 375 degrees F. Using a sharp butcher knife or cleaver, cut the pumpkin into three inch cubes, peeling on. Scoop out all of the seeds and stringy pulp from the cubes. In a two gallon stock pot, place pumpkin in enough water to cover by two inches. Add sugar, bring to a rolling boil and reduce heat to simmer. Cook until pumpkin is tender to the touch. Remove from heat and strain one cup of poaching liquid. Cool pumpkin under cold running water. Using a paring knife or large spoon, scrape the softened pulp into a large mixing bowl. Once all the pulp has been removed, drain off excess water and set aside. In a heavy bottom black iron pot, melt butter over medium high heat. Add apples and saute two to three minutes. Add pumpkin, cane syrup, honey, cinnamon, nutmeg and allspice. Stir to blend all of the ingredients well. Add raisins and sherry and cook on medium high heat until mixture is heated thoroughly. Ladle a small amount of the poaching liquid as needed to keep the mixture moist. Once well blended, pour the mixture into an oven-proof casserole dish and top with marshmallows. Cover and bake twenty to thirty minutes or until slightly browned around the edges. Serve as a starch accompaniment to any entree or add three whole eggs and use as a pie or turnover filling.

Changes

BAKED CUSHAW SQUARES

PREP TIME: 1 1/2 Hours
SERVES: 6-8
COMMENT:

Cushaw, the striped crooked neck pumpkin, is commonplace along the highways of Louisiana. Though this pumpkin is normally peeled, boiled and cooked casserole-style with brown sugar for the holiday table, this simple recipe is good all year long.

INGREDIENTS:

1 medium size cushaw
2 cups sugar
1 pound butter
1/4 cup cane syrup
1 tsp allspice
pinch of cinnamon
pinch of nutmeg
1/2 cup brown sugar

The Antique Barn at Loyd Hall

METHOD:

Preheat oven to 400 degrees F. Using a very sharp butcher knife, cut cushaw in half and remove the seeds and stringy pulp. Cut each half into three inch squares, leaving the hard shell intact. In a one gallon stock pot, boil the cushaw in lightly sweetened water until tender but not mushy. Use the blade of a paring knife to test for tenderness. Once tender, remove and place the squares on a large cookie sheet or pan. Set aside. In a heavy bottom sauce pot, place one half cup of the poaching liquid along with sugar, butter and cane syrup. Bring to a low boil, stirring constantly until a bubbly syrup is achieved. Do not scorch. Add allspice, cinnamon and nutmeg. Top the cushaw pieces with the sugar mixture and sprinkle with brown sugar. Bake until thoroughly heated. When eating, scoop the sweetened meat from the shell as a snack or serve as a starch accompaniment to any entree.

Changes

BLACKEYED PEAS WITH SMOTHERED OKRA

PREP TIME: 2 Hours
SERVES: 6-8
COMMENT:

Smothered okra and tomatoes are often combined with blackeyed peas, crowder peas and purple hull peas. Normally, they are cooked separately and then combined into a casserole, as I am doing here. Please feel free to cut your cooking time by combining them into one pot, if you wish.

INGREDIENTS:

1 pound dried blackeyed peas
1 pound fresh okra, sliced or
1-10 ounce frozen package
1 pound sliced smoked sausage
1/4 cup oil
1 cup chopped onions
1/2 cup chopped celery
1/2 cup chopped green bell pepper
1 tbsp diced garlic
1-16 ounce can whole tomatoes, drained
1 cup chopped onions
1 cup chopped red bell pepper
1 tbsp diced garlic
salt and cracked black pepper to taste
Louisiana Gold Pepper Sauce to taste

METHOD:

Soak the blackeyed peas overnight in cold water in the refrigerator. Drain and rinse prior to cooking. In a one gallon sauce pot, heat oil over medium high heat. Add onions, celery, bell pepper and garlic. Saute three to five minutes or until vegetables are wilted. Add sausage and continue to saute until sausage is lightly browned. Remove approximately one fourth cup excess oil and reserve for sauteing okra. Add blackeyed peas, blending well into the vegetable mixture. Add enough cold water to cover the beans by two inches, bring to a rolling boil and reduce to simmer. Cook one and a half to two hours or until peas are tender. In a heavy bottom black iron skillet, heat reserved oil over medium high heat. Add onions, bell pepper and garlic. Saute three to five minutes or until vegetables are wilted. Add okra and tomatoes, blending well into vegetable mixture. Simmer approximately one hour, stirring occasionally to keep from scorching. Once the peas and okra are cooked, combine and season to taste using salt, pepper and Louisiana Gold. Place in a casserole dish and serve. You may wish to reheat peas by baking at 375 degrees for fifteen to twenty minutes.

Changes

STUFFED ARTICHOKES

PREP TIME: 2 Hours
SERVES: 6
COMMENT:

At one time, stuffed artichokes were the Italians' best kept secret. There are many flavor variations to this dish, especially the addition of fresh herbs such as basil, rosemary and oregano to the bread crumb mixture. This recipe, however, is a very simple rendition that is packed with flavor.

INGREDIENTS:

6 whole artichokes
6 cups seasoned Italian bread crumbs
3 cups grated Romano cheese
2 tbsps finely minced garlic
3 cups olive oil
salt and cracked pepper to taste

METHOD:

It is always best to grate fresh Romano cheese for this recipe. The pre-packaged variety looses a lot of its flavor on the shelf, so you should avoid it when preparing this dish. In a large mixing bowl, combine all dried ingredients. Stir to blend the cheese and garlic into the bread crumb mixture. Season to taste using salt and cracked pepper. Clean artichokes by clipping the tips of the leaves with sharp scissors. Cut large stems from the bottom so the artichokes will sit flat. Rinse artichokes well and press firmly down to spread open the leaves. Scrape the inside center of the artichoke down to the bottom, removing all purple leaves and pulp with a tablespoon. Once the center is open, you may begin stuffing. Place one artichoke at a time into a bowl with the mixed seasonings. Start by filling the center, then each leaf from the top down, pushing as much into the leaves as possible. Continue until all six artichokes have been stuffed with equal amounts of the breading mixture. Place the stuffed artichokes in a large roasting pan with lid. Add enough water into the pot to rise about one inch off the bottom. Slowly pour half a cup of olive oil over each artichoke to coat well. Cover, bring water to a boil and reduce to simmer. Allow artichokes to steam in olive oil/water mixture for one to one and a half hours. Be careful that artichokes do not stick and scorch during the cooking process. Test for tenderness by removing one leaf from the center and tasting for doneness. Serve one artichoke as an entree or split in half and serve as an appetizer.

Changes

VEGETABLE CHILI

PREP TIME: 2 Hours
SERVES: 10-12
COMMENT:

The Spanish influence in Northeast Louisiana is readily apparent when one visits that section of the state. The Spanish came over from Texas, across the Sabine River, and brought with them many of their wonderful flavors and techniques. This vegetable chili is one such dish.

INGREDIENTS:

1/2 pound white navy beans
1/2 pound red kidney beans
1 cup diced zucchini
1 cup diced summer squash
1/2 cup chopped broccoli
1/4 cup vegetable oil
1 cup diced onions
1/2 cup chopped celery
1/4 cup chopped green bell pepper
1/4 cup diced garlic
2 tsps chili powder
1-4 ounce can diced green chilies
1-14 ounce can peeled tomatoes, reserve juice
salt and cracked pepper to taste
Louisiana Gold Pepper Sauce to taste
sprig of fresh cilantro
1/4 cup chopped parsley

METHOD:

Combine navy and kidney beans in a colander and rinse under cold water. Place the beans in a ceramic bowl, cover with cold water and keep in refrigerator overnight. This will cut the cooking time by one third. When ready to cook, rinse the beans once again under cold water. In a heavy bottom black iron pot, heat oil over medium high heat. Add onions, celery, bell pepper and garlic. Saute three to five minutes or until vegetables are wilted. Add beans and stir well into the vegetable mixture. Sprinkle in chili powder, chilies, tomatoes and juice. Stir well to incorporate all ingredients. Add five cups of cold water and bring to a rolling boil. Reduce heat to simmer and cook approximately one and a half hours or until beans are tender. Add remaining vegetables and season to taste using salt, pepper and Louisiana Gold. Finish the flavors by adding cilantro and parsley and allow to cook until squash is tender but not mushy. Serve with hot garlic bread or cornbread sticks.

LAGNIAPPE

Today, when referring to chili many think of the red, spicy stew made with tomatoes, beans and ground beef. In reality, chili refers to all of the cone-shaped peppers coming from South and Central America and Mexico. Though none of these were known in Europe, Asia and Africa before the discovery of America, these chili peppers have found their way into pots across the globe. In Brazil and Peru, Indians began eating wild chilies over six thousand years before Christ. The Incas and Aztecs received the peppers as tribute from conquered peoples of the south. It was the Spanish however, who brought the chili peppers to North America.

Changes

BUTTERED VEGETABLE CASSEROLE

PREP TIME: 2 Hours
SERVES: 6-8
COMMENT:

In today's world, we are constantly looking for new and innovative ways to create recipes that not only taste good, but are good for us. Vegetable casseroles have been around for a long time, however, this new twist is certain to gain rave reviews.

INGREDIENTS:

2 cups chopped broccoli
2 cups chopped cauliflower
1 cup sliced carrots
1 cup sliced potatoes
1 cup sliced sweet potatoes
1 cup sliced mushrooms
1 cup sliced red onions
1/2 cup sliced green onions
1/4 pound margarine or butter
salt and cracked pepper to taste
1/4 cup diced garlic
1/4 cup chopped basil
1/4 cup chopped thyme
3/4 cup chicken stock (see recipe)

METHOD:

Preheat oven to 350 degrees F. In a three quart casserole dish, layer all ingredients beginning with potatoes and carrots on the bottom and ending with broccoli and cauliflower. Between each colored layer, place one or two small pats of butter. Season each layer with salt, pepper, garlic, thyme and basil. Continue until all layers are complete and the casserole has a multi-colored look from top to bottom. Finish with two to three pats of butter on top and pour in chicken stock. Cover and bake for one to one and a half hours or until all vegetables are tender. Serve by scooping a generous serving of all layers as a vegetable accompaniment to any entree.

Hand Painted 1859 Dresden Porcelain Doorknob and Keyhole Cover original to Nottoway

Changes

HONEY MINT GLAZED CARROTS

PREP TIME: 30 Minutes
SERVES: 6
COMMENT:

If you ever need a quick vegetable dish, this is the answer. Normally, carrots are available all year long and are very inexpensive. With a quick flavor change, an ordinary carrot dish becomes a sought after delicacy.

INGREDIENTS:

3 cups diagonally sliced carrots
3 slices cooked bacon, crumbled
3 tbsps butter
3 tbsps honey
pinch of cinnamon
pinch of nutmeg
3 tbsps freshly chopped mint
1/2 ounce brandy
sprig of mint (optional)

METHOD:

In a one quart sauce pot, poach carrots in lightly salted water six to eight minutes or until tender. Remove from heat, strain one half cup of the poaching liquid and set aside. Cool carrots under cold running water. In a heavy bottom saute pan, melt butter over medium high heat. Add honey, blending well into the butter. If mixture becomes too thick, you may add two or more tablespoons of the poaching liquid. Add bacon, cinnamon and nutmeg. Once blended, add brandy.

NOTE: *When pouring brandy into a hot pan, you may wish to remove it from any open flame, as it may flare up for ten to fifteen seconds before extinguishing itself.*

Stir well to incorporate the flavors . Stir in mint and carrots and toss gently until glazed. Continue to cook until thoroughly heated. Place in a serving bowl and garnish with a sprig of fresh mint.

Changes

Layton Castle

Layton Castle

"A Louisiana Chateau"

It's been said that every man's home is his castle. No matter how simple or elegant the structure may be, a man feels like a king in his domain. However, it's not often that one carries this emotion into the physical construction of a home. When Judge Henry Bry's daughter married Robert Layton in the late 1800s, they continued work on his beautiful Mulberry Grove Plantation. When Robert died tragically at the early age of 29, his wife, Eugenia, packed up their three children and headed off in grief to Europe. Having been inspired by the chateaus and large estates there, she returned home to Monroe to convert Mulberry Grove into the most unique mansion in North Louisiana.

The Tomb of the Builder, Judge Henry Bry, at Layton Castle

Born in 1781, Henry Bry came from Geneva, Switzerland, to the Ouachita River area in 1803 at the time of the Louisiana Purchase. He acquired this high land and built a typical raised cottage in 1814. He served as parish judge and was a member of the Louisiana House of Representatives, sitting on the first State Constitutional Convention committee. Although he never aspired to political position, his personality and intelligence often intervened and he served on numerous government boards.

On May 1, 1819, residents of his community were startled by the appearance of the first steamboat to ascend the Ouachita River. The name of the boat was the President James Monroe. Bry headed an impromptu celebration in honor of this event and unanimously convinced the people to name their village Monroe, after this historical visit. Bry was a man of many interests, but his main hobby at the plantation was silkworm production. He brought in Mulberry trees and grew them especially for the silkworms, thus the name of his home. The small building which housed these worms still stands and is thought to be the oldest structure in Ouachita Parish.

At the turn of the century, Eugenia Layton began extensive remodeling of the home. Her desire was to recreate an old world castle similar to those she had admired during her years in Switzerland. The new building stood three stories high and was accented by a round watch tower similar to those found in European castles. Today, the home is owned by Carol Layton Parsons, the great granddaughter of Judge Bry.

To reach Layton Castle, take Highway 165 North to Monroe. The Castle stands at 300 South Grand Street. 318-325-1952.

At left, clockwise from bottom left, Sautéed Celery Almandine (page 148), Tomato Braised Pork Cutlets (page 192), and Pecan Ambrosia (page 292)

SAUTÉED CELERY ALMANDINE

PREP TIME: 30 Minutes
SERVES: 6
COMMENT:

Celery, like onions, is normally considered one of the trinity of flavors here in Louisiana. In the very early days, the wild thistle replaced the celery in our cooking. Sauteed thistles with almonds or roasted pecans were often served for special occasions and holidays.

INGREDIENTS:

4 cups diagonally sliced celery, one inch long
1/2 cup butter, divided
1/4 cup diced onions
1/4 cup diced red bell pepper
1 tbsp diced garlic
1/4 cup sliced green onions
1 tsp flour
1/4 cup white wine
1/2 cup chicken stock
salt and cracked pepper to taste
1/2 cup slivered almonds or pecans

METHOD:

In a large black iron skillet, melt one fourth cup butter over medium high heat. Add onions, bell pepper, garlic and green onions. Saute three to five minutes or until vegetables are wilted. Add celery and cook ten to twelve minutes or until celery is tender. Do not overcook. Sprinkle in flour, deglaze with white wine and add chicken stock. Bring to a low boil and simmer until sauce is thickened. Season to taste using salt and cracked pepper. In a separate saute pan, melt the remaining butter over medium high heat. Add almonds or pecans and saute one to two minutes. Do not over-brown as the nuts may become bitter. Add nuts to the sauteed celery and pour into a serving dish.

Changes

ASPARAGUS WITH LEMON SAUCE

PREP TIME: 30 Minutes
SERVES: 6
COMMENT:

Asparagus has been called the aristocrat of vegetables and with just cause. Though many feel that asparagus must be peeled prior to serving, it is certainly not necessary. Asparagus cooks quickly with simple boiling or steaming but will also cook in approximately nine minutes in the microwave.

INGREDIENTS:

1 1/2 pounds fresh asparagus
salt to taste
1 tbsp butter
1 gallon hot water
1 1/2 tbsps butter
1 1/2 tbsps flour
3/4 cup milk
1/2 tsp ground ginger
1 tbsp grated lemon peel
1 tbsp lemon juice
salt and cracked pepper to taste
Louisiana Gold Pepper Sauce to taste
2 drops yellow food coloring
lemon slices for garnish

METHOD:

In a two gallon stock pot, place one tablespoon of butter, one gallon of water and salt to taste over medium high heat. While water is heating, trim asparagus to a uniform length. Discard any of the tough, brittle end pieces. Place asparagus in the boiling water and gently separate using a fork. Allow to boil uncovered for five minutes, then cover for seven to ten minutes longer, or until stalk ends are tender. While asparagus is cooking, prepare the lemon sauce. Place one and a half tablespoons of butter in a sixteen ounce measuring cup. Melt butter in the microwave for forty-five seconds. Stir in flour and cook one minute longer on high setting or until flour is bubbly. Stir in milk and ginger and cook until thickened, approximately two minutes. Blend in lemon peel and juice and season to taste using salt, pepper and Louisiana Gold. Add food coloring, blending well into the sauce. To serve, remove asparagus from boiling water and drain. Place equal amounts of asparagus on six serving plates and top with a generous amount of the lemon cream sauce.

Changes

BEET MARMALADE

PREP TIME: 1 Hour
SERVES: 6
COMMENT:

Since beets are grown as both a winter and a summer crop in Louisiana, it is obvious that there are many recipes for this versatile vegetable. This marmalade allows the beets to be used not only as a vegetable but also as a flavoring ingredient for other dishes on the table.

INGREDIENTS:

8 medium beets, julienned
1 1/2 cups reserved stock
1 1/2 tbsps sugar
1 1/2 tbsps honey
1/2 tsp salt
1 1/2 tbsps cornstarch, (dissolved in water)
cracked black pepper to taste
pinch of ginger
1/4 cup red wine vinegar

The Pigeonnaire at Magnolia Mound

METHOD:

Place beets in a one quart stock pot and cover with water by one inch. Bring to a rolling boil, reduce to simmer and cook, testing frequently, until beets are tender. Do not overcook. Strain, reserving one and a half cups of the boiling liquid. Cool beets under cold running water. Set aside. In a heavy bottom saute pan, combine stock, sugar, honey, salt and dissolved cornstarch. Bring to a rolling boil and reduce to simmer as mixture thickens. Season to taste using salt, pepper and ginger. Add red wine vinegar and fold in the beets. Continue cooking until beets resemble a marmalade or preserve, approximately fifteen to twenty minutes.

Changes

WHIPPED POTATO CLOUDS

PREP TIME: 1 Hour
SERVES: 6
COMMENT:

Great mashed potatoes are hard to make! How often have you had runny, watery potatoes or on the other hand, dried, chalky potatoes. When following this recipe, you are assured a potato that warrants its name.

INGREDIENTS:

6 large russet potatoes
8 tbsps butter
1 cup heavy whipping cream
salt and white pepper to taste
pinch of nutmeg
2 pats of butter for garnish
1/4 cup chopped parsley

METHOD:

In a one gallon stock pot, place enough salted water to cover the six potatoes by three inches. Always use a pot large enough to allow the potatoes enough room when boiling. Make sure that you salt the water liberally, being careful not to over salt. Peel the potatoes, removing any discolored spots or "eyes". Cut each potato in half lengthwise and each half in thirds. This will yield six half moons per potato. Make sure that the pieces are equal in size to guarantee even cooking. Place potatoes in boiling water and when water returns to a full boil, reduce heat to medium. Allow potatoes to boil fifteen to twenty minutes or until the tip of a knife or fork can easily pass through the potato. NOTE: Do not overboil. The result will be mushy, pasty potatoes. When cooked, drain in a colander and toss to remove all cooking liquid. In a heavy bottom saute pan, melt butter over medium high heat. Add cream, salt, pepper and nutmeg. Bring to a low simmer, stirring occasionally. Place drained potatoes in a large mixing bowl and mash with a fork or potato masher only until the major pieces are well mashed. It is acceptable to have a small lump here or there because this tells the guest that the potatoes were made from scratch and not from a box. Blend in the milk/butter mixture and adjust seasonings for taste. Serve in a warmed bowl and top with a couple pats of butter and a sprinkle of parsley.

LAGNIAPPE

With the exception of bread, the potato ranks first among the world's most important foods. Only wheat is produced in greater quantity than potatoes around the world. Its great success is due to two factors: its neutral taste allows it to accompany almost any other food and its bulky, starchy nature helps to satisfy the appetite more quickly and at less expense than any other vegetable. Chefs, cooks and food experts all agree that along with the tomato, the potato is the most useful gift that America has made to the world.

Changes

BACON AND POTATO BEIGNETS

PREP TIME: 1 1/2 Hours

SERVES: 6

COMMENT:

Beignets, the light, airy donuts of the French Market, are a perfect description for these bacon-potato croquettes. The whipping cream and eggs tend to lighten up these fritters, so you may wish to serve them with a heavier main course.

INGREDIENTS:

8 medium white potatoes, baked
2 eggs, beaten
3 tbsps whipping cream
salt and cracked pepper to taste
pinch of nutmeg
1/2 cup cheddar cheese
2 tbsps sliced green onions
2 tbsps minced parsley
4 slices bacon
1/2 cup finely diced onions
1 tsp diced garlic
1/2 cup milk
2 eggs, beaten
1/2 cup flour
3 cups seasoned Italian bread crumbs
oil for frying
1/2 cup sour cream

METHOD:

Preheat oven to 350 degrees F. Into a large mixing bowl, scrape potato pulp and discard shells. Add eggs, whipping cream, salt, pepper, nutmeg, cheese, green onions and parsley. Using a large serving spoon, mix all ingredients well into the potatoes. In a black iron skillet, fry bacon over medium high heat. Once crisp, remove and crush into potato mixture. Discard all but one tablespoon of bacon drippings from the skillet and saute onions and garlic. Once wilted, pour vegetables into potatoes. Mix all seasonings well and roll potatoes into golf ball size patties. In the same black iron skillet, heat one inch of oil to 350 degrees F. In a large mixing bowl, combine egg and milk into an eggwash. Dust beignets in flour. Dip into eggwash and then into bread crumbs. Pan fry beignets until golden brown but not too dark. Remove, drain, place on a cookie sheet and bake for six minutes. Serve hot with sour cream.

Changes

SWEET POTATO PECAN BALLS

PREP TIME: 1 1/2 Hours
SERVES: 6
COMMENT:

It amazes me how one finds methods of presenting everyday foods in very elegant ways. These sweet potato pecan balls are not only great tasting but are a wonderful addition to any buffet table.

INGREDIENTS:

5 baked sweet potatoes
2 egg yolks
1/2 tsp salt
1/2 cup brown sugar
8 tbsps melted butter
pinch of ground cloves
pinch of ground cinnamon
pinch of ground nutmeg
12 tbsps mayhaw jelly
2 cups roasted, chopped pecans

METHOD:

Preheat oven to 400 degrees F. Scoop the meat from the baked sweet potatoes, place into a mixing bowl and mash. The five potatoes should produce two full cups of mashed sweet potatoes. Add egg yolks, salt, brown sugar and melted butter. Blend well into the sweet potato mixture. Add cloves, cinnamon and nutmeg, stirring well to incorporate the flavors into the potatoes. Using a large cooking spoon, divide the mixture into six equal parts and roll each into a ball shape. Once shaped, use your thumb to press a hole down into the center of the ball. Fill this indention with one teaspoon of mayhaw jelly. Close the hole by pushing the potato over the jelly. Roll potatoes in the roasted pecans to coat evenly. Place pecan balls on a buttered cookie sheet. Bake ten to twelve minutes. Remove from oven, place on a serving plate and top each potato with an additional spoonful of the mayhaw jelly. Serve immediately.

Changes

BRAISED RED CABBAGE IN APPLE CIDER

PREP TIME: 1 Hour
SERVES: 6
COMMENT:

The braising of red cabbage with fresh fruit is very common in the German communities of Louisiana. Though often thought of as a holiday dish, I prefer this vegetable when serving any wild game entree.

INGREDIENTS:

3 pounds shredded red cabbage
1 cup apple cider
1/4 cup butter
1/2 cup diced onions
1/4 cup diced celery
1 tsp diced garlic
2 cups julienned red apples
1/2 cup chicken stock (see recipe)
1 tbsp sugar
2 bay leaves
salt and cracked pepper to taste

leRosier Restaurant & Bed and Breakfast Stands Directly Across from Shadows

METHOD:

In a heavy bottom black iron pot, melt butter over medium high heat. Add onions, celery and garlic. Saute three to five minutes or until vegetables are wilted. Add shredded cabbage and cook for thirty minutes until cabbage begins to wilt, stirring occasionally. Add apples, chicken stock, cider and sugar, blending well. Add bay leaves and continue cooking, uncovered, fifteen to twenty minutes. Season to taste using salt and pepper. Remove bay leaves and serve as an accompaniment to lamb, beef or game.

Changes

TOMATO BASIL PIE

PREP TIME: 45 minutes
SERVES: 6-8
COMMENT:

I remember one Saturday afternoon when Patti Fullilove, owner of Fullilove Herb Farm in Shreveport, Louisiana, and I spent time discussing her famous tomato and basil pie. She remarked that any Cajun addition to the pie would make it better. I never knew the origin of the dish until I found a similar version served at Magnolia Plantation in Natchitoches. It's definitely Creole.

INGREDIENTS:

4-5 medium size ripe tomatoes
1/2 cup torn basil leaves
1 cup grated Monterrey Jack
1/2 cup olive oil
1/2 cup julienned andouille sausage
1 cup crawfish tails
1/2 cup cheddar cheese
1/2 cup Parmesan cheese
1 small bermuda onion, sliced
salt and cracked pepper to taste
1 cup seasoned Italian bread crumbs
1-9 inch pre-baked pie shell

METHOD:

Preheat oven to 350 degrees F. Cut tomatoes into one quarter inch slices. Drain for approximately one hour on paper towels. You must remove the excess liquid, otherwise the pie will be soggy. Generously layer Monterrey Jack into the bottom of the pre-baked crust. Place a layer of sliced tomatoes, paint with olive oil and sprinkle with basil, andouille, crawfish, cheddar and Parmesan cheese. Season with salt and pepper. Add two to three slices of bermuda onion and continue until the pie is filled. Once the top layer has been added, sprinkle generously with a mixture of bread crumbs and Parmesan cheese. Add the remaining Monterrey Jack and basil. Bake fifteen to twenty minutes or until cheese is melted and bread crumbs are well browned. Allow pie to cool slightly before serving. You may place the finished pie in the refrigerator and serve cold or freeze for later use.

LAGNIAPPE

When the tomato was discovered in America, it was thought to be poisonous by the early botanists. However, it was not long before they came to realize its worth and began to write about it worldwide. In 1544, a naturalist writing about the plant referred to it as "a sort of egg-plant" and called it "mala aurea or golden apple". This leads us to believe that the original tomato was the yellow or golden variety grown today. Though this delicate fruit became well known worldwide, it was the Italians who quickly incorporated it into their cuisine. It is difficult to imagine Italian cooking today without the "red or golden apple"!

Changes

WHITE BEANS WITH HAM AND SALT MEAT

PREP TIME: 1 1/2 Hours
SERVES: 6
COMMENT:

White beans were referred to at one time as "poor man's meat". I guess that's why they were a staple on the battlefield of Chalmette, when the British came to claim New Orleans. You probably remember the words of the song, "We took a little bacon and we took a little beans and we met the bloody British at the town of New Orleans."

INGREDIENTS:

1 pound Great Northern navy beans
1/2 cup Crisco or bacon drippings
1 cup chopped onions
1 cup chopped celery
1/2 cup chopped bell pepper
1/4 cup diced garlic
1 cup sliced green onions
2 cups diced smoked ham
1 pound salt meat or pickled pork
1/2 cup chopped parsley
1 cup sliced green onions
salt and cracked pepper to taste
Louisiana Gold Pepper Sauce to taste

METHOD:

The cooking time of the beans will be cut about one third if the beans are soaked overnight in cold water. This will help soften the outer shell and naturally the cooking time will be shortened. In a four quart sauce pot, melt Crisco or bacon drippings over medium high heat. Add onions, celery, bell peppers, garlic, green onions and smoked ham. Saute approximately five to ten minutes or until vegetables are wilted. Add salt meat and beans. Blend well with vegetables and cook two to three minutes. Add enough cold water to cover beans by approximately one to two inches. Bring to a rolling boil and allow to cook thirty minutes, stirring occasionally to avoid scorching. Reduce heat to simmer and cook approximately one hour or until beans are tender. Stir from time to time, as beans will settle to the bottom of the pot as they cook. Add chopped parsley and additional green onions. Season to taste using salt, pepper and Louisiana Gold. Using a metal spoon, mash approximately one third of the beans against the side of the pot to create a creaming effect. Once beans are tender and creamy, they are ready to be served. In order for the maximum flavor to develop, this dish should be cooked one day before it is to be served. Serve over steamed white rice.

Changes

Chapter Six

Poultry

The Myrtles Plantation

The Myrtles Plantation

"Ghostly Apparitions"

Grapevine Pattern Wrought Iron Railing at The Myrtles

One of the great things about living in Louisiana is being able to walk out onto those great plantation verandas. Here, you can sit in a rocking chair, enjoy a slice of freshly baked cake and take in the scenery of this great state. It was on one such day back in 1834 that Mrs. Clark Woodruff, owner of the Myrtles, sat on her veranda with her two daughters, Sarah and Matilda. They were enjoying the scenery and eating a slice of pound cake. The only difference was that their dessert was laced with oleander poisoning. Within two days, the family was dead. The crime was blamed on a slave girl who had poisoned the Woodruffs because of a reprimand a few days earlier. Often, visitors at the Myrtles claim they hear the girls playing and see them frolicking under the oaks.

The Myrtles takes its name from the grove of crepe myrtle trees surrounding the property. The original 650 acre land grant was awarded to General David Bradford, a veteran of the 1794 Whiskey Rebellion. According to legend, Bradford cleared an ancient Indian burial ground to build his magnificent home. Because of this desecration, Bradford and his home were cursed. Those unfortunate souls who met their untimely deaths at the plantation were destined to remain there and roam the grounds forever. The story and a half wooden home with its wide gallery is embellished by a New Orleans style cast iron banister. Details inside the home are exquisite. From elaborate ceiling medallions to friezes and fretwork, which decorate all of the rooms, the decor is second to none. The mantles are made of Carrara marble and the doorknobs are mercury enclosed in glass, designed never to need polishing. Surprisingly, some of the rooms contain closets, an unusual extravagant feature in early plantations. The ladies' and gentlemen's parlors, located on the main floor, are a mirrored reflection of each other. The dining and gaming rooms are also located on this downstairs floor.

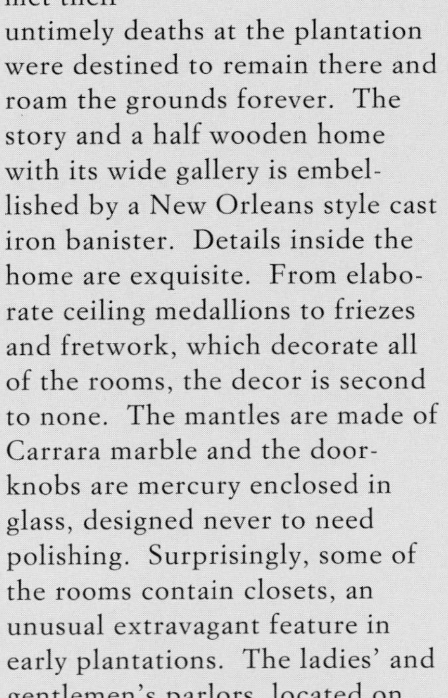

The home was purchased in 1992 by John and Teeta Moss. It is open daily as a bed and breakfast and a full-service restaurant is located on the property. One might try securing reservations for one of the ever popular ghost tours offered Friday and Saturday nights, beginning at 9:30 pm. There is also a special event held on Halloween night each year.

To reach The Myrtles, take Highway 61 North from Baton Rouge to St. Francisville. 504-635-6277.

At left, Oven Roasted Guinea Hen with Mixed Vegetables (page 160) and Cane River Pound Cake (page 280)

OVEN ROASTED GUINEA HEN WITH MIXED VEGETABLES

PREP TIME: 1 1/2 Hours
SERVES: 6-8
COMMENT:

It is hard to believe that a bird once referred to as "Hen of the Pharaohs" was also quite common on the Louisiana plantations. I find guineas to be tender, delicate and full-flavored. They taste somewhat like a cross between chicken and pheasant. Don't wait for a special occasion to try this recipe. Why not Sunday?

INGREDIENTS:

2-2 1/2 pound guinea hens
1 orange, halved
2 onions, quartered
2 celery stalks, quartered
2 carrots, sliced
10 cloves of garlic
6 sprigs of thyme
8 sage leaves
6 new potatoes
3 sliced carrots
6 tiny beets, unpeeled
1/2 cup melted butter
1/2 cup Madeira wine
salt and pepper to taste
Louisiana Gold Pepper Sauce to taste

METHOD:

Preheat oven to 375 degrees F. Wash birds well inside and out. Squeeze one half orange into the center cavity of each bird. Season cavity generously with salt, pepper and Louisiana Gold. Stuff each bird with equal parts of onion, celery, carrots, garlic and thyme. Place birds, breast side up, in a roasting pan and continue to season. Place four sage leaves under the breast skin of each bird and remaining vegetables in the bottom of the roaster. Top hens with melted butter and Madeira wine. Cover tightly and roast for one hour. Remove cover and allow to brown for approximately thirty minutes. Birds should set thirty minutes before carving. Prior to serving, peel beets and arrange around the base of a serving platter. Carve hens and serve with hot pan drippings.

LAGNIAPPE

Farmers in many ways have succeeded in taking the natural flavor out of chickens and turkeys through methods of raising and processing. However, they have not been able to duplicate this negative venture with the guineas. This is perhaps because the guinea lives on farms and has not resigned itself to domestication. The guinea hasn't lost the dark flesh of most game birds and is frequently compared to pheasant. Even on the farm, they like to roost on the top branches of trees. They will only descend when grain is offered, however, they can get along without it. Though the guinea fowl originated in Africa, and made its way to America in the late 1700s, today it outsells chicken in France.

Changes

CANE SYRUP GLAZED CORNISH HEN

PREP TIME: 1 1/2 Hours
SERVES: 6
COMMENT:

It was in the late 1700s that sugar was first crystallized on a Louisiana Plantation. Prior to that time, honey and syrup were used not only as sweeteners but also as glazes in cooking. This recipe is a great example of that technique.

INGREDIENTS:

6 cornish game hens
3 small onions, quartered
3 celery stalks, quartered
12 cloves of garlic
1/2 cup cane syrup
1/4 cup orange juice
1/4 cup butter
1/4 cup chopped thyme
1/4 cup chopped sage
2 oranges, sectioned
salt and cracked pepper to taste
Louisiana Gold Pepper Sauce to taste
paprika for color
1/2 cup white wine
2 cups chicken stock (see recipe)

METHOD:

Preheat oven to 375 degrees F. Wash birds well and season inside cavity generously with salt, pepper and Louisiana Gold. Stuff each cavity with onion, celery and garlic. Place birds, breast side up, in a roasting pan and continue to season. In a mixing bowl, combine syrup, orange juice, butter, thyme and sage. Brush birds lightly with glaze and sprinkle with paprika to ensure even browning. Surround the birds with remaining vegetable seasonings and orange sections. Cover tightly and roast for forty-five minutes. Uncover and allow birds to brown evenly. Continue to glaze with cane syrup mixture during the browning process. Once cooked, remove birds and deglaze baking pan with white wine. Add chicken stock and reduce over medium high heat for a wonderful sauce accompaniment.

Changes

BAKED CHICKEN WITH HERBED BUTTER

PREP TIME: 2 Hours
SERVES: 6
COMMENT:

In the plantation days, the most popular method of cooking chicken was stewing. For special occasions and holidays, baking or French roasting was preferred. With an herb garden planted next to the kitchen, I can imagine how flavorful this table centerpiece must have been.

INGREDIENTS:

2-3 pound broilers
1/4 pound butter
1/4 cup chopped basil
1/4 cup chopped thyme
1/4 cup chopped sage
1 tbsp chopped tarragon
1 tbsp chopped garlic
salt to taste
1 tbsp cracked black pepper
Louisiana Gold Pepper Sauce to taste
1 head of garlic, split
4 bay leaves

METHOD:

Preheat oven to 375 degrees F. Soften butter at room temperature and place in a large mixing bowl. Add all remaining ingredients except chicken, garlic and bay leaves. Using a wire whisk, whip until all ingredients are well blended. Season inside cavity of chickens generously with salt and pepper. Place chickens in a roasting pan and, using your fingertips, separate the skin from the breast. Rub a small amount of the herbed butter between the breast and skin. Continue this seasoning process completely until chickens are well coated and all butter has been used. Place half of the garlic and two bay leaves in the cavity of each chicken. Tie legs to keep them in place during the cooking process. Season with additional salt and pepper, if desired. Bake, uncovered, one to one and a half hours, basting occasionally with the pan drippings. When done, remove to a serving platter and sprinkle with fresh herbs. Serve over dirty rice (see recipe).

A Vase of Flowers at Magnolia

Changes

CASSEROLE OF BAKED CHICKEN & OYSTERS

PREP TIME: 1 1/2 Hours
SERVES: 6
COMMENT:

Oyster dishes were found everywhere in bayou country. From the delicate oyster stew made with cream to the hearty roux-based oyster soup, many wonderful creations used oysters as a main ingredient. Here, we incorporate gulf oysters with a young chicken to create a definite masterpiece.

INGREDIENTS:

1-3 pound fryer
2 pints oysters, reserve liquor
1/2 cup butter
1/2 cup chopped onions
1/2 cup chopped celery
1/4 cup chopped red bell pepper
1 tbsp diced garlic
1/2 cup flour
1 quart chicken stock (see recipe)
1 cup heavy whipping cream
salt and cracked pepper to taste
Louisiana Gold Pepper Sauce to taste
pinch of thyme
pinch of basil
1 cup grated Parmesan cheese
1/4 cup chopped parsley
paprika for garnish

METHOD:

Preheat oven to 350 degrees F. Cut chicken into eight serving pieces. Season to taste using salt, pepper and Louisiana Gold. In a ten inch saute pan, melt butter over medium high heat. Brown chicken lightly on all sides, remove and place in an oven-proof baking dish. Set aside. In the same saute pan, add onions, celery, bell pepper and garlic. Saute three to five minutes or until vegetables are wilted. Sprinkle in flour and using a wire whisk, stir until blonde roux is achieved (see roux techniques). Add oyster liquor and stock, one ladle at a time, until all is incorporated. Blend ingredients until sauce like consistency is achieved. Add cream and one pint of oysters. Bring to a rolling boil and reduce to simmer. Season to taste using salt, pepper, thyme, basil, and Louisiana Gold. Place remaining oysters in casserole dish, pour in oyster sauce and top with cheese. Garnish with parsley and paprika. Bake, covered, until chicken is tender, approximately thirty to forty-five minutes. Remove cover and brown slightly.

Changes

CAPTAIN JIM'S STEAMBOAT CHICKEN

PREP TIME: 1 1/2 Hours
SERVES: 6
COMMENT:

Legend has it that a riverboat captain ate this dish in the Far East and brought it back to the Marmillion family at San Francisco. This is just another example of how Creole cuisine developed.

INGREDIENTS:

1-4 pound broiler
1 cup seasoned flour
1/2 cup vegetable oil
2 cups chopped onions
1 cup chopped green bell pepper
1 tbsp diced garlic
1-32 ounce can stewed tomatoes
1/2 cup chicken stock (see recipe)
1 tsp curry powder
1 tbsp chopped thyme
2 tbsps chopped parsley
1/4 cup sliced green onions
1/2 cup currants
salt and cracked pepper to taste
Louisiana Gold Pepper Sauce to taste
12 whole roasted pecans
4 cups cooked white rice

METHOD:

Preheat oven to 375 degrees F. Using a sharp boning knife, debone chicken and cube into one inch pieces. Season lightly with salt, pepper and Louisiana Gold. Dust in flour, shaking off all excess and set aside. In a heavy bottom dutch oven, heat oil over medium high heat. Saute chicken until golden brown on both sides, approximately ten to twelve minutes. Remove and keep warm. Add onions, bell pepper and garlic. Saute three to five minutes or until vegetables are wilted. Pour in tomatoes and chicken stock. Bring to a rolling boil, reduce to simmer and cook for fifteen minutes, stirring occasionally. Add curry, thyme, parsley and green onions. Continue to cook an additional fifteen minutes. Season to taste using currants, salt, pepper and Louisiana Gold and cook an additional five minutes. Place chicken in an oven-proof casserole dish and top with sauce. Cover and bake for forty-five minutes. Remove, garnish with roasted pecans and serve over rice.

Changes

CASSEROLE OF CHICKEN & EGGPLANT

PREP TIME: 1 1/2 Hours
SERVES: 6
COMMENT:

The Italians arrived in South Louisiana in the late 1800s seeking work on the sugar plantations. They not only proved to be skilled laborers, but they also brought wonderful cooking techniques to bayou country. This interesting casserole was created near Opelousas, Louisiana.

INGREDIENTS:

6 chicken breasts, deboned
2 eggs, beaten
1 cup seasoned Italian bread crumbs
1/2 cup olive oil
1 medium size eggplant
1 cup chopped onions
1/2 cup chopped celery
1/2 cup chopped bell pepper
2 tbsps diced garlic
1/2 cup sliced green olives
2-16 ounce cans stewed tomatoes
1 tsp sugar
1 tsp sweet marjoram
1 tsp chopped thyme
1 tbsp chopped basil
1 tsp chopped oregano
salt and cracked pepper to taste
1/2 cup sliced green onions
1/4 cup chopped parsley
1/4 cup grated Parmesan cheese
1 cup shredded Mozzarella cheese

METHOD:

Preheat oven to 375 degrees F. Cut eggplant into six equal slices. Set aside. Remove skin from breasts and pound lightly. Season to taste using salt and pepper. Dip chicken breasts in egg and coat in bread crumbs. Place on a baking sheet, cover and chill in the refrigerator ten to fifteen minutes. In a heavy bottom dutch oven, heat oil over medium high heat. Saute breasts three to five minutes on each side. Remove and place in oven-proof casserole dish. Saute eggplant until golden brown on both sides. Remove, drain and place one slice on top of each chicken breast. In the same oil, add onions, celery, bell pepper, garlic and olives. Saute three to five minutes or until vegetables are wilted. Add tomatoes, sugar, marjoram, thyme, basil and oregano. Blend ingredients well, bring to a rolling boil and reduce to simmer. Season to taste using salt and pepper. Allow sauce to cook approximately thirty minutes. Add green onions and parsley and adjust seasonings if necessary. Spoon the sauce over chicken breasts and top evenly with cheeses. Bake fifteen to twenty minutes or until Mozzarella melts and sauce is bubbly. You may wish to serve over hot pasta.

Changes

BREAST OF CHICKEN VIALA

PREP TIME: 1 Hour
SERVES: 6
COMMENT:

The Viala Plantation, home of Lafitte's Landing Restaurant today, was originally a working indigo plantation. The Vialas were Spanish and created this tasty chicken entree.

INGREDIENTS:

6 chicken breast quarters
3/4 cup seasoned Italian bread crumbs
1/2 cup grated Parmesan cheese
2 tbsps chopped sage
1 tsp chopped thyme
1 tsp chopped rosemary
1/2 cup milk
1/4 pound butter
1 tbsp chopped garlic
juice of one lemon
paprika for color
salt and cracked pepper to taste
Louisiana Gold Pepper Sauce to taste

METHOD:

Preheat oven to 350 degrees F. In a large mixing bowl, combine bread crumbs, cheese, sage, thyme and rosemary. Season to taste using salt and pepper. Dip each breast quarter in milk and coat generously with bread crumb mixture. Arrange breasts on greased baking sheet. Set aside. In a large measuring cup, combine butter, garlic, lemon juice and Louisiana Gold. Melt in microwave for one minute, blend thoroughly and drizzle garlic butter over breasts. Coat with paprika and bake, uncovered, until chicken is golden brown, approximately forty-five minutes. Any leftover chicken is wonderful in the Chunky Chicken Plantation Style Salad (see recipe).

Changes

MARGARET SHAFFER'S CHICKEN PIE

PREP TIME: 2 Hours
SERVES: 8
COMMENT:

Entree type pies were prevalent in all cultures in Louisiana. The English had their shepherd's pies and the Cajuns had their meat pies. This cooking technique enabled the plantation kitchen to make use of leftovers while creating hearty, flavorful dishes.

INGREDIENTS:

2-3 pound broilers
1 large onion, quartered
2 celery stalks, chopped
6 cloves of garlic
1 bay leaf
sprig of thyme
10 black peppercorns
3/4 cup butter
1 cup chopped onions
1 cup chopped celery
1/2 cup chopped red bell pepper
1/4 cup diced garlic
3/4 cup flour
1 1/2 quarts reserved stock
1 tbsp chopped thyme
1 tbsp chopped basil
1 tsp chopped sage
1/2 cup diced carrots
1 cup frozen peas
salt and cracked pepper to taste
Louisiana Gold Pepper Sauce to taste
4-9 inch prepared pie crusts

METHOD:

Preheat oven to 400 degrees F. Cut chicken into quarters and place in a two gallon stock pot over medium high heat. Add onions, celery, garlic, bay leaf, thyme and peppercorns. Cover chicken with lightly salted water by one inch. Bring to a rolling boil, reduce to simmer and allow to cook until chicken is tender, approximately forty-five minutes. Remove chicken, debone and return bones to stock pot. Continue to simmer stock for fifteen minutes, strain and reserve six cups. Cube chicken and set aside. In a heavy bottom dutch oven, melt butter over medium high heat. Add onions, celery, bell pepper and garlic. Saute three to five minutes or until vegetables are wilted. Sprinkle in flour and using a wire whisk, stir constantly until blonde roux is achieved (see roux techniques). Add stock, one ladle at a time, until all is incorporated. Add thyme, basil, sage, carrots and peas. Blend well and season to taste using salt, pepper and Louisiana Gold. Allow sauce to simmer approximately thirty minutes. Remove and allow to cool slightly. Add chicken meat to sauce, blending well. Place pie crusts in two nine inch pie pans. Bake five to ten minutes or until lightly browned. Remove from oven and fill with chicken mixture. Cover each pie with remaining pastry, seal edges of pie and pierce with fork to allow steam to vent during cooking. Bake until golden brown, approximately twenty minutes. Any remaining chicken and gravy should be heated and served in a casserole dish along with the pie.

Changes

CHICKEN & BROCCOLI CASSEROLE

PREP TIME: 1 1/2 Hours
SERVES: 6
COMMENT:

In 1835, Martha Turnbull noted that chickens, turkeys and ducks were served at Rosedown's grand opening. Knowing that this English plantation featured a fabulous vegetable garden, I'm sure this chicken casserole was part of the day's menu.

INGREDIENTS:

3 whole chicken breasts
2 cups cooked broccoli florets
1 cubed carrot
1 cubed onion
2 cloves garlic
1/4 cup butter
1/2 cup chopped onions
1/4 cup chopped celery
1/4 cup chopped red bell pepper
1 tbsp diced garlic
1/4 cup flour
1 cup reserved chicken stock
1 cup milk
1/2 tsp grated lemon peel
pinch of nutmeg
salt and cracked pepper to taste
Louisiana Gold Pepper Sauce to taste
1 cup sour cream
1/2 cup grated Parmesan cheese
paprika for color

1770 Chippendale Style Birdcage at Rosedown

METHOD:

Preheat oven to 350 degrees F. Place chicken, carrots, onion and garlic in a stock pot over medium high heat. Cover chicken with lightly salted water by one inch. Bring to a rolling boil, reduce to simmer and cook until chicken is tender, approximately twenty minutes. Remove chicken, cool and reserve one cup of stock. Debone chicken, cube meat and set aside. In a heavy bottom dutch oven, melt butter over medium high heat. Add onions, celery, bell pepper and garlic. Saute three to five minutes or until vegetables are wilted. Sprinkle in flour and using a wire whisk, stir constantly until blonde roux is achieved (see roux techniques). Add chicken stock and milk. Continue to stir, blending well into the vegetable mixture. Add lemon peel and nutmeg. Season to taste using salt, pepper and Louisiana Gold. Remove from heat and allow to cool slightly. Fold in sour cream and adjust seasonings if necessary. In a two quart casserole dish, layer chicken, broccoli and sauce. Top with Parmesan cheese and paprika. Bake, uncovered, twenty-five to thirty minutes or until cheese is golden brown.

Changes

DANIEL TURNBULL'S STUFFED TURKEY

PREP TIME: 4 Hours
SERVES: 8-10
COMMENT:

Today, it's easy to cook a good turkey. The quality of the birds is great and they are available all year long. When Daniel and Martha built Rosedown, it was a different story. Only wild birds were available and they had to be prepared properly, if they were going to be good. Daniel certainly knew how to do it.

INGREDIENTS:

1 10-12 pound turkey with giblets
1 pound bulk pork sausage
1/4 cup butter
1/2 cup chopped onions
1/2 cup chopped celery
1/2 cup chopped red bell pepper
1/2 cup chopped yellow bell pepper
2 tbsps garlic
1/4 cup sliced green onions
2 apples, cubed
1 cup chopped pecans
6 slices bread, crumbled
1 tbsp chopped thyme
2 tbsps chopped sage
salt and cracked pepper to taste
Louisiana Gold Pepper Sauce to taste
granulated garlic to taste
paprika for color
4 apples, quartered
3 celery stalks, quartered
3 carrots, quartered
2 onions, quartered

METHOD:

Preheat oven to 375 degrees F. Wash bird thoroughly, drain and reserve giblets. Set aside. In a heavy bottom dutch oven, melt butter over medium high heat. Add onions, celery, bell peppers, garlic and green onions. Saute three to five minutes or until vegetables are wilted. Add sausage, chop into vegetable mixture and cook until golden brown, approximately twenty minutes. Drain all excess fat from sausage mixture and add cubed apples and pecans. Season to taste using salt, pepper and Louisiana Gold. Remove from heat, add bread and blend thoroughly into stuffing mixture. Add thyme and sage, stir well and allow to cool slightly. Stuff bird and truss close the cavity. Season thoroughly using salt, pepper, Louisiana Gold and granulated garlic and top with paprika for even browning. Place turkey in a large roasting pan and surround with remaining ingredients. Cover tightly with foil and bake two and a half hours. Check for doneness, remove foil and brown for thirty minutes. Remove and allow bird to sit thirty minutes prior to slicing. Any additional stuffing may be served as an accompaniment to the turkey.

Changes

LAGNIAPPE

Benjamin Franklin stated that the turkey is a true and original bird of America. He went on to say, "I wish the eagle had not been served as the representative of our country. The turkey is a much more respectable bird and is a true native of our shores." Franklin was right and though turkey was consumed throughout the Americas as far back as recorded history, it was Thanksgiving that made it famous. The birds were so heavily consumed by the Pilgrims and the Indians that by 1708 some counties in New York declared closed season on the turkey, thus beginning the farm-raised turkey industry in America.

RATATOUILLE STUFFED CHICKEN

PREP TIME: 1 Hour
SERVES: 6
COMMENT:

The use of multiple vegetables in casseroles and stuffings was prevalent throughout the English, Spanish and German sections of North Louisiana. Large gardens guaranteed an ample supply of the needed ingredients for casseroles, soups and stuffings. This vegetable stuffing was often used in the kitchens of Creole Louisiana.

INGREDIENTS:

6 large deboned chicken breasts, skin-on
1/4 cup butter
1/4 cup chopped onions
1/4 cup chopped celery
2 tbsps chopped red bell pepper
2 tbsps chopped yellow bell pepper
1 tsp diced garlic
1/4 cup diced tomatoes
1/4 cup chopped black olives
1/2 cup diced yellow squash
1/2 cup diced zucchini
1 cup diced eggplant
pinch of thyme
pinch of basil
1 cup seasoned Italian bread crumbs
1-8 ounce can cream of celery soup
1/2 cup water
salt and pepper to taste
Louisiana Gold Pepper Sauce to taste
1/4 cup sliced green onions
1/4 cup chopped parsley

METHOD:

Preheat oven to 375 degrees F. In a large saute pan, melt butter over medium high heat. Add onions, celery, bell peppers and garlic. Saute three to five minutes or until vegetables are wilted. Add tomatoes, black olives, squash, zucchini and eggplant. Continue to saute until vegetables are cooked but not mushy. Season to taste using thyme, basil, salt, pepper and Louisiana Gold. Sprinkle in bread crumbs and stir well into the vegetable mixture. Remove from heat and allow to cool. Once the mixture is cool, divide into six equal portions. Season chicken thoroughly using salt and pepper. Stuff ratatouille beneath the skin of each chicken breast and cover tightly with the skin. Combine soup and water in a mixing bowl and blend thoroughly. Pour over the chicken and sprinkle with green onions and parsley. Adjust seasonings with salt and pepper if necessary. Cover and bake for thirty minutes. Remove cover and allow chicken to brown slightly for an additional fifteen minutes.

Changes

Blythewood Plantation

Blythewood Plantation

"A New York Influence"

Just the fact that the New York architects, Drake and Anderson, were called upon to design this plantation in Southeast Louisiana indicates that this mansion is a little different. Designed for Daniel Hardy Sanders in 1885, this colonial revival home is not quite victorian but certainly not your usual Greek revival. There is no plaster, no Louisiana cypress and no red clay brick. Instead, this twelve thousand square foot home was constructed totally out of beautiful heart pine which was grown, milled and cured on the property.

The original Blythewood was built by Reliegh Self on a three thousand acre Spanish land grant prior to the Civil War. The home was totally burned and it was Daniel's dream to rebuild. The famous New York architects were also responsible for many other fine homes and buildings in this area. The well known contractor, James Dalstrum, of New Orleans was called in to oversee the building project. It took about three years to complete the eighteen room restoration with much detail and care given to the beaded ceilings and intricate wainscotting. Unlike most Louisiana plantations, this home had closets in every room and fireplaces and mantles galore. The double staircase in the central hallway is one of the most unique in plantation architecture.

Late 1800s Gilded, Black Marble Victorian Mantle Clock (above)
German Woodcarved Lamp Base (left)

When approaching Blythewood, visitors encounter an elaborate white fence surrounding the home. Walkways lead from the street to the steps and are made of historic Amite brick, gouged thin by the footsteps of time. Today, Blythewood is not only open for tours but is also available to overnight guests seeking bed and breakfast in a plantation atmosphere. Guests may also arrange to dine by candlelight in Blythewood's magnificent dining room.

To reach the plantation, take I-55 to the Amite Exit. Travel Highway 16 to Duncan Street and then on to 300 Elm Street in Amite. 504-345-6419.

At left, clockwise from bottom left, Strawberry Shortcake (page 279), Rosemary Stuffed Leg of Pork (page 191), and Blackeyed Peas with Smothered Okra (page 140)

STRAWBERRY COQ AU VIN

PREP TIME: 1 1/2 Hours
SERVES: 6-8
COMMENT:

This classical chicken stew is always made with a large baking hen or rooster. The increased cooking time ensures much better flavor because of the marriage of meat, vegetables and wine. Should you choose to use a spring chicken, be careful of the cooking time. The bird tends to fall apart, and the full flavor does not quite develop.

INGREDIENTS:

1 large baking hen
1 cup whole strawberries
1/2 cup bacon fat
1/2 cup flour
1 cup chopped onions
1 cup chopped celery
1/4 cup diced garlic
1 cup pearl onions
1 cup strawberry or rose wine
2 cups chicken stock (see recipe)
20 button mushrooms
1 cup fresh green peas
1 tsp chopped thyme
1 tsp chopped oregano
1 bay leaf
salt and cracked pepper to taste
Louisiana Gold Pepper Sauce to taste

LAGNIAPPE

Chicken is singularly the most versatile meat in the world. It can be broiled, roasted, baked, steamed, fried, boiled, fricasseed and barbecued. It may be made into a soup or a stew such as the sought after Coq Au Vin. This "chicken in wine" dish originated in France and has many variations from region to region. In Alsace, it is finished with cream and eggs but in Provence, black olives are added. In Normandy, cider replaces the wine while in Strasbourg, beer is used in the dish. In Burgundy, where the dish was created, it is still made with red burgundy, mushrooms and pearl onions.

METHOD:

Cut hen into eight serving pieces. In a heavy bottom dutch oven, heat bacon fat over medium high heat. Season chicken with salt, pepper and Louisiana Gold. Dust in flour, shaking off all excess. Brown on both sides, remove and set aside. Add onions, celery, garlic and pearl onions. Saute three to five minutes or until vegetables are wilted. Return chicken to pot and add strawberry wine and chicken stock. Bring to a rolling boil and reduce to simmer. Add strawberries, mushrooms, peas, thyme, oregano and bay leaf and adjust seasonings if necessary. Cover and braise for one hour and check for tenderness. You may need to skim any fats that rise to the surface during the cooking process. When done, serve with a generous portion of the strawberry sauce.

Changes

CRABMEAT STUFFED BREAST OF CHICKEN WITH ARTICHOKE SAUCE

PREP TIME: 1 1/2 Hours
SERVES: 6
COMMENT:

Crabs have always been a major ingredient in Louisiana cuisine. From the crab boil to the corn and crab bisque, they go from one end of the spectrum to the other. Here, the crab is formed into a stuffing and used to enhance an otherwise simple dish.

INGREDIENTS:

6 chicken breasts, deboned, skin-on
1 pound lump crabmeat
1/4 cup butter
1/4 cup diced onions
1/4 cup diced celery
1/4 cup diced red bell pepper
1 tbsp chopped garlic
1 ounce white wine
2 eggs
1/2 cup seasoned Italian bread crumbs
salt and cracked pepper to taste
dash of Louisiana Gold Pepper Sauce
1/4 cup melted butter
1-15 ounce can artichoke hearts
1/4 cup sliced green onions
1 tbsp chopped parsley
3 tbsps flour
3 cups chicken stock
1 cup heavy whipping cream

METHOD:

Preheat oven to 375 degrees F. In a heavy bottom saute pan, melt butter over medium high heat. Add onions, celery, bell pepper and garlic. Saute three to five minutes or until vegetables are wilted. Add crabmeat and deglaze with white wine. Season to taste using salt, pepper and Louisiana Gold. Remove from heat and allow to cool slightly. In a small mixing bowl, whip eggs and add to crabmeat stuffing while stirring constantly. Sprinkle in bread crumbs to absorb any liquid and adjust seasonings if necessary. Divide stuffing into six equal portions and season the chicken breasts well on all sides using salt and pepper. Lift the skin from the center of the breast, keeping the ends intact, and place the stuffing between the meat and skin to form a mound. Once all six breasts are stuffed, place in an 8" x 11" baking dish and set aside. In a heavy bottom sauce pot, heat remaining butter over medium high heat. Cut artichokes in half and saute in butter three to five minutes. Add green onions and parsley and sprinkle in flour, stirring into vegetable mixture. Slowly pour in the chicken stock and heavy whipping cream, bring to a rolling boil and reduce to simmer. Season the sauce with salt, pepper and a dash of Louisiana Gold. Once the sauce is thickened slightly, pour over the chicken breasts and bake, uncovered, approximately one hour.

Changes

CHICKEN & OKRA STEW

PREP TIME: 1 Hour
SERVES: 6
COMMENT:

Okra was one of the new-found delicacies which offered cooks variety and versatility in the kitchens of New Orleans in the late 1700s. Not only was it a main ingredient in the gumbo pots of Louisiana, often it was added to other soups and stews. No okra dish was better known than the chicken and okra stew of bayou country.

INGREDIENTS:

1 whole chicken, cut in pieces
1 cup sliced okra
1 cup vegetable oil
1 cup flour
1 cup chopped onions
1 cup chopped celery
1/2 cup chopped green bell pepper
1/4 cup diced yellow bell pepper
1/4 cup diced red bell pepper
1/4 cup diced garlic
1/2 cup diced tomatoes
1/2 cup tomato sauce
1 cup sliced smoked sausage
pinch of thyme
pinch of basil
2 quarts chicken stock (see recipe)
1/2 cup sliced green onions
1/4 cup chopped parsley
1 bay leaf
salt and cracked pepper to taste
Louisiana Gold Pepper Sauce to taste

METHOD:

In a heavy bottom black pot, heat oil over medium high heat. Add flour and stir constantly until golden brown roux is achieved (see roux techniques). Add onions, celery, bell peppers, garlic and diced tomatoes. Saute three to five minutes or until vegetables are wilted. Add chicken and blend into roux mixture. Add tomato sauce, sausage, thyme and basil. Continue to cook three to five additional minutes. Slowly pour in chicken stock, a little at a time, stirring into the roux mixture. Add enough stock to achieve a stew like consistency. Add green onions, parsley and bay leaf. Season to taste using salt, pepper and Louisiana Gold and cook ten to fifteen minutes. Add okra and continue to cook until chicken is tender. You may wish to add a little more chicken stock as needed to maintain consistency. Serve over steamed rice.

Changes

BRUNSWICK STEW

PREP TIME: 2 Hours
SERVES: 6-8
COMMENT:

Here in North Louisiana there is an ongoing dispute as to the origin of Brunswick Stew. Was it the English, Irish or Scottish who first introduced it to our area? I don't know, but the flavor certainly pleases our Louisiana palates.

A Pump Organ at Caspiana

INGREDIENTS:

1-3 pound broiler
1 pound cubed beef
1 pound cubed pork
2 onions, cubed
2 celery stalks, quartered
3 carrots, sliced
2 bay leaves
sprig of thyme
15-20 black peppercorns
2 cups diced tomatoes
2 cups cubed potatoes
2 cups diced carrots
4 ears of corn, halved
2 cups lima beans
2 cups sliced okra
1 cup diced onions
1 cup diced celery
2 tbsps diced garlic
2 cups tomato sauce
1/2 cup sherry
1 tbsp Worcestershire Sauce
salt and cracked pepper to taste

Changes

METHOD:

Cut chicken into eight serving pieces. In a large stock pot, place chicken, beef, pork, onions, celery, carrots, bay leaves, thyme and peppercorns. Cover chicken with lightly salted water by two inches. Bring to a rolling boil, reduce to simmer and allow to cook until meat is tender, approximately one hour. Drain, reserve three quarts of stock and discard vegetables. Debone chicken and finely chop all meats. Pour reserved stock into a two gallon dutch oven and bring to a rolling boil over medium high heat. Add tomatoes, potatoes, carrots, corn, lima beans, okra, onions, celery and garlic. Reduce heat to simmer and allow to cook fifteen minutes. Add meat, tomato sauce and sherry. Season to taste using Worcestershire sauce, salt and pepper. Cook an additional thirty minutes to allow flavors to develop.

CHICKEN SAUCE ROBERT

PREP TIME: 2 1/2 Hours
SERVES: 6-8
COMMENT:

Sauce Robert is the rich tomato-based brown sauce from which sauce piquante was developed. The French lay claim to the sauce. However, most people in Louisiana feel that it was definitely a Spanish creation.

INGREDIENTS:

1-5 pound stewing hen
3/4 cup oil
3/4 cup flour
2 cups chopped onions
1 cup chopped celery
1/2 cup chopped bell pepper
1/4 cup diced garlic
1 cup diced tomatoes
1-8 ounce can tomato sauce
1/4 cup diced jalapenos, seeded
2 1/2 quarts chicken stock (see recipe)
1 cup sliced mushrooms
2 bay leaves
1/4 cup chopped basil
1/4 cup chopped sage
1 tbsp chopped thyme
salt and cracked pepper to taste
Louisiana Gold Pepper Sauce to taste
1/2 cup sliced green onions
1/4 cup chopped parsley

METHOD:

Cut baking hen into eight pieces and divide each breast in half. Today, many people choose to boil the stewing hen first. This will result in removing the fat and bones from the finished product. I still like to do it the old fashioned way which somehow gives the dish more flavor. In a heavy bottom dutch oven, heat oil over medium high heat. Sprinkle in flour and using a wire whisk, stir constantly until dark brown roux is achieved (see roux techniques). Should black specks appear, discard and begin again. Add onions, celery, bell pepper and garlic. Saute three to five minutes or until vegetables are wilted. Add tomatoes, sauce and jalapenos. Blend ingredients well into roux mixture and cook five additional minutes. Add chicken stock, one ladle at a time, stirring constantly until sauce consistency is achieved. Add chicken, mushrooms, bay leaves, basil, sage and thyme. Bring to a rolling boil, reduce to simmer and allow to cook one and a half hours, stirring occasionally. Add additional stock if necessary to maintain sauce consistency. Cooking time will vary depending on the size of the bird. Normally, two to three hours is required. Once chicken becomes tender, season to taste using salt, pepper and Louisiana Gold. Add green onions and parsley and cook an additional five to ten minutes. Serve over steamed white rice or pasta.

Changes

CHICKEN & DUMPLINGS RANDOLPH

PREP TIME: 2 Hours
SERVES: 6-8
COMMENT:

We all have memories of chicken and dumplings simmering in a pot, ready to serve. It really is sad how those great old dishes from yesterday seem to slip by the way side and are literally forgotten. Personally, I feel we ought to resurrect this dish to its prominent place on the Sunday dinner table.

INGREDIENTS:

2-3 pound broilers
2 medium onions, cubed
2 celery stalks, quartered
1 bell pepper, quartered
1 head of garlic, halved
4 carrots, sliced
2 bay leaves
2 sprigs of thyme
15-20 black peppercorns
1/2 cup diced carrots
1/2 cup sliced celery
1/4 cup sliced green onions
1/4 cup chopped parsley
2 cups flour
1 1/2 tsps baking powder
3 tbsps shortening
3/4 cup buttermilk
salt and cracked pepper to taste

METHOD:

Cut each chicken into eight serving pieces. In a large stock pot, place chicken, onions, celery, bell pepper, garlic, carrots, bay leaves, thyme and peppercorns. Cover chicken with lightly salted water by two inches. Bring to a rolling boil, reduce to simmer and cook until chicken is tender, approximately one hour. Remove chicken from stock and allow to cool. Debone and tear the meat into irregular serving pieces. Set aside. Return the bones to the stock and cook an additional thirty minutes. Strain and reserve three quarts of the stock. In a separate mixing bowl, combine flour, baking powder and shortening. Cut the shortening into the flour until mixture resembles a coarse meal. Add buttermilk, stirring with a fork until the ingredients are moist. Season to taste using salt and pepper. Turn the dough out onto a floured surface and knead gently four to five times. Cover with a dry cloth and set aside. Return chicken stock to a low boil. Add chicken, carrots, celery, green onions and parsley. While the vegetables are poaching, roll the dumplings one quarter inch thick and slice one inch square or pinch the dough into one and a half inch pieces. Drop the dumplings into the boiling broth, stirring gently after each addition. Reduce heat to low and cook until dumplings are tender, approximately eight to ten minutes. Season the broth to taste and serve in large soup bowls with chicken, vegetables and dumplings. Garnish with chopped parsley.

Changes

CACCIATORE PLANTATION STYLE

PREP TIME: 1 Hour
SERVES: 6
COMMENT:

Normally, cacciatore is a braised chicken dish taking hours to create. In the City of New Orleans, the Italians prepared this recipe to speed up the process a bit while retaining the great flavor.

INGREDIENTS:

6 chicken breasts, deboned
1 cup flour
1/4 cup olive oil
1 cup chopped onions
1 cup chopped celery
1/2 cup chopped bell pepper
2 tbsps chopped garlic
2 cups sliced mushrooms
2-16 ounce cans stewed tomatoes
1/2 cup white wine
2 bay leaves
1 tsp sweet marjoram
1 tsp chopped thyme
1 tbsp chopped basil
1 tsp chopped oregano
salt and cracked pepper to taste
1/2 cup sliced green onions
1/4 cup chopped parsley
6 cups cooked spaghetti

METHOD:

I always boil my spaghetti in chicken stock when making cacciatore. Season breasts lightly using salt and pepper. Dust in flour, shaking off all excess. In a heavy bottom dutch oven, heat olive oil over medium high heat. Saute chicken breasts until golden brown on both sides. Remove and keep warm. Into the oil add onions, celery, bell pepper, garlic and mushrooms. Saute three to five minutes or until vegetables are wilted. Add tomatoes, wine, bay leaves, marjoram, thyme, basil and oregano. Blend well into the vegetable mixture. Season to taste using salt and pepper. Allow sauce to simmer thirty minutes. Add chicken breasts and cook ten additional minutes. Add green onions and parsley and adjust seasonings if necessary. Serve over hot spaghetti.

LAGNIAPPE

There is nothing new in cooking under the sun! This is certainly evidenced by the similarity of dishes in different cultures, especially the braised tomato dishes. In bayou country, there is nothing more famous than Shrimp Creole - Gulf shrimp slowly braised in a rich roux-based tomato sauce. In France, there is the sauce piquante-meats, game or seafood slowly braised in a spicy tomàto stew. The Italians would argue that none is superior to their cacciatore. This hunter-style tomato dish incorporates a multitude of vegetables, herbs and spices smothered in olive oil and tomatoes and served over spaghetti. You know, I think the Italians have an argument.

Changes

CREOLE CHICKEN & GRITS

PREP TIME: 1 Hour
SERVES: 6
COMMENT:

Since this Creole style chicken is served over grits, I have to assume that it was originally a breakfast dish. This isn't surprising because the Planter's Breakfast was served around 10:00 am. In many cases this was the main meal of day. In fact, it was the origin of our present day brunch.

INGREDIENTS:

6 boneless chicken breasts
1/2 cup oil
1/2 cup flour
3/4 cup chopped onions
1/2 cup chopped celery
1/4 cup chopped bell pepper
1/4 cup diced garlic
2 bay leaves
1-8 ounce can tomato sauce
1 quart chicken stock (see recipe)
1 tbsp chopped oregano
1 tbsp chopped basil
1 tsp chopped thyme
salt and cracked pepper to taste
Louisiana Gold Pepper Sauce to taste
1/4 cup sliced green onions
1/4 cup chopped parsley
6 cups cheese garlic grits

The Creole Mantle at Magnolia Mound

METHOD:

In a heavy bottom dutch oven, heat oil over medium high heat. Season chicken breasts with salt and pepper. Saute in oil until lightly browned on both sides, remove and set aside. Sprinkle in flour and using a wire whisk, stir constantly until dark roux is achieved (see roux techniques). Should black specks appear, discard and begin again. Add onions, celery, bell pepper and garlic. Saute three to five minutes or until vegetables are wilted. Add bay leaves and tomato sauce, blending well into the vegetable mixture. Pour in chicken stock, one cup at a time, until sauce consistency is achieved. Add oregano, basil and thyme. Season to taste using salt, pepper and Louisiana Gold. Bring mixture to a rolling boil and reduce to simmer. Add chicken breasts to the sauce and allow to cook thirty minutes. Add more stock should sauce become too thick. Add green onions and parsley and adjust seasonings if necessary. Place one cup serving of hot cheese garlic grits in the center of a ten inch plate, add one chicken breast and top with generous serving of Creole sauce.

Changes

PECAN CRUSTED CHICKEN

PREP TIME: 1 Hour

SERVES: 6

COMMENT:

Cajuns relish the flavor of pecans, whether served in pies and desserts or as a breading on meats and fish. Here, the crushed pecans are combined with flour to create a batter that is certain to excite the Cajun palate.

INGREDIENTS:

1 cup crushed pecans
6 chicken breasts, cleaned and deboned
1/2 cup oil
1 cup flour
1 tsp chopped thyme
1 tsp chopped basil
1 egg
1/2 cup water
1/2 cup milk
1/4 cup chopped pecans
1/4 cup praline liqueur
2 cups heavy whipping cream
salt and pepper to taste
Louisiana Gold Pepper Sauce to taste

METHOD:

In a heavy bottom saute pan, heat oil over medium high heat. Combine flour and pecans and season to taste using salt, pepper, thyme and basil. In a mixing bowl, combine egg, water and milk. Using a wire whisk, whip until ingredients are well blended. Season eggwash with salt, pepper and Louisiana Gold. Dip chicken in eggwash and then in pecan flour, shaking off all excess. Pan fry chicken until golden brown on both sides, approximately seven to ten minutes. Remove and keep warm. Drain all but one tablespoon of oil from skillet and retain pan drippings. Add pecans and saute one minute. Remove from flame and deglaze with praline liqueur. Return to the flame, being careful as liqueur will ignite. Add heavy whipping cream, bring to a rolling boil and reduce to simmer. Allow praline cream to reduce to one half volume. Season to taste using salt and pepper. Place chicken breast in the center of a ten inch plate and top with two ounces of the praline cream.

Changes

MASON DIXON FRIED CHICKEN WITH CREAM GRAVY

PREP TIME: 1 Hour
SERVES: 6-8
COMMENT:

Alexandria, Louisiana, is considered the "Mason Dixon Line" of the bayou state. The French Creoles influenced the lower half of the state, while the Northern part was considered more English. It is at this dividing line that foods have a tendency to reflect both cultures. This French fried chicken with English style gravy is such a dish.

INGREDIENTS:

2-2 1/2 pound fryers
2 eggs, beaten
1 cup milk
4 cups all purpose flour
salt and cracked pepper to taste
granulated garlic to taste
Louisiana Gold Pepper Sauce to taste
oil for frying
1/4 cup flour
3 cups hot cream
dash of nutmeg

METHOD:

Cut each chicken into eight serving pieces. Place in a large mixing bowl and season to taste using salt, pepper, garlic and Louisiana Gold. In a separate bowl, combine egg and milk. Using a wire whisk, whip until all ingredients are well blended. Place four cups of flour in a large paper bag. Season lightly with salt, pepper and granulated garlic. Heat one inch of oil in a black iron skillet over medium high heat. The ideal frying temperature is 350 degrees F. Dip chicken in egg batter and place in seasoned flour. Close bag tightly and shake vigorously to coat chicken well. Fry chicken twenty to twenty-five minutes or until golden brown, turning occasionally. Remove chicken, drain and keep warm. Pour all but one quarter cup of oil from skillet, retaining pan drippings. Add remaining flour and using a wire whisk, stir constantly to blend into the drippings. Slowly pour in hot cream, stirring constantly to create a cream gravy. Sprinkle with nutmeg and season to taste using salt, pepper and Louisiana Gold. To serve, spoon a generous portion of the cream gravy over chicken.

LAGNIAPPE

When making great Southern fried chicken, the most important element is a good black iron skillet. We've all had chicken cooked in those crusted-over black skillets, handed down from grandmother's house. I was even warned never to clean the crust from the skillet, otherwise the chicken would never be as good as hers. Whether you clean it or not, I agree that a black iron skillet is imperative to the success of this dish. It not only protects the chicken from scorching over that hot fire, but it also imparts an even heat around the meat. If you don't have an heirloom skillet, buy one at the hardware store. Season it and you'll have your own, ready to hand down to the next generation.

Changes

PLANTATION FRIED CHICKEN WITH GARLIC AND HERBS

PREP TIME: 1 Hour
SERVES: 4-6
COMMENT:

Every culture has its version of "sticky" fried chicken. In this recipe we pan-fry seasoned, unfloured chicken in a small amount of oil over low heat until the meat is golden brown and extremely tender. My grandmother was a master at this pan frying technique, and this is her version.

INGREDIENTS:

1 large fryer
1/4 cup butter
1/4 cup olive oil
salt and cracked pepper to taste
Louisiana Gold Pepper Sauce to taste
granulated garlic to taste
paprika for color
12 small cloves of garlic
1 sprig rosemary
1 cup chicken stock

A Veilleuse (First Light of Day) Coffee Pot

METHOD:

Using a sharp boning knife, cut chicken into eight serving pieces. If the breasts are large, you may leave a large portion attached to each wing. This will provide two additional serving pieces. In a large mixing bowl, season chicken generously with salt, pepper, Louisiana Gold, granulated garlic and paprika. Allow the chicken to marinate approximately one hour prior to frying. In a large black iron skillet, heat butter and oil over medium high heat. Saute chicken until golden brown on both sides. Add garlic and rosemary and lower heat to simmer. Cover, turn occasionally and allow to cook approximately thirty minutes. The chicken will release its own juices in the pan creating a natural sauce. Should you wish to have more of a gravy once the chicken is fried, remove from skillet and add chicken stock. Bring mixture to a rolling boil and reduce to one half volume. Season to taste and serve along with chicken.

Changes

SOUTHERN FRIED CHICKEN

PREP TIME: 30 Minutes

SERVES: 6

COMMENT:

Of all chicken dishes cooked in America, none is more famous than the Southern fried chicken of Louisiana. There are literally hundreds of recipes for this dish. This one comes from the head cook at Madewood, Thelma Parker.

INGREDIENTS:

2-2 1/2 pound fryers
salt and cracked pepper to taste
Louisiana Gold Pepper Sauce to taste
granulated garlic to taste
1/2 cup milk
4 cups seasoned flour
oil for frying

METHOD:

Cut fryers into eight serving pieces each. Place chicken in a large mixing bowl and season generously with salt, pepper, Louisiana Gold and granulated garlic. Add milk and coat chicken well. Allow to sit at room temperature approximately one hour. In a heavy bottom black iron skillet, heat one inch of oil over medium high heat. The ideal frying temperature should be 350 degrees F. Pour seasoned flour into a brown paper bag, add chicken and seal tightly. Shake vigorously to coat chicken. Place chicken in skillet, being careful not to overcrowd. Fry until golden brown on each side, approximately ten to fifteen minutes, turning occasionally. You may check for doneness by inserting a fork into the heavier pieces of chicken to see if clear juices run from the centers. It is best to always fry chicken at a slightly lower temperature to ensure thorough cooking on the inside without over-browning the outside. Drain on paper towels and keep warm in a 250 degree F oven. Serve piping hot.

Changes

POACHED CHICKEN BURNSIDE

PREP TIME: 2 1/2 Hours
SERVES: 6
COMMENT:

Nothing was simpler to prepare in the plantation open hearth than poached chicken. This forefather of chicken noodle soup had many variations, depending on the time of year and the nationality preparing the dish.

INGREDIENTS:

1-4 pound stewing hen
2 onions, quartered
2 celery stalks, quartered
3 carrots, halved
1 head of garlic, split
2 bay leaves
2 sprigs of thyme
salt and cracked pepper to taste
6 new potatoes
6 pearl onions
6 cauliflower florets
4 carrots, quartered
1/2 cup sliced green onions
1/4 cup chopped parsley

METHOD:

Rinse chicken well inside and out. Tie legs to keep together during the cooking process. In a large stock pot, place chicken, onions, celery, carrots, garlic, bay leaves and thyme. Cover chicken with lightly salted water by two inches. Bring to a rolling boil and reduce heat to simmer. Cook until chicken is tender but not falling apart, approximately two to two and a half hours. Carefully remove chicken from stock and keep warm. Discard all vegetables and return stock to a low boil. Adjust seasonings using salt and pepper. Add potatoes, onions, cauliflower, carrots, green onions and parsley and poach until tender. When cooked, place equal portions of chicken, vegetables and stock in a soup bowl and serve with hot garlic bread.

Changes

Chapter Seven

Meat

Ardoyne Plantation

Ardoyne Plantation

"Plantation Treasurers"

A Handpump in the Garden at Ardoyne

Today, it's not easy to find a Louisiana plantation that has remained in the same family since it was originally built. If you should be lucky enough to find one, what a wealth of information, family history and memorabilia you are sure to find. Near the banks of Bayou Lafourche, I've discovered such a place. Just as I suspected all along, it's all right here, untouched for the past 100 years - everything from daily journals on sugar production to the annual receipts from the General Store. There's even an original copy of the Code Noir, the law governing the ownership and treatment of slaves.

Ardoyne is a Scottish word meaning "little knoll". The Victorian home was built for Mr. John Dalton Shaffer and his wife, Julia Richardson Cutliff. The unique home, designed by New Orleans architect John Williams, was begun in 1897 and completed in 1900. The massive structure has 21 rooms, all with 16 foot ceilings. Cypress was used to build the home and it was harvested and cured from the nearby swamplands. In the 60 foot hallway that ends with a beautiful carved staircase, there are original Gilbert Stuart paintings of George Washington and his stepdaughter, Nellie Curtis. Original Audubons are also on display in this entrance way.

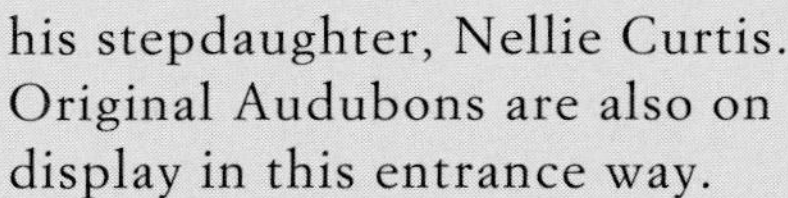

In the parlor, one can view a huge mirror from an old New Orleans hotel. Beautiful antiques, as well as a concert piano, may also be seen. The octagonal room was used as the plantation office, where the day to day business was conducted. In the master bedroom there are two huge, half-tester beds and a day bed. The latter was used by the lady of the house to lie down during the day to keep from disturbing the larger beds. The home has twin porches. The side porch with walk-in windows contains several gas lamps which were used to light the mule barns. The second porch is totally screened in and this mosquito porch, as it's called, is used mainly in the summer to enjoy the early evening breezes.

Ardoyne was a vast highly productive sugar plantation. Of the 350 acres still remaining today, most are dedicated to the cultivation of sugar cane.

The home is located near Houma, Louisiana on Highway 331 in Schriever. This private residence is not open to the public.

At left, clockwise from bottom left, Whipped Potato Clouds (page 151), Turtle Soup Terrebonne (page 92), and Baked Country Ham with Cane Syrup and Beer (page 190)

BAKED COUNTRY HAM WITH CANE SYRUP AND BEER

PREP TIME: 4 days
SERVES: 20-30
COMMENT:

There are only two problems with a good country ham. The first is the inconvenience of soaking it three days before cooking. The second is finding a roasting pan big enough to hold the thing. When all is said and done, there is no center of the table dish better then a baked country ham.

INGREDIENTS:

1 10-12 pound Smithfield or other country ham
1 gallon weak tea, cooled
1 cup Louisiana cane syrup
1 quart beer
1 cup brown sugar
1/2 cup Creole or Dijon mustard
1/4 cup chopped thyme
1/4 cup chopped sage
1/4 cup chopped tarragon
1 tbsp file powder
cracked black pepper to taste
Louisiana Gold Pepper Sauce to taste
20 kumquat halves

METHOD:

In a sink of cold water, scrub the ham to remove mold which accumulates during the curing process. This mold is not harmful but must be removed before cooking. In a large pan, soak the ham in tea. If more liquid is needed to cover the ham, simply use cold tap water. I prefer to use tea in this process because it helps to counteract the heavy salt used in the curing process. Soak the ham in a cool place two to three days, turning the ham once a day. Preheat oven to 500 degrees F. Drain off tea, rinse and place ham in a large baking pan. Pour cane syrup over the ham and beer in the bottom of the roasting pan. Cover tightly with foil to ensure that steam will not escape. Bake thirty to forty-five minutes at 500 degrees F. Reduce temperature to 275 degrees F and bake two hours longer. Remove foil and turn ham in the liquid. Recover and continue to bake approximately one and a half hours more. Remove from oven and let ham cool in its own liquid. Once cool, remove the rind and all but a thin layer of the fat. Before making glaze, preheat oven to 400 degrees F. Using a sharp paring knife, score the ham. In a large mixing bowl, combine sugar, mustard, thyme, sage, tarragon, file, black pepper and Louisiana Gold. Using a wire whisk, whip until all ingredients are well blended. Add one to two tablespoons of the cooking liquid to the glaze mixture and spread over the top of the ham. Place twenty kumquat halves across the top of the ham and secure with toothpicks. Bake for thirty minutes to set the glaze. Most people prefer to allow the ham to cool thoroughly prior to slicing.

Changes

____

____

____

ROSEMARY STUFFED LEG OF PORK

PREP TIME: 3 Hours
SERVES: 6-8
COMMENT:

The fresh pork ham has been a tradition on the New Year's Day table for generations here in Louisiana. Normally, it is stuffed with fresh seasonings and spices prior to roasting. Various fruits and glazes should also be considered when baking this centerpiece.

INGREDIENTS:

1 5-7 pound fresh pork ham
1/2 cup chopped rosemary
1/4 cup chopped thyme
1/4 cup chopped basil
1/4 cup chopped sage
1/2 cup chopped green onions
1/2 cup chopped parsley
1/2 cup minced garlic
1/2 cup melted butter
3 apples, quartered
1 large onion, quartered
10 garlic cloves
salt and cracked pepper to taste
Louisiana Gold Pepper Sauce to taste

METHOD:

Preheat oven to 375 degrees F. Have your butcher remove the heavy skin covering the outer portion of the leg. You may wish to remove the lower portion of the shank to ensure that the roast will fit in a homestyle oven. Using a sharp paring knife, cut approximately fifteen to twenty one-inch slits throughout the roast. In a small mixing bowl, combine rosemary, thyme, basil, sage, green onions, parsley and garlic. Season the mixture generously with salt and pepper. Blend all ingredients well and stuff a generous portion of the seasoning mixture into the slits. Place the roast in a large baking pan and drizzle with the melted butter. Coat the roast with remaining seasoning mixture. Surround with apples, onions and garlic. Sprinkle the entire roast with additional salt, pepper and Louisiana Gold. Cover and bake until internal temperature reaches 145 degrees F, approximately two and a half hours. Remove cover and allow roast to brown evenly. Allow to sit and rest thirty minutes prior to slicing.

LAGNIAPPE

Pork has been called the most important butcher's meat in the world. The first pigs to enter what is now the United States came in 1542 near Tampa, Florida. Hernando DeSoto brought 13 animals knowing that pigs were self-sustaining and could take care of themselves. Cortez and his conquistadors had already introduced pigs to North America at a feast of roasted pig in what is now Mexico City. There is certainly no meat with the versatility of pork. Once a farmer remarked, you can do anything with a pig except milk it or ride it!

Changes

TOMATO BRAISED PORK CUTLETS

PREP TIME: 1 Hour
SERVES: 6
COMMENT:

Many of us in Louisiana will debate at a moments notice the origin of our famous grillades. This pan grilled pork or veal cutlet was often served in a rich gravy over grits for breakfast or lunch. I think that the following recipe is as close to the original as any I've found.

INGREDIENTS:

1 cup chopped tomatoes
6 pork shoulder steaks
1/4 cup vegetable oil
1 cup seasoned flour
1 cup chopped onions
1/2 cup chopped celery
1/2 cup chopped bell pepper
1/4 cup diced garlic
1 cup sliced mushrooms
1 ounce cognac or brandy
1 tbsp Worcestershire Sauce
1 cup tomato sauce
2 cups chicken stock (see recipe)
salt and cracked pepper to taste
Louisiana Gold Pepper Sauce to taste

A Garden in Bloom at Layton

METHOD:

Have your butcher cut six shoulder blade steaks to equal about two pounds total weight. Season the steaks well using salt and pepper. In a large black iron skillet, heat oil over medium high heat. Dredge steaks in flour, shaking off all excess. Place in oil and pan fry until golden brown on both sides. Remove steaks and set aside. Into the same pan, add onions, celery, bell pepper and garlic. Saute three to five minutes or until vegetables are wilted. Add mushrooms and chopped tomatoes, blending well into the vegetable mixture. Carefully add the cognac or brandy.

NOTE: *Take care when pouring cognac into the skillet as the alcohol will ignite for just a second before extinguishing itself.*

Add Worcestershire, tomato sauce and chicken stock. Season to taste using salt, pepper and Louisiana Gold. Place the steaks in the sauce and cover. Reduce heat to simmer and cook until steaks are tender, approximately forty-five minutes. Serve over rice or cheese garlic grits.

Changes

CANE SYRUP GLAZED CROWN ROAST

PREP TIME: 2 hours
SERVES: 6
COMMENT:

I love to experiment with stuffings and dressings. The only difference between the two is a matter of placement. A stuffing goes into a bird. A dressing goes into a bowl. This recipe uses fruit and French bread as its main ingredients.

INGREDIENTS:

1 crown roast of pork
1/2 cup butter
1 cup chopped onions
1 cup chopped celery
1/2 cup chopped red bell pepper
1/2 cup chopped yellow bell pepper
1/4 diced garlic
1/4 cup diced andouille sausage
1 green apple, diced
1 red apple, diced
2 cups French bread, cubed
1 cup chicken stock (see recipe)
1 tbsp chopped thyme
1 tbsp chopped basil
1 tbsp chopped sage
1/4 cup sliced green onions
1/4 cup chopped parsley
salt and cracked pepper to taste
Louisiana Gold Pepper Sauce to taste
1/2 cup Louisiana cane syrup

METHOD:

Preheat oven to 375 degrees F. Tie roast together using butcher's twine to form a crown and secure with skewers. Season roast with salt, pepper, Louisiana Gold and half of the thyme, basil and sage. In a ten inch saute pan, melt butter over medium high heat. Add onions, celery, bell peppers, garlic and andouille. Saute three to five minutes or until vegetables are wilted. Add apples and bread and chop into the vegetable mixture. Cook five to ten minutes, adding chicken stock to keep stuffing moist. Season with remaining thyme, basil, sage, green onions, parsley, salt, pepper and Louisiana Gold. Remove from heat and allow to cool slightly. Spoon stuffing mixture into the center of the roast. Cover roast completely with foil and bake for one and a half hours. Remove foil, allow to brown evenly and glaze with pan drippings and cane syrup.

Changes

CORNBREAD STUFFED PORK CHOPS

PREP TIME: 1 1/2 hours
SERVES: 6
COMMENT:

In the 1800s, pork was preferred to other meats because of its availability and versatility. Crown roast was the most sought after dish but was too much for a small family. Instead, many simply stuffed the center cut chops with a variety of local fillings.

INGREDIENTS:

6-1 inch center cut pork chops
3 cups crumbled cornbread
1/2 cup butter
1 cup chopped onions
1/2 cup chopped celery
1/4 cup chopped red bell pepper
1/4 cup diced garlic
1 cup (150-200 count) shrimp
1/4 cup sliced green onions
1/4 cup chopped parsley
1 tbsp chopped sage
1 tbsp chopped thyme
1 tbsp chopped basil
1 quart hot chicken stock (see recipe)
salt and cracked pepper to taste
Louisiana Gold Pepper Sauce to taste

METHOD:

Preheat oven to 375 degrees F. Have your butcher split the chops down the center to form a pocket for the stuffing. Season chops inside and out with salt, pepper and Louisiana Gold. Set aside. In a heavy bottom black iron skillet, melt butter over medium high heat. Add onions, celery, bell pepper and garlic. Saute three to five minutes or until vegetables are wilted. Add shrimp, green onions, parsley, sage, thyme and basil. Blend well into the vegetable mixture and cook until shrimp are pink, approximately ten minutes. Sprinkle in cornbread and blend well into the shrimp mixture. Add chicken stock, one ladle at a time, to keep stuffing moist and prevent it from sticking. Season to taste using salt, pepper and Louisiana Gold. Once stuffing is full-flavored, remove from heat and allow to cool. Stuff equal amounts of cornbread mixture into the center of the chops. Place the chops in an oven-proof casserole dish and top with four cups of Nantua sauce (see recipe), or substitute two cans of cream of shrimp soup. Bake, covered, one and a half hours or until chops are tender.

Changes

____
____
____
____
____
____

SMOTHERED PORK CHOPS CLEMENTINE

PREP TIME: 1 Hour
SERVES: 6
COMMENT:

In the early days of Louisiana cooking, smoking pork was natural. Often no time was allowed for smoking, when meals were needed in a rush. The innovative cooks of North Louisiana would do the next best thing - smother the chops with smoked sausage to impart the flavor. The addition of peaches in this recipe made an ordinary dish spectacular.

INGREDIENTS:

6 loin chops
1/2 cup flour
1/4 cup vegetable oil
1 cup chopped onions
1 cup chopped celery
1/4 cup chopped red bell pepper
1/4 cup chopped yellow bell pepper
1 tbsp diced garlic
1 pound heavy smoked sausage
2 peaches, sliced
1/2 cup sliced mushrooms
pinch of thyme
pinch of basil
2 cups chicken stock (see recipe)
1/2 cup sliced green onions
1/2 cup chopped parsley
salt and cracked pepper to taste
Louisiana Gold Pepper Sauce to taste

METHOD:

Have your butcher cut three-quarter inch chops from the center of a pork loin. The heavy chops will hold up during the long braising period. Season the chops with salt, pepper and Louisiana Gold. Dust lightly in flour, shaking off all excess. In a large black iron skillet, heat oil over medium high heat. Saute chops until golden brown on both sides. Add onions, celery, bell peppers and garlic. Saute three to five minutes or until vegetables are wilted. Slice smoked sausage, add to chops and blend well. Add peaches, mushrooms, thyme, basil and chicken stock. Bring to a rolling boil and reduce heat to simmer. Cover and cook until chops are tender, approximately forty-five minutes. Add green onions and parsley and adjust seasonings if necessary. Once chops are tender, remove to a serving platter and top with the sausage/peach sauce. Serve over pasta or seasoned rice.

Changes

SMOTHERED PORK SAUSAGE IN APPLE CIDER

PREP TIME: 1 Hour

SERVES: 6

COMMENT:

Although the early settlers did not find apple trees growing in Louisiana, many families cherished the flavor and always had a tree or two. In north and central Louisiana, they were more prominent than in the south and thus, this wonderful recipe.

INGREDIENTS:

2 pounds fresh pork sausage links
1/2 cup chicken stock (see recipe)
1 cup chopped onions
1/2 cup chopped celery
1/2 cup chopped red bell pepper
1 tbsp diced garlic
1 cup diced apples
1 cup apple cider
1/2 cup sliced green onions
1/4 cup chopped parsley
salt and cracked pepper to taste
Louisiana Gold Pepper Sauce to taste

A Civil War Fork and Spoon

METHOD:

Preheat oven to 375 degrees F. Using a fork, prick sausage at intervals and place in a heavy black iron skillet. Add stock and cook over medium high heat, covered, turning sausage occasionally until fat is rendered. Once browned, remove sausage and pour all but one fourth cup of the drippings from the skillet. Add onions, celery, bell pepper, garlic and apples. Saute three to five minutes or until vegetables are wilted. Return sausage to the skillet and add cider, green onions and parsley. Season to taste using salt, pepper and Louisiana Gold. Cover, place in oven and bake thirty to forty-five minutes. Serve on a large platter surrounded by honeyed apple rings (see recipe).

Changes

PORK SAUSAGE SOUFFLÉ

PREP TIME: 1 1/2 Hours
SERVES: 8-10
COMMENT:

Smoked or fresh pork sausage is incorporated into many Louisiana dishes such as jambalayas, gumbos and soufflés. This simple dish is served for breakfast at Loyd Hall and has received accolades from visitors around the world.

INGREDIENTS:

1 1/2 pounds bulk pork sausage
1 cup finely diced onions
1/2 cup finely diced celery
1/2 cup finely diced red bell pepper
1/4 cup diced garlic
8 whole eggs
2 1/2 cups half and half cream
6 slices bread
1/4 pound melted butter
1 1/2 cups grated cheddar cheese
1/2 cup chopped parsley
1/2 cup sliced green onions
salt and pepper to taste
pinch of dry mustard
Louisiana Gold Pepper Sauce to taste

METHOD:

NOTE: This dish is better when prepared and allowed to sit in the refrigerator overnight prior to cooking. However, when serving as a luncheon item, it must sit a minimum of two hours. In a large heavy bottom skillet, saute sausage over medium high heat until golden brown. Drain all but two tablespoons of rendered fat and add onions, celery, bell pepper and garlic. Saute ten minutes or until vegetables are wilted. Remove from heat and set aside. In a large mixing bowl, combine eggs and half and half. Using a wire whisk, whip until ingredients are well blended. Season the egg mixture with salt, pepper, dry mustard and Louisiana Gold. In the bottom of a 9" x 13" baking dish, place the six slices of bread. Using a pastry brush, coat bread with butter. Evenly spread the sausage mixture over the bread and top with cheese, parsley and green onions. Pour in seasoned egg mixture, cover and allow to sit in the refrigerator overnight. When ready to cook, preheat oven to 350 degrees F. and bake approximately forty-five minutes. When done, allow to rest five to ten minutes and cut into squares for service.

Changes

OUACHITA STUFFED PEPPERS

PREP TIME: 1 1/2 Hours
SERVES: 6
COMMENT:

The Indians of Louisiana were instrumental in helping to develop the cuisines of the Cajuns and Creoles. Corn, squash, beans and cornmeal were part of their daily repertoire and quickly found their way into the black iron pots. Here, we combine the Native American ingredients with pork and beef to create an entree out of this world.

INGREDIENTS:

2 each red, green and yellow bell peppers
2 pounds ground pork
2 pounds ground beef
1/4 cup butter
1 cup chopped onions
1 cup chopped celery
1/4 cup diced red bell pepper
1/4 cup diced yellow bell pepper
1/4 cup diced garlic
1 cup beef stock (see recipe)
1/2 cup sliced green onions
1/4 cup chopped parsley
1 cup whole kernel corn
2 cups crushed corn bread
salt and cracked pepper to taste
Louisiana Gold Pepper Sauce to taste
4 cups prepared tomato sauce

METHOD:

Preheat oven to 375 degrees F. In a large black iron skillet, melt butter over medium high heat. Add pork and beef and cook until golden brown, approximately thirty minutes. Drain off all but two tablespoons of oil. Add onions, celery, bell peppers and garlic. Saute three to five minutes or until vegetables are wilted. Add beef stock to keep mixture moist while meat is sauteing. Once tender, add green onions, parsley and corn. Sprinkle in crushed corn bread and blend well into meat mixture. Season to taste using salt, pepper and Louisiana Gold. Remove the top from the bell peppers and clean all pulp from the inside. Stuff with the meat dressing, place in a large casserole dish and surround with a prepared tomato sauce. Bake for thirty minutes or until peppers are tender.

Changes

____
____
____
____
____

LAGNIAPPE

There are many varieties of peppers growing in the world and sweet peppers are among the most common. It is interesting to note that peppers, especially the peppercorn variety, were used as money for some 2,000 years. During the Middle Ages, a pound of peppercorns was equivalent to two weeks salary for an English farm hand. In Ancient and Medieval times, the same pound of peppercorns was equal to the value of a pound of gold. Pepper served not only as payment of rent, but it was also used to buy land. By the end of the 14th century, a man's wealth, in many parts of the world, was no longer measured in terms of land or estate, but in the amount of pepper stored in his pantry or cellar.

ROLLED VEGETABLE AND POTATO MEATLOAF

PREP TIME: 2 Hours
SERVES: 8-10
COMMENT:

The Creole settlement of Natchitoches is famous worldwide for its meat pies. Slow braised meat, flavored with vegetables and herbs, made into a loaf or pie is traditional in many cultures. However, in this old Louisiana settlement it is more than a tradition – it is a way of life.

INGREDIENTS:

2 pounds ground chuck
1 pound lean ground pork
1/2 cup finely diced onions
1/4 cup finely diced celery
1/4 cup finely diced red bell pepper
2 tbsps diced garlic
1/4 cup finely sliced green onions
1/4 cup chopped parsley
3 whole eggs
1/3 cup heavy whipping cream
salt and cracked pepper to taste
Louisiana Gold Pepper Sauce to taste
1/4 cup chopped basil
1/2 cup diced white potatoes
1/2 cup cooked whole kernel corn
3 cups tomato sauce

METHOD:

Preheat oven to 350 degrees F. In a large mixing bowl, combine ground chuck, pork, onions, celery, bell pepper, garlic, green onions and parsley. Using your hands, mix the ingredients thoroughly until all seasonings are well blended. Add eggs, whipping cream, salt, pepper and Louisiana Gold. Continue to blend until the liquids are well incorporated. On a large sheet of wax paper, press the ground meat mixture into a rectangle, 12" x 10". Make sure that the rectangle is of equal height throughout, approximately one quarter inch. Beginning one half inch from the edge of the meat, top evenly with the basil, potatoes and whole kernel corn. Using the tips of your fingers, gently press the ingredients into the meat. Using the wax paper, roll the meat like a jelly roll until it is thoroughly sealed. Place in a large casserole dish, top with the tomato sauce and sprinkle with a pinch of salt and cracked pepper. Bake, uncovered, approximately one to one and a half hours.

Changes

PORCUPINE BALLS

PREP TIME: 1 Hour

SERVES: 6

COMMENT:

Meatballs, or as the French say, boullettes, seem to find their way into many creative dishes. Crowley, the rice capital of the world, has incorporated rice into its meatballs. Once cooked, children refer to them as "porcupine balls" because the rice sticks out from the meatballs in a bristly fashion.

INGREDIENTS:

2 pounds ground meat
1 cup finely diced andouille
1 cup minced onions
1 cup minced celery
1/2 cup minced bell pepper
1/4 cup diced garlic
1/4 cup sliced green onions
1/4 cup chopped parsley
1 tsp chopped thyme
1 tsp chopped basil
2 eggs
1 cup seasoned Italian bread crumbs
1 cup cooked rice
salt and cracked pepper to taste
Louisiana Gold Pepper Sauce to taste
4 cups hunter sauce (see recipe)

METHOD:

Preheat oven to 350 degrees F. In a large mixing bowl, combine ground meat, andouille, onions, celery, bell pepper, garlic, green onions and parsley. Using your hands, mix all ingredients well. Add thyme, basil and eggs. Season to taste using salt, pepper and Louisiana Gold. Continue to mix until ingredients are well blended. Sprinkle in bread crumbs to absorb liquid and hold meatballs together during cooking. Blend in cooked rice and form into twelve meatballs. Place on a cookie sheet and bake until golden brown, approximately twenty minutes. Remove, place in an oven-proof casserole dish and top with hunter sauce or your favorite tomato gravy. Bake, covered, for an additional thirty minutes. Serve over rice or pasta.

Changes

CORNED BEEF AND CABBAGE

PREP TIME: 3 Hours
SERVES: 6
COMMENT:

I remember when corned beef and cabbage was considered a "winter dish". But today I can think of nothing better than a platter of this delicacy, especially when the cabbage and fixings are slowly simmered in the corned beef poaching liquid.

INGREDIENTS:

1 5-6 pound corned beef
1-3 pound green cabbage
3 large onions, quartered
6 carrots, peeled and halved
3 celery sticks, halved
6 whole cloves
12 black peppercorns
2 bay leaves
12 new potatoes
6 carrots, peeled and halved
12 whole cloves of garlic
salt and cracked black pepper to taste
Louisiana Gold Pepper Sauce to taste
chopped parsley for garnish

The Yellow Garden with its Contemporary Fountain was Mrs. Stern's Favorite

METHOD:

In a large stock pot, place corned beef, onions, carrots, celery, cloves, peppercorns, bay leaves and Louisiana Gold. Cover the contents with lightly salted water by four inches. Bring to a rolling boil, reduce heat to simmer and cook until beef is tender, approximately two and a half hours. Remove and keep warm. Strain broth and return it to the stock pot. Add potatoes, carrots and garlic. Season to taste using salt and pepper. Bring to a rolling boil, reduce to simmer and allow to cook approximately ten minutes. Slice the cabbage into six equal wedges and add to the stock. The vegetables and cabbage should be cooked perfectly in twenty to thirty minutes. To serve, arrange the beef on a warm serving platter and surround with cabbage and vegetables. Ladle hot broth over the beef and vegetables and garnish with chopped parsley. I always serve a sauce boat of horseradish cream with this dish (see recipe).

Changes

ST. FRANCISVILLE CORNED BEEF HASH

PREP TIME: 1 Hour
SERVES: 6
COMMENT:

The English were extremely fond of corned beef. This process of curing beef in pickling spice with brown sugar and saltpeter, prior to boiling or baking, was quite common in English households. When they came to settle the "Rolling Felicianas" of Louisiana, corned beef quickly found its way to their menus.

INGREDIENTS:

4 cups cooked corned beef
1 large white potato
1/2 cup butter
1/2 cup finely diced onions
1/2 cup finely diced celery
1/4 cup finely diced red bell pepper
1/4 cup diced garlic
1/4 cup sliced green onions
1 tsp chopped thyme
salt and cracked pepper to taste
Louisiana Gold Pepper Sauce to taste
6 poached eggs

METHOD:

Using a paring knife, cut the potato into one quarter inch cubes. Poach in lightly salted water until tender but not overcooked. Drain, cool and set aside. In a large saute pan, melt butter over medium high heat. Add onions, celery, bell pepper, garlic, green onions and thyme. Saute three to five minutes or until vegetables are wilted. Add corned beef and potatoes and blend well into the vegetable mixture. Season to taste using salt, pepper and Louisiana Gold. Saute an additional two to three minutes. Using the bottom of a cooking spoon, mash the contents of the skillet into a large patty. Reduce heat to low, cover and cook until corned beef has browned slightly, approximately ten minutes. Uncover and turn hash with a large spatula. Continue to cook until browned, approximately five additional minutes. Divide hash into six equal servings and top with poached eggs.

Changes

Caspiana Plantation

Caspiana Plantation

"A Family Devoted"

The Hutchinson family migrated to America from Ireland in the late 1600s seeking fame and fortune. They arrived in North Louisiana in the early 1800s Here they built their neo-classical cottage and called it the "Big House". They were a God-fearing, very religious family who, along with nine children, built the first Methodist Church in this area. Tradition had it that the entire family met at the house every Sunday after services. It was a steamboat captain sailing the Caspian Sea many years before who gave the house its present name.

The plantation is one of a dwindling number of antebellum frame houses remaining in Northwest Louisiana. Its architecture is, in one sense, typical of these houses.
In another sense, it is unique, reflecting a local experiment in farming and living. Architecturally, Caspiana House has the form found most often among frame pioneer homes of this area. Derived from folk housing of the eastern Piedmont, it reveals the origins of the people for whom it was built. The uniqueness of this home lies in the fact that it is built on extra high piers because it is located in the low bottom lands of the Red River. While tall pier river plantations were commonplace, no other example has been found of this type in the northwest part of the state. This home should not be confused with the traditional raised cottages of South Louisiana.

The General Store at Caspiana

Before being moved to the Pioneer Heritage Center on the campus of LSU Shreveport, the home had been moved twice on the plantation site to escape encroachment by the Red River. Colored glass in the transom and side lights of the front door has been left in place even though it appears to have been a later addition. The interior walls are covered with muslin under wallpaper. In many rooms, wallboard was left exposed and painted.

Today, the house is used to teach regional folk history at Louisiana State University. Tours are designed to show school children how people lived on late 19th century plantations.

To reach Caspiana, take I-49 North to Shreveport. The University is located on Youree Drive. 318-797-5332.

At left, clockwise from bottom left, Caspiana Fried Catfish (page 221), Vegetable Chili (page 142), and Italian Style Oven-Fried Squash (page 131)

LUMBERJACK STEW

PREP TIME: 2 Hours
SERVES: 6
COMMENT:

This hearty meat and vegetable stew originated in the lumber camps of North Louisiana. Not only did it provide nourishment to the hard working lumberjacks, but the incredible flavor enhanced an otherwise boring camp menu.

INGREDIENTS:

1 veal shank
1 pound stew meat
1 heavy baking hen
1/4 cup vegetable oil
1 cup diced onions
1 cup diced celery
1 cup diced bell pepper
1 tbsp diced garlic
1 cup red kidney beans
1 cup white beans
1 cup lima beans
1 cup whole kernel corn
3 sliced carrots
3 diced potatoes
1 tsp chopped thyme
1 tsp chopped basil
salt and black pepper to taste
Louisiana Gold Pepper Sauce to taste

METHOD:

Cut baking hen into eight serving pieces. In a large dutch oven, heat oil over medium high heat. Add veal shank, stew meat and baking hen. Brown lightly on all sides. Add onions, celery, bell pepper and garlic. Blend well into the meats and saute three to five minutes or until vegetables are wilted. Add all remaining vegetables, thyme and basil and stir well. Add enough water or chicken stock to cover ingredients by two inches. Bring to a rolling boil, reduce to simmer and allow ingredients to cook until shank is tender and beans are cooked thoroughly, approximately two hours. Season to taste using salt, pepper and Louisiana Gold. The potatoes and beans will act as a thickening agent in the liquid. This dish should be served in vegetable soup fashion with hot garlic bread.

Changes

POOR MAN'S STEW

PREP TIME: 3 1/2 Hours
SERVES: 10-12
COMMENT:

Some variety of this simple vegetable soup was the mainstay on many battlefields in the 1800s. When no meat was available, a poor quality sausage or seafood would be substituted. Often, however, nothing but the vegetables and broth would flavor the pot.

INGREDIENTS:

1-2 pound beef roast
1 pound smoked sausage, cut into one inch links
1 cup chopped onions
1 cup chopped celery
1 cup chopped bell pepper
6 whole cloves of garlic
2 bay leaves
2 cups cubed potatoes
2 cups diced carrots
3 ears corn, halved
2 cups chopped tomatoes
1 cup sliced okra
salt and cracked pepper to taste
Louisiana Gold Pepper Sauce to taste

METHOD:

In a heavy bottom stock pot, place roast, sausage, onions, celery, bell pepper, garlic and bay leaves. Cover with lightly salted water by two inches. Season to taste using salt, pepper and Louisiana Gold. Bring to a rolling boil, reduce to simmer and cook until roast is tender, approximately two to three hours. Remove roast from pot and tear into small serving pieces. Return meat and all remaining vegetables to the stock. Bring to a low boil and cook until vegetables are tender. Adjust seasonings if necessary. Serve in a soup bowl with hot French bread.

Changes

HERB AND GARLIC STUFFED LEG OF LAMB

PREP TIME: 2 Hours
SERVES: 6-8
COMMENT:

Leg of lamb is best when prepared from an animal that is six months to one year old. It has a very mild flavor and is tender when roasted. Though lamb was not often used in Louisiana plantation cooking, it seems to have been a real specialty at Rosedown. When flavored with rosemary, sage and garlic, there is nothing better.

INGREDIENTS:

1-5 pound leg of lamb
1/4 cup minced rosemary
1/4 cup minced sage
1 tbsp minced tarragon
1 tbsp minced thyme
1/4 cup chopped garlic
1/4 pound melted butter
salt and cracked pepper to taste
1/2 cup chopped rose petals

METHOD:

Preheat oven to 450 degrees F. Using a sharp paring knife, remove the fell or white papery membrane covering the leg of lamb. In a small mixing bowl, combine all of the herbs and garlic and blend to incorporate well. Season to taste using salt and pepper. Cut a one inch hole at intervals around the roast and stuff with equal portions of the seasoning mixture. Fill a minimum of one dozen holes. Place the lamb, fat side up, in a large baking pan and drizzle with butter. Rub remaining herb mixture over the lamb and season to taste using salt and pepper. Place in the oven, uncovered, and cook ten to fifteen minutes. Reduce temperature to 375 degrees F. Roast thirty minutes per pound or until internal temperature reaches 140 degrees F for medium, basting occasionally. Allow the roast to sit thirty minutes before carving and serve with pan drippings. Garnish with rose petals.

LAGNIAPPE

Garlic is indisputably one of the oldest spices known to man. It is one of the few, if not the only, spices mentioned in the Bible. Remember Moses coming down from the mountain with the 10 commandments in hand? It is here that the Israelites mentioned that they left Egypt without their garlic. Shakespeare hated garlic while Gandhi, Henry VIII and Eleanor Roosevelt loved the spice. It's even rumored to chase off vampires. Obviously, garlic is hated by some and loved by many. I would hate to think what our Louisiana cooking would be today without the great flavor of garlic.

Changes

LAFITTE'S PEPPER SEARED LAMB CHOPS

PREP TIME: 45 Minutes

SERVES: 6

COMMENT:

The Creoles of New Orleans were great fanciers of lamb. When the Viala family left New Orleans to construct their plantation in Donaldsonville, their love for lamb accompanied them to this city. The old Viala Plantation is home to my Lafitte's Landing Restaurant today.

INGREDIENTS:

12 lamb chops, 1/2 inch thick
1/2 cup ground pink peppercorns
1/2 cup ground black peppercorns
1 cup seasoned flour
1/2 cup oil
1/2 cup sliced green onions
1 tbsp diced garlic
1 cup oyster mushrooms
1/2 tsp chopped rosemary
1 tsp chopped thyme
1 ounce dark rum
2 cups demi-glace (see recipe)
1/4 cup heavy whipping cream
salt and cracked pepper to taste
3 cups cooked spinach fettucine

The Cypress Smokehouse at Viala

METHOD:

Place the lamb chops on a large platter and evenly coat both sides with crushed peppercorns. Set aside. In a heavy bottom saute pan, heat oil over medium high heat. Dust chops in flour, shaking off all excess. Saute until golden brown on both sides or medium rare. Remove chops and set aside. Into the saute pan, add onions, garlic, mushrooms, rosemary and thyme. Saute three to five minutes or until vegetables are wilted. Remove the pan from burner and add rum.

NOTE: *Be careful as alcohol will ignite and burn a few minutes until flame extinguishes itself.*

Add demi-glace and whipping cream and season to taste using salt and pepper. Swirl the skillet above the burner until the demi-glace and cream are well incorporated. Bring to a rolling boil, reduce sauce until slightly thickened and return chops to pan. Heat two to three minutes and serve with hot fettucine.

Changes

VEAL SHANKS AUDUBON

PREP TIME: 3 hours
SERVES: 6
COMMENT:

Shanks were very important in early plantation cooking. Pork shanks were the most popular and readily available. However, often when young calves were slaughtered, the shanks were reserved for that special event. Here is John James Audubon's favorite shank recipe, prepared during his stay at Oakley Plantation in 1821.

INGREDIENTS:

4 - 1 pound veal shanks
1/2 cup oil
1 cup flour
1 cup chopped onions
1 cup chopped celery
1 cup chopped bell pepper
1/4 cup diced garlic
1 cup pearl onions
2 sliced carrots
2 quarts beef stock (see recipe)
1 yam, cubed
1 pkg frozen peas
20 button mushrooms
1 cup oyster mushrooms
pinch of thyme
pinch of basil
1 sprig of rosemary
salt and cracked pepper to taste
Louisiana Gold Pepper Sauce to taste

METHOD:

Preheat oven to 400 degrees F. In a large dutch oven, heat oil over medium high heat. Season veal shanks with salt, pepper, thyme and basil. Dust the shanks in flour, shaking off all excess. Place shanks in dutch oven and brown on all sides. Remove and set aside. Add onions, celery, bell pepper, garlic, pearl onions and carrots. Saute three to five minutes or until vegetables are wilted. Add shanks and beef stock. Bring to a rolling boil and add all remaining ingredients. Season to taste using salt, pepper and Louisiana Gold. Cover, bake two and a half hours and check for tenderness. Remove shanks and reduce cooking liquid over medium high heat to a thickened sauce consistency. Serve over pasta.

Changes

____

____

____

____

____

LAGNIAPPE

This dish is named in honor of the artist and naturalist, John James Audubon. It was in 1803 that he left art lessons in Paris to come in search of adventure in America. In 1820, after marrying in Pennsylvania, Audubon set out for New Orleans by flatboat without a cent in his pocket. He carried a flute, a violin and a bird book. He soon met the Pirrie family of St. Francisville who needed a tutor for their daughter, Eliza. They hired the temperamental Frenchman to teach dancing, music, drawing and hair platting to Eliza. The arrangements were simple. He would teach in the morning and devote his afternoon to drawing birds. For this, he received free room and board. The family agreed but thought the time spent in the woods was a waste and the drawings certainly had no value!

BRAISED OSSO BUCCO

PREP TIME: 30 minutes
SERVES: 6
COMMENT:

Osso bucco or "long bone" is the shank portion of the leg in beef, veal and lamb. This bone is surrounded by a large portion of meat that is perfect for slow braising. Though inexpensive, when cooked properly, it becomes one of the finest cuts of meat you've ever eaten.

INGREDIENTS:

12 osso bucco, one inch thick
1 cup seasoned flour
1/2 cup olive oil
2 cups chopped onions
1 cup chopped celery
1/2 cup chopped bell pepper
1/4 cup diced garlic
1 tbsp chopped thyme
1 tbsp chopped basil
1 tbsp oregano
1/2 cup red wine
1-28 ounce can plum tomatoes, drained
2 cups beef stock (see recipe)
1 cup sliced mushrooms
1 cup pearl onions
salt and cracked pepper to taste
Louisiana Gold Pepper Sauce to taste
4 cups cooked angel hair pasta

METHOD:

Preheat oven to 375 degrees F. In a heavy bottom dutch oven, heat oil over medium high heat. Dust shanks in seasoned flour, shaking off all excess, and brown on both sides. Remove and set aside. Add onions, celery, bell peppers, garlic, thyme, basil and oregano. Saute three to five minutes or until vegetables are wilted. Deglaze with red wine and add tomatoes and beef stock. Bring to a rolling boil and reduce to simmer. Add mushrooms and pearl onions and season to taste using salt, pepper and Louisiana Gold. Return shanks to sauce, cover and bake until tender, approximately forty-five minutes. Serve over angel hair pasta.

Changes

BRUCCIALUNA

PREP TIME: 4 Hours
SERVES: 6-8
COMMENT:

The Italians arrived in and around Donaldsonville in the late 1800s. They settled on Bayou Lafourche, where many Italian families opened grocery stores, vegetable stands and meat markets. This classic recipe is still found on menus in that area today.

INGREDIENTS:

2 large round steaks
1 pound ground pork
1/2 cup chopped onions
1/2 cup chopped bell pepper
1/4 cup diced garlic
1/4 cup sliced green onions
1 tbsp chopped oregano
1 tbsp chopped thyme
1 tbsp chopped basil
2 eggs
1/4 cup grated Parmesan cheese
1 cup seasoned Italian bread crumbs
1/2 cup olive oil
1 cup chopped onions
1 cup chopped celery
1/2 cup chopped bell pepper
1/4 cup diced garlic
2 cups diced tomatoes
4-8 ounce cans tomato sauce
1 cup chicken stock (see recipe)
1 tbsp chopped oregano
1 tbsp chopped basil
1 tbsp sugar
salt and cracked pepper to taste
Louisiana Gold Pepper Sauce to taste
1/2 cup sliced green onions
1/4 cup chopped parsley

METHOD:

In a large mixing bowl, combine pork, onions, bell pepper, garlic, green onions, oregano, thyme, basil, eggs, cheese and bread crumbs. Using your hands, mix all ingredients thoroughly. Season to taste using salt, pepper and Louisiana Gold. Stuff round steaks with equal portions of the seasoned pork. Roll into a jelly roll and tie securely with butcher's twine. In a large black iron dutch oven, heat olive oil over medium high heat. Season stuffed round steak with salt and pepper and saute until golden brown on all sides. Remove and set aside. In the same oil, add onions, celery, bell pepper and garlic. Saute three to five minutes or until vegetables are wilted. Add tomatoes, tomato sauce, stock, oregano, basil and sugar. Bring sauce to a rolling boil, reduce to simmer and season to taste using salt, pepper and Louisiana Gold. Return the bruccialuna to sauce and cook until round steak is tender, approximately two to three hours. Add green onions and parsley and cook ten additional minutes. When ready to serve, remove twine, slice and serve over pasta.

The Servants' Rear Staircase at Madewood

Changes

BRAISED SKIRT STEAK ASHLAND

PREP TIME: 1 hour
SERVES: 6
COMMENT:

Skirt steak, often referred to as butcher steak, is one of those lean healthy cuts of meat. It is excellent when properly cooked and is located in the beef section running from the rib to the loin. Skirt steak is best when cooked quickly over a hot fire or slowly braised in a rich sauce. This recipe is my favorite.

INGREDIENTS:

6-6 ounce skirt steaks
1/4 cup vegetable oil
1 cup unseasoned flour
1 cup chopped onions
1/2 cup chopped celery
1/2 cup chopped bell pepper
1/4 cup diced garlic
1 cup sliced carrots
1 cup diced tomatoes
1 cup sliced mushrooms
1-8 ounce can tomato sauce
4 cups beef stock (see recipe)
1/2 cup sliced green onions
1/4 cup chopped parsley
salt and cracked pepper to taste
Louisiana Gold Pepper Sauce to taste

METHOD:

In a heavy bottom dutch oven, heat oil over medium high heat. Season skirt steaks with salt, pepper and Louisiana Gold. Dust the steaks in flour, shaking off all excess. Saute steaks until golden brown on both sides. Remove and set aside. Add onions, celery, bell pepper and garlic. Saute three to five minutes or until vegetables are wilted. Add carrots, tomatoes and mushrooms and continue to saute an additional five minutes. Pour in tomato sauce and beef stock, bring to a rolling boil and reduce to simmer. Return steaks to dutch oven and add green onions and parsley. Allow to braise until tender, approximately one to one and a half hours. Adjust seasonings to taste using salt, pepper and Louisiana Gold. Serve over rice or egg noodles.

Changes

HONEY GLAZED BARBECUED RIBS

PREP TIME: 1 hour
SERVES: 10
COMMENT:

Though pork ribs are the most popular in South Louisiana cooking, nothing is meatier or tastier than properly barbecued beef short ribs. When glazed with honey and cane syrup and smoked over pecan wood, these ribs are worth fighting for.

INGREDIENTS:

4 pounds beef short ribs
1 large onion, quartered
1 stick of celery, quartered
1 carrot, sliced
1 head of garlic, split
1 tbsp black peppercorns
2 bay leaves
2 tbsps Creole mustard
1/4 cup honey
1/4 cup cane syrup
1/2 cup tomato sauce
1/2 cup ketchup
pinch of chile powder
1 tbsp diced garlic
salt and cracked pepper to taste
Louisiana Gold Pepper Sauce to taste

METHOD:

In a large stock pot, combine onions, celery, carrot, garlic, peppercorns and bay leaves. Cut short ribs into six inch sections and place in stock pot. Cover with lightly salted water by four inches. Bring to a rolling boil, reduce to simmer and cook until ribs are tender, approximately forty-five minutes. Remove from water and set aside. This may be done one day prior to grilling. Preheat barbecue pit according to manufacturer's directions and soak a few pieces of pecan wood chips in water. In a large mixing bowl, combine all remaining ingredients. Using a wire whisk, whip until all ingredients are well blended. Place ribs on pit, with a few chips of the wood, and cook until thoroughly heated and browned. Glaze with the sauce mixture and continue to cook until ribs are to your liking. Serve with cajun ratatouille and old maid's potato salad (see recipe).

The Billiard Room at San Francisco

Changes

BOEUF EN DAUBE

PREP TIME: 2 1/2 Hours
MAKES: 2 - 4" x 8" terrine pans
COMMENT:

Daube is the French term for slowly braised beef combined with fresh vegetables and seasonings. This dish was normally served on Sunday. The leftovers were mixed with red wine, bacon and seasonings. The dish was placed in a terrine mold, chilled and jelled, similar to hogs head cheese. It was considered a delicacy and served as a salad or hors d'oeuvre.

INGREDIENTS:

3 pounds round steak
3 quarts beef stock (see recipe)
1 onion, quartered
2 stalks celery, halved
1 bell pepper, quartered
2 carrots, halved
6 cloves of garlic
1 bay leaf
1 tbsp whole peppercorns
4 whole cloves
1 cup dry red wine
salt and cracked pepper to taste
1 sprig of thyme
1 tbsp chopped sage
Louisiana Gold Pepper Sauce to taste
1/4 cup minced onions
1/4 cup minced red bell peppers
1/2 cup minced carrots
1/4 cup chopped parsley
3 strips cooked bacon, crushed
4 envelopes unflavored gelatin

METHOD:

In a stock pot, combine round steak, beef stock, onion, celery, bell pepper, carrots, garlic, bay leaf, peppercorns, cloves and red wine. Season to taste using salt, pepper, thyme, sage and Louisiana Gold. Bring to a rolling boil, reduce to simmer and allow to cook until tender, approximately one and a half hours. Remove the round steak from liquid and allow to cool. Strain approximately two and a half quarts of stock for the terrine. In a sauce pot, combine minced onions, bell pepper, carrots and parsley. Add stock, bring to a low boil and reduce to simmer. Allow to cook until vegetables are wilted but not overcooked. Remove from heat and set aside. Using a paring knife, chop the meat into very small pieces. Place meat and bacon in the bottom of two 4" x 8" terrine pans. Dissolve gelatin in one cup of the stock and return to pot. Adjust seasonings using salt, pepper and Louisiana Gold. Ladle the hot stock over the meat in the terrine pans until filled three fourths of an inch from the top. Allow to cool, cover with clear wrap and refrigerate overnight for flavors to develop. Serve on a decorated platter with garlic croutons or crackers.

Changes

SAUTEED LIVER AND ONIONS

PREP TIME: 1 Hour
SERVES: 6
COMMENT:

Although many people tend to dislike the flavor of liver today, this item was in high demand during the plantation days. After all, there was only one liver to every cow and customers stood in line for this delicacy.

INGREDIENTS:

2 pounds sliced calves liver
8 ounces bacon
2 large onions, thinly sliced
1 cup seasoned flour
salt and cracked pepper to taste
1/4 cup chicken stock (see recipe)

METHOD:

In a heavy bottom black iron skillet, cook bacon over medium high heat. Continue to cook until bacon is crispy. Remove, chop and set aside. Season liver using salt and pepper. Dust in flour, shaking off all excess. Saute until golden brown on each side, approximately ten minutes. Set aside and keep warm. Into skillet, add onions and cook over medium high heat. Stir constantly until onions are wilted and caramelized, approximately twenty minutes. When done, push onions to one side of the skillet and add bacon and liver. Pour in chicken stock, bring to a rolling boil and cook for five minutes. To serve, place liver in the center of the plate and top with caramelized onions and bacon.

Changes

Chapter Eight

Seafood

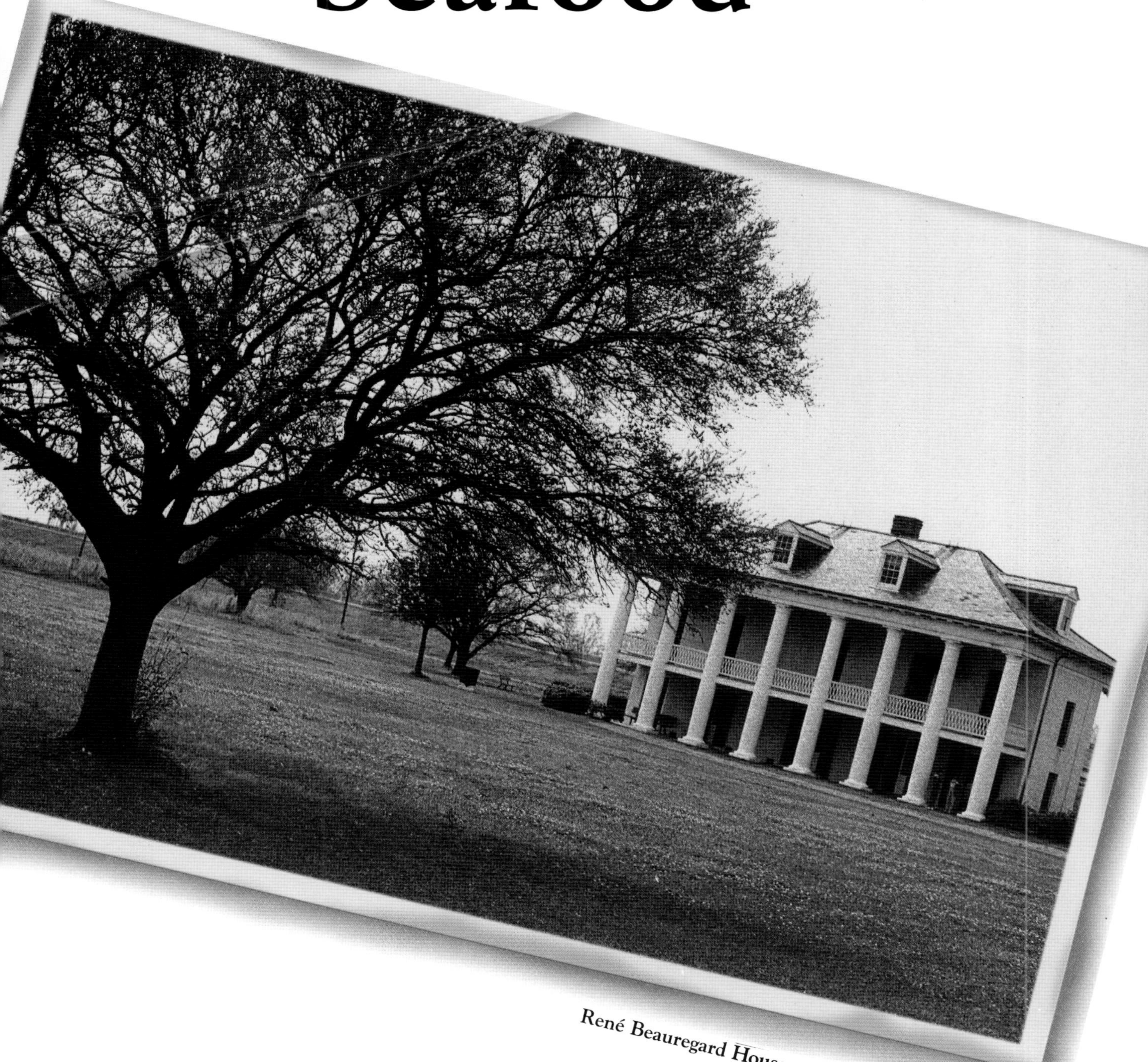
René Beauregard House

Rene Beauregard House

"The Battle of New Orleans"

We've all heard the words of the song..."in 1814, we took a little trip, along with Colonel Jackson down the mighty Mississip...". That trip ended six miles below the city of New Orleans in Chalmette. On the cold, foggy morning of January 8, 1815, ten thousand British troops arrived to reclaim Louisiana for England. General Andrew Jackson answered the call, amassing his army of five thousand. They were made up of soldiers, free men of color, Indians and pirates. The battle ensued and when the smoke cleared, two thousand British soldiers lay dead. The victorious Americans claimed only thirteen casualties and General Andrew Jackson was off to the White House.

The Beauregard house stands next to the monument in Chalmette National Historic Park, the site of the Battle of New Orleans. Records show that the house was built on land purchased by Alexandre Baron, the Marquis de Trana, in April 1832, seventeen years after the famous battle. For years it has been called Beauregard, after its last private occupant, Judge Rene Beauregard, son of the famous Confederate General P.G.T. Beauregard. The house is built in the French Creole style with no hallways. It was originally designed as a summer cottage for wealthy New Orleans planters instead of the center of a great plantation. The home was originally built without columns but they were added in the 1850s for a more impressive look.

One of the most interesting construction details of this house is the two fireplace chimneys that come together as one in the attic by means of a large arch. The central chimney then projects through the roof just below the ridge. This design allows for symmetry between the dormer windows.

To reach the home, park and battlefield monument, head to Chalmette, Louisiana. Take Paris Road to West St. Bernard Highway and follow the signs to Chalmette National Historic Park. 504-589-4428

The Chalmette Monument Honoring Those Who Died at the Battle of New Orleans

At left, Shrimp and Catfish Fricassee (page 220) and White Beans with Ham and Salt Meat (page 156)

SHRIMP AND CATFISH FRICASSEE

PREP TIME: 1 1/2 Hours
SERVES: 6-8
COMMENT:

A fricassee or stew is usually a mixture of whatever is at hand. I've discovered many combinations in Louisiana fricassees from seafoods and meats to vegetables and game. In the city of Chalmette, below New Orleans, the hunters and trappers combine blue channel catfish with river shrimp to create an incomparable fricassee.

INGREDIENTS:

1 pound peeled river or gulf shrimp
3 pounds cubed catfish
1 cup oil
1 cup flour
1 cup chopped onions
1 cup chopped celery
1 cup chopped bell pepper
2 tbsps diced garlic
1 tbsp diced cayenne peppers
4 bay leaves
pinch of thyme
pinch of basil
3 quarts fish stock (see recipe)
1 cup chopped parsley
1 cup sliced green onions
6 eggs
salt and cracked pepper to taste
Louisiana Gold Pepper Sauce to taste

METHOD:

In a two gallon heavy bottom stock pot, heat oil over medium high heat. Sprinkle in flour and using a wire whisk, stir constantly until dark brown roux is achieved (see roux techniques). Should black specks appear, discard and begin again. Add onions, celery, bell pepper and garlic. Saute three to five minutes or until vegetables are wilted. Add cayenne peppers, bay leaves, thyme and basil, blending well into roux mixture. Add approximately two cups of the cubed fish and stir into roux. Slowly add fish stock, one ladle at a time, until a rich stew consistency is achieved. Remember, the remaining fish are ninety percent water and will thin the stew considerably when added. You may wish to keep the stew just a little thicker until the remaining fish are incorporated. Reserve the remaining stock for later use. Bring to a rolling boil, reduce to simmer and cook approximately thirty minutes. Add the remaining fish, shrimp, green onions and parsley. Stir into the stew mixture and continue to cook until fish is tender, approximately ten to fifteen minutes. Crack the eggs into the simmering stew and allow to poach for ten minutes. Season to taste using salt, pepper and Louisiana Gold. Serve over steamed rice or pasta.

Changes

CASPIANA FRIED CATFISH

PREP TIME: 30 Minutes
SERVES: 6
COMMENT:

There are literally thousands of "family recipes" for fried catfish. Every now and again a special recipe will emerge that is worthy of taking note. This is definitely one!

INGREDIENTS:

12 3-5 ounce whole catfish fillets
1 cup prepared mustard
1/4 cup Worcestershire sauce
salt and cracked black pepper to taste
granulated garlic to taste
1 tbsp dried thyme
1 tbsp dried basil
Louisiana Gold Pepper Sauce to taste
3 cups yellow corn flour
vegetable oil for deep frying
2 small bermuda onions, thinly sliced
1 cup sliced green onions
1/2 cup red wine vinegar

METHOD:

In a homestyle deep fryer, such as Fry Daddy, heat oil according to manufacturer's directions. If using a dutch oven, heat oil to 375 degrees F. In a large mixing bowl, place mustard and Worcestershire sauce. Season to taste using salt, pepper, granulated garlic, thyme, basil and Louisiana Gold. Using a wire whisk, whip until all ingredients are well blended. Add fillets and toss fish in marinade until well coated. Allow to sit at room temperature fifteen minutes. Place the corn flour in a large paper bag and season to taste using salt, pepper and granulated garlic. Remember not to over-season, since the fish has been seasoned in the marinade. Place fish fillets in paper bag with corn flour. Seal the bag tightly and shake vigorously until fish are well coated. You may also bread the fish in a large pan, if a paper bag is not available. Fry fish, two to three fillets at a time, until it is golden brown and floats to the top of the oil. When cooked, remove and drain. Stack the fish on a large serving platter and top each layer with green onions, bermuda onions and a sprinkle of vinegar. This will create a steaming effect and the flavor will permeate the fish. However, no strong onion or mustard flavor will be prevalent in this dish.

Changes

THELMA PARKER'S SHRIMP PIE

PREP TIME: 1 1/2 Hours
SERVES: 6
COMMENT:

I first met Thelma Parker on a visit to Madewood Plantation. Thelma has been the cook there for over 25 years and is famous for her Shrimp Pie. Though she makes the recipe using canned shrimp soup, I have created the recipe using a more traditional method.

INGREDIENTS:

2 lbs (70-90 count) shrimp, peeled
1/4 pound butter
1 cup chopped onions
1 cup chopped celery
1/2 cup chopped green bell pepper
1/2 cup chopped red bell pepper
2 tbsps diced garlic
1/2 cup diced tomatoes
2 bay leaves
1/2 cup tomato sauce
1 cup flour
1 1/2 quarts shellfish stock (see recipe)
Worcestershire Sauce to taste
1 cup sliced green onions
1/2 cup chopped parsley
salt and cracked pepper to taste
Louisiana Gold Pepper Sauce to taste
3-9 inch prepared pie shells
1 egg
1/2 cup milk
1/2 cup water

METHOD:

Preheat oven to 350 degrees F. Place pie shells in refrigerator to chill. In a one gallon stock pot, melt butter over medium high heat. Add onions, celery, bell peppers, garlic, tomatoes and bay leaves. Saute three to five minutes or until vegetables are wilted. Add shrimp and tomato sauce, blending well into the vegetable mixture. Sprinkle in flour and using a wire whip, stir constantly until blonde roux is achieved (see roux techniques). Slowly add shrimp stock or water, a little at a time, until sauce consistency is achieved. Bring to a low boil, reduce to simmer and cook thirty minutes, stirring occasionally. Add Worcestershire sauce, green onions and parsley and cook an additional five minutes. Season to taste using salt, pepper and Louisiana Gold. Remove from heat and allow to cool thoroughly. Remove pie shells from refrigerator and cut in two. Place a generous portion of shrimp filling in the center of each half. In a small mixing bowl, combine egg, milk and water. Using a wire whisk, stir until all ingredients are well blended. Paint the edges of the dough with the eggwash. Fold dough in a triangle shape and seal the edges by pressing together with a fork. Pierce two or three holes in the top of the dough to allow steam to escape during the cooking process. Coat the top of the pie with eggwash and place on a baking sheet. Bake twenty to twenty-five minutes or until golden brown. The shrimp pies may be made in advance and frozen. When cooking, remove from the freezer and place in a 375 degree F oven for approximately one hour.

Changes

OPEN HEARTH GRILLED FISH

PREP TIME: 1 Hour
SERVES: 6
COMMENT:

There was only one way to roast a fish in the open hearth prior to the reflector oven. The cook would place a seasoned, whole fish on an oak, pecan or cedar plank. Then the plank would be placed standing upright on the side wall of the hearth. The reflective heat from the coals cooked the fish. Here is a similar version for the home oven.

Black Iron Cookware at Magnolia Mound

INGREDIENTS:

1 3-4 pound large mouth bass
1/4 cup olive oil
1/4 cup chopped thyme
1/4 cup chopped basil
1/4 cup chopped tarragon
1/4 cup chopped dill
1 bunch whole mixed herbs
salt and cracked pepper to taste
Louisiana Gold Pepper Sauce to taste

METHOD:

Have the local lumber company cut a piece of oak, pecan or cedar eight inches wide and twenty inches long. Be sure to measure your oven width before cutting the length of the plank. Oil the plank thoroughly with olive oil, rubbing well into the pores of the wood. To season, place in a 200 degree F oven for thirty minutes. Remove and allow to cool. Preheat oven to 275 degrees F. Completely scale the fish, leaving the head and tail intact. Remove the gills and rinse the inside cavity. Using a sharp paring knife, cut three slits on each side of the fish to the bone. These slits will be used for seasoning, but also to ensure proper cooking. Rub the fish with olive oil and season inside and out with salt, pepper and Louisiana Gold. Place the chopped herbs in a small mixing bowl and blend thoroughly. Rub the herb mixture in each of the six slits and completely over the fish. Fill the belly cavity with the whole mixed herbs. Rub the plank thoroughly with olive oil and preheat in oven for fifteen minutes. Remove and place the fish lengthwise on the hot plank. Put the plank on a cookie sheet to catch any drippings that may run off during cooking. Bake on center rack of the oven for approximately twenty minutes or until fish is flaky. There is no need to turn the fish during the cooking process. Remove and serve on the plank for a unique presentation.

Changes

CREOLE CRAB AND RICE CASSEROLE

PREP TIME: 1 Hour
SERVES: 6
COMMENT:

Duncan Kenner, the builder of this magnificent Greek temple, often spoke of his love for crab. With the Germans living ten miles down river, a variety of cheeses were available. Kenner would combine this cheese with lump crab and seasoned rice to create his favorite dish.

INGREDIENTS:

1 cup jumbo lump crabmeat
2 cups cooked white rice
1 pound sharp cheddar cheese or Velveeta
1 cup milk
4 tbsps butter
1/2 cup finely diced onions
1/2 cup finely diced celery
1/2 cup finely diced green bell pepper
1/2 cup finely diced red bell pepper
1/4 cup diced garlic
1/2 cup sliced green onions
1/4 cup chopped parsley
salt and cracked pepper to taste
Louisiana Gold Pepper Sauce to taste
2 eggs, well beaten

METHOD:

Preheat oven to 350 degrees F. The perfect formula for cooked rice is one part rice to one and a half parts water with a pinch of salt and a pat of butter. Bring the liquid to a rolling boil and add rice. Reduce heat to lowest setting, cover and allow to cook thirty minutes without stirring. The rice will be perfect every time. In a small dutch oven, melt butter over medium high heat. Add cheese and milk and stir constantly until cheese has melted. Remove from heat and add onions, celery, bell peppers, garlic, green onions and parsley, blending well into the cheese mixture. Season to taste using salt, pepper and Louisiana Gold. You may wish to over-season since the rice will need the additional flavor. Fold in the lump crabmeat and rice and gently stir until well incorporated. Add eggs, cover and bake until casserole is firmly set, approximately forty-five minutes.

Changes

Kent House Plantation

Kent House Plantation

"Word Travels Fast"

Although there were no telephones or televisions back in the 1800s, communication was necessary and did take place. If the message was urgent, pony express or dispatch could be used. With the advent of steamboats and trains, communication tended to speed up just a little. In the rural areas, as well as in the cities, a card or placard could be nailed to a tree or post announcing an event. When there was a message of sorrow, such as a death in the family, a simple black bow or ribbon nailed to the gate post told the entire story.

Kent House is the oldest known structure still standing in Central Louisiana. Completed in 1800, it was built by Pierre Baillio II. His land grant had been received in 1794 from the Spanish Governor Carondelet. In 1842, Robert Hynson purchased the home and having come from Kent County, Maryland, he named the home for that area.

The separate outdoor kitchen was often the first building constructed on the plantation after completion of the main house. The kitchens were always separated because of the constant threat of fire or excess heat during the summer. The original kitchen at Kent House was destroyed by a tornado and never rebuilt. However, in 1979, a kitchen from Augusta Plantation near Bunkie, Louisiana was moved to the site. Today, open-hearth cooking is featured in this structure. Kent House not only survived the ravages of time, but also the Civil War. In 1963, the home was planned for demolition. Once again, the home was spared from destruction, and was renovated and placed on the National Register. Today, the home is completely furnished with museum quality antiques and on the grounds are appropriate gardens and out buildings depicting plantation life.

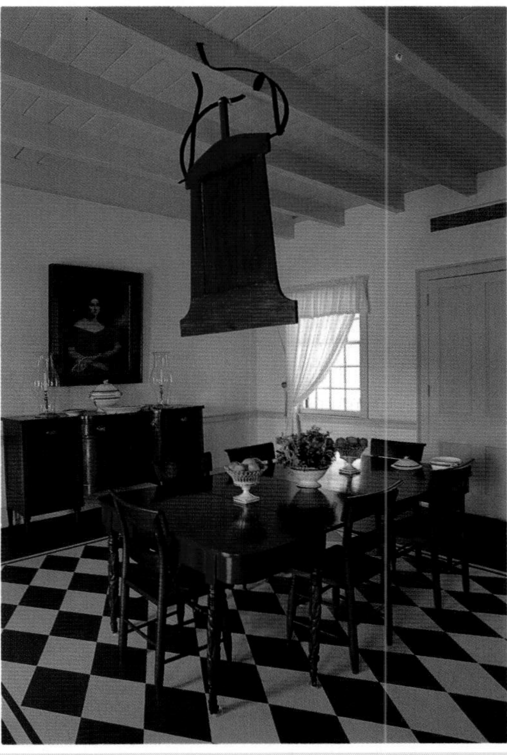

The Dining Room at Kent House

One of the most unique events at Kent House is the "Wakes of the Past" exhibit. Since death was such a significant aspect of daily life, this mourning tour accurately depicts details of a plantation death scene. The exhibit takes place the entire month of October.

To reach Kent House, take I-49 North to Alexandria. Follow Highway 71 to Bayou Rapides Road. 318-487-5998.

At left, clockwise from bottom left, Creamed Radishes (page 132), Poach Brandied Pears (page 282), Smothered Pork Sausage in Apple Cider (page 196), and Honeyed Apple Rings (page 305)

PAN-FRIED STRIPED BASS WITH GARLIC DEMI-BORDELAISE

PREP TIME: 1 Hour

SERVES: 6

COMMENT:

Lake Bruin, in Tensas Parish, is known for the best striped bass fishing in Louisiana. When caught fresh and pan fried, this fish will match the taste and texture of any fine fish available in the world. Flavoring with a quick garlic demi-bordelaise sauce turns this campfire delight into a delicacy.

INGREDIENTS:

6-1 pound striped bass
1 egg
1 cup milk
2 tbsps Creole mustard
1 cup water
3 cups seasoned yellow corn flour
oil for sauteing
1/4 pound butter
18 cloves garlic
1/4 cup chopped parsley
1/4 cup sliced green onions
juice of one lemon
1 ounce dry white wine
Worcestershire Sauce to taste
salt and cracked pepper to taste
Louisiana Gold Pepper Sauce to taste

METHOD:

In a black iron skillet, heat oil over medium high heat. Using a sharp paring knife, cut slits in each side of the bass to ensure quick frying. Season the fish inside and out using salt, pepper and Louisiana Gold. In a mixing bowl, combine egg, milk, mustard and water. Using a wire whisk, stir until all ingredients are well blended. Dip the fish into the eggwash and then into the yellow corn flour, shaking off all excess. Pan fry three to five minutes on each side or until fish is golden brown. Place in a 250 degree F oven to keep warm. Pour off the excess oil from the black iron skillet except for pan drippings. Add butter and melt over medium high heat. Add garlic and saute until tender but not over-browned. Add all other ingredients, swirling the pan constantly to blend well. Remove fish from oven and place on a large serving platter. Top with garlic demi-bordelaise sauce.

Changes

HERB BAKED LARGE MOUTH BASS

PREP TIME: 1 Hour
SERVES: 6
COMMENT:

The Spanish influence around Toledo Bend Lake gave origin to this tomato-based fish stew. The Spanish settled Sabine Parish prior to the Louisiana Purchase and many of their great fish dishes became a major part of our Louisiana cuisine. Keeping the fish whole and stuffing it with fresh herbs, prior to baking, makes this dish a perfect table centerpiece.

INGREDIENTS:

1 3-4 pound large mouth bass
1 cup fresh basil
1 cup fresh thyme
1 cup fresh dill
4 bay leaves
4 lemon slices
8 slices purple onions
1/4 cup olive oil
1 cup chopped onions
1 cup chopped celery
1/2 cup chopped bell pepper
1/4 cup chopped garlic
1 cup diced tomatoes
2 cups V-8 or tomato juice
2-8 ounce cans tomato sauce
1 tbsp chopped thyme
1 tbsp chopped basil
2 bay leaves
salt and cracked pepper to taste
Louisiana Gold Pepper Sauce to taste
4 lemon slices
1/4 cup sliced green onions
1/4 cup chopped parsley

METHOD:

Preheat oven to 375 degrees F. Remove gills and eyes from the fish and make sure the cavity is well cleaned. It is best to cook the fish with the head on. This will make for a beautiful table presentation. Season the inside cavity well with salt, pepper and Louisiana Gold. Stuff fish with thyme, basil, dill, bay leaves and lemon slices. Using a sharp knife, cut three diagonal slits across the top fillet of the fish. This will assist in the flavoring as well as the presentation of the dish. Place purple onions on the bottom of a large baking pan. Add fish and season to taste using salt, pepper and Louisiana Gold. Set aside. In a black iron dutch oven, heat olive oil over medium high heat. Add onions, celery, bell pepper and garlic. Saute three to five minutes or until vegetables are wilted. Add tomatoes, tomato juice and sauce. Bring to a rolling boil, reduce to simmer and cook ten to fifteen minutes. Add basil, thyme and bay leaves. Season to taste using salt and pepper. Remove from heat and pour hot sauce over the stuffed fish. Garnish with lemon slices, green onions and parsley. Cover with foil and bake approximately thirty minutes. When cooked, remove to a large serving platter and top with sauce. Garnish with fresh herbs.

Changes

MUSTARD-FRIED WHITE PERCH

PREP TIME: 30 Minutes
SERVES: 6
COMMENT:

The white perch of North Louisiana is not only a prize game fish, but it is also revered as the best eating fish around. In South Louisiana, it is referred to as either crappie or sac-a-lait. Many people fillet the fish because of the small bones, but most prefer it whole and crispy.

Yucca House at Melrose, One of the Oldest Structures in America

INGREDIENTS:

24 crappie fillets
oil for deep frying
2 eggs
1 cup milk
2 tbsps Creole mustard
juice of one lemon
1/4 cup chopped dill
salt and cracked pepper to taste
Louisiana Gold Pepper Sauce to taste
4 cups seasoned corn meal

METHOD:

In a homestyle deep fryer, such as Fry Daddy, heat oil according to manufacturer's directions. If using a dutch oven, heat oil to 375 degrees F. The oil should cover the fish by two inches. In a mixing bowl, combine eggs, milk, mustard, lemon juice, dill, salt, pepper and Louisiana Gold. Place fillets in mustard batter and allow to marinate at room temperature for thirty minutes. Place the corn meal in a large paper bag, add fillets and seal tightly. Shake vigorously to coat fillets thoroughly. Deep fry a few fillets at a time until fish are golden brown and rise to the surface. Remove, drain and keep warm. Serve fillets with tartar or cocktail sauce (see recipe).

Changes

____

____

____

____

LAGNIAPPE

I remember one night sitting around a table at Griffin's Lodge on Toledo Bend Lake. Patsy Havard served a cornmeal dish that I experienced for the first time. The locals called it "stirrup" and after hearing the history of the dish, that name made sense. Just as we eat hushpuppies in the southern part of Louisiana, stirrup is eaten up North. After the fish is cooked, drain all oil from the fryer and scrape the cornmeal residue that has fallen to the bottom. Place this in a black iron pot with a little fresh cornmeal, green onions and parsley. Saute the mixture until the vegetables are wilted and add two eggs and fresh chopped tomatoes. "Stir-rup" the mixture until it resembles couscous. The dish is already full flavored from the seasoning of the fish. Serve one spoon of the stirrup with fish fillets.

REDFISH COURTBOUILLON

PREP TIME: 1 Hour
SERVES: 8-10
COMMENT:

The courtbouillon of South Louisiana differs greatly from that of its forefather, the courtbouillon of the Mediterranean coast of France. Here in bayou country, we begin with the dark brown roux of the Cajuns. In the South of France, the soup begins with olive oil and layers of vegetables and shellfish. I do believe the Cajun version is far superior.

INGREDIENTS:

1 3-5 pound redfish
1 onion, quartered
2 celery stalks, quartered
1 head of garlic, split
2 bay leaves
20 black peppercorns
1 cup oil
1 cup flour
2 cups chopped onions
2 cups chopped celery
1/2 cup chopped red bell pepper
1/2 cup chopped yellow bell pepper
1/2 cup chopped green bell pepper
2 tbsps chopped garlic
1/2 cup chopped fish pieces
1 cup diced tomatoes
1-8 ounce can Rotel tomatoes
1-8 ounce can tomato sauce
3 quarts reserved fish stock
juice of one lemon
3 bay leaves
pinch of thyme
pinch of basil
1/2 cup sliced green onions
1/4 cup chopped parsley
salt and pepper to taste
Louisianan Gold Pepper Sauce to taste

METHOD:

Fillet the redfish, cut into two inch square cubes and set aside. In a black iron pot, place fish bones, head, onions, celery, garlic, bay leaves and peppercorns. Cover with slightly salted water by two inches. Bring to a rolling boil and cook thirty minutes, skimming the impurities that rise to the surface. Strain and reserve three quarts for the courtbouillon. In a large dutch oven, heat oil over medium high heat. Add flour and using a wire whip, stir constantly until dark brown roux is achieved (see roux techniques). Should black specks appear, discard and begin again. Add onions, celery, bell peppers and garlic. Saute three to five minutes or until vegetables are wilted. Add chopped fish, tomatoes and tomato sauce and continue to saute until fish is cooked into the roux mixture. Add fish stock, one ladle at a time, until all is incorporated. Add lemon juice, bay leaves, thyme and basil. Bring to a rolling boil, reduce to simmer and allow to cook thirty minutes. Add green onions and parsley and season to taste using salt, pepper and Louisiana Gold. Place cubed fillets in sauce, allow to cook three minutes and remove. Adjust seasonings if necessary. Serve over steamed white rice.

Changes

DEEP FRIED HARDSHELL CRABS

PREP TIME: 30 Minutes
SERVES: 6
COMMENT:

This is another great example of a recipe created out of necessity. Normally, crabs are either boiled or made into patties, but never deep fried whole. Since there is an abundance of crabs in South Louisiana, many recipes have been developed to use them.

INGREDIENTS:

2 dozen hardshell crabs, cleaned
2 eggs
1 cup milk
1 cup beer
2 tbsps Creole mustard
1 tbsp Old Bay seasoning
2 tbsps granulated garlic
salt and cracked pepper to taste
Louisiana Gold Pepper Sauce to taste
3 cups seasoned yellow corn flour
oil for deep frying

METHOD:

Have your seafood supplier remove the outer shell from the crab and clean away the organs, eyes, etc. Leave the claws and feet attached to the body and split each crab in half. In a homestyle deep fryer, such as a Fry Daddy, preheat oil according to manufacturer's directions. If using a dutch oven, preheat oil to 375 degrees F. In a large mixing bowl, combine eggs, milk, beer and mustard. Using a wire whisk, blend ingredients well to form beer batter. Season the batter with Old Bay, garlic, salt, pepper and Louisiana Gold. Place the crabs in beer batter and coat well with seasonings. Place corn flour in a brown paper bag, add crabs and seal tightly. Shake vigorously until crabs are coated thoroughly. Deep fry three to five minutes or until crabs are golden brown. Remove and drain on paper towels. Serve with cocktail or tartar sauce.

Changes

____

____

____

LAGNIAPPE

There are over 4,400 species of crabs in the world today. Although different, most have one thing in common - all true crabs are edible. The smallest crab can live in an oyster shell while the Japanese giant crab, the largest, spans ten feet and weighs over thirty pounds. Though we have been eating crabs for thousands of years, most of us know nothing about how crabs eat. Some are hunters, pursuing live prey. Others, like the lobster, are scavengers. Others eat only vegetables, and the robber crab will climb a palm tree to eat coconut for its dinner. Here in America, we prefer the Louisiana and Chesapeake Bay blue crab for boiling or steaming. We fancy the dungeness of the West Coast for eating cold with a dipping sauce. The Alaskan King crab is beyond a doubt the premier seafood to serve alongside a steak.

COUSHATTA GARFISH STEW

PREP TIME: 1 1/2 Hours
SERVES: 6-8
COMMENT:

The tribal symbol of the Coushatta Indians is the garfish. This fish not only symbolizes sustenance and nourishment, but it also plays an important part in tribal customs. The bones are used for jewelry and costuming, while the hide is used for shoes and dress. This prehistoric fish also symbolizes strength and survival.

INGREDIENTS:

4 cups poached garfish meat
1/2 cup chopped onions
1/2 cup chopped celery
1/4 cup chopped red bell pepper
1/4 cup chopped yellow bell pepper
1 tbsp diced garlic
2 eggs
1/4 cup sliced green onions
1 cup seasoned Italian bread crumbs
1/2 cup melted butter
1 cup oil
1 cup flour
1 cup chopped onions
1 cup chopped celery
1/4 cup chopped red bell pepper
1/4 cup chopped yellow bell pepper
1/4 cup diced garlic
1/2 cup reserved fish meat
1/2 cup tomato sauce
2 quarts shellfish stock (see recipe)
1 cup sliced green onions
1 cup chopped parsley
pinch of thyme
pinch of basil
2 bay leaves
Worcestershire Sauce to taste
salt and cracked pepper to taste
Louisiana Gold Pepper Sauce to taste

METHOD:

Preheat oven to 375 degrees F. In a large mixing bowl, combine first eight ingredients. Using your hands, mix all ingredients until well blended. Remove one half cup of seasoned meat for use in the stew. Slowly add the bread crumbs to pick up all excess moisture in the patty mixture. Form into twelve two and a half inch patties. Place patties on a cookie sheet, drizzle with butter and bake fifteen to twenty minutes. Remove and set aside. In a large dutch oven, heat oil over medium high heat. Add flour and using a wire whisk, stir until golden brown roux is achieved (see roux techniques). Add onions, celery, bell peppers and garlic. Saute three to five minutes or until vegetables are wilted. Add fish and tomato sauce and blend well into the vegetable mixture. Slowly add fish stock, a little at a time, until a heavy cream-like consistency is reached. Bring mixture to a rolling boil, reduce to simmer and allow to cook thirty minutes. Add green onions, parsley, thyme, basil and bay leaves. Blend well into the stew. Add the patties and when stirring, be careful not to break. After a few minutes of cooking, the patties will become firm. Season to taste using Worcestershire, salt, pepper and Louisiana Gold. If mixture becomes too thick, thin sauce by using a little more of the fish stock. Serve over steamed white rice or pasta.

Changes

CRAWFISH SAUSAGE CASSEROLE

PREP TIME: 30 Minutes
SERVES: 6
COMMENT:

This casserole originated when leftover boiled crawfish was combined with sausage and rice to create a unique breakfast item. This ingenious marriage of ingredients may be served as an entree, a side dish or an accompaniment to meat and seafood.

INGREDIENTS:

1 cup crawfish tails
2 cups sliced heavy smoked sausage
1/4 pound butter
1/2 cup diced onions
1/2 cup diced celery
1/4 cup diced red bell pepper
1/4 cup diced yellow bell pepper
1/4 cup diced green bell pepper
1 tbsp diced garlic
1/2 cup sliced green onions
4 whole eggs
6 cups cooked white rice
pinch of thyme
pinch of basil
1/4 cup chopped parsley
salt and cracked pepper to taste
Louisiana Gold Pepper Sauce to taste

METHOD:

In a twelve inch black iron skillet, melt butter over medium high heat. Add smoked sausage and cook three to five minutes, browning well on all sides. Add onions, celery, bell peppers and garlic. Saute three to five minutes or until vegetables are wilted. Add crawfish and green onions and blend well into the vegetable mixture. Add eggs and allow the whites to cook slightly. Spoon in rice and stir into sausage/egg mixture until all ingredients are well blended. Add thyme, basil, parsley, salt, pepper and Louisiana Gold. Continue to stir until all ingredients are well blended and the eggs are cooked in the rice. You may wish to serve the casserole in the black iron skillet or remove it to a serving bowl.

LAGNIAPPE

Rice was being cultivated in China 2,800 years before Christ. It was considered one of the five sacred crops along with soy beans, wheat, barley and millet. Prior to importing rice into America, the Native Indians were harvesting a wild rice around the Great Lakes region. Though it was not really rice, this "crazy oats", as the French explorers called it, grew from water exactly as true rice does. In plantation days, North Carolina grew sixty percent of all rice in the United States. By 1877, Louisiana took the lead and today raises twice as much rice as any other two states combined. The obvious reason for this is our lowlands, bayous and rivers, which provide an ideal environment for the production of rice.

Changes

PRAIRIE CRAWFISH STEW

PREP TIME: 1 Hour

SERVES: 6-8

COMMENT:

Crawfish were always in the bayous and swamplands of South Louisiana. In Central Louisiana, the addition of boiled eggs and crawfish claws extended recipes for those larger families of the prairie. Eggs were not only plentiful in the community, but they were also an excellent source of protein.

INGREDIENTS:

2 lbs cleaned crawfish tails
1 cup vegetable oil
1 cup flour
2 cups chopped onions
1 cup chopped celery
1 cup chopped bell pepper
2 tbsps diced garlic
1/2 cup diced tomatoes
1/4 cup tomato sauce
3 quarts shellfish stock (see recipe)
1 tbsp chopped thyme
1 tbsp chopped basil
1 cup sliced green onions
1 cup chopped parsley
1 cup crawfish claws
salt and cracked pepper to taste
Louisiana Gold Pepper Sauce to taste
6 whole eggs

METHOD:

A rich crawfish stock will certainly make this dish a winner. Any shellfish stock or fish stock may be substituted, but the dish will be good even if plain water is used. In a two quart dutch oven, heat oil over medium high heat. Add flour and using a wire whip, stir constantly until dark brown roux is achieved (see roux techniques). Add onions, celery, bell pepper, garlic and tomatoes. Saute three to five minutes or until vegetables are wilted. Add crawfish tails, blending well into the vegetable mixture. Add tomato sauce and slowly add shellfish stock, stirring constantly until all is incorporated. Add thyme, basil, green onions, parsley and claws. Bring to a low boil, reduce to simmer and cook thirty minutes, stirring occasionally. Season to taste using salt, pepper and Louisiana Gold. Break one egg at a time into the simmering stew, allowing the whites to set in the liquid before breaking the next egg. Continue until all have been added. Adjust seasonings if necessary. Serve over steamed white rice.

The Cypress Swamps at Magnolia Ridge

Changes

LAKE DES ALLEMANDS CORN AND CRAB CAKES

PREP TIME: 1 Hour
SERVES: 8
COMMENT:

Lake Des Allemands was the first home of the Cajuns once they moved into the swamplands of Louisiana. In addition to some of the finest hunting and fishing, this lake is known for its blue crab harvest each year. Crabs are most often boiled in season, but pan-fried crab cakes are wonderful and can be served all year long.

INGREDIENTS:

1 pound jumbo lump crabmeat
1 pound claw crabmeat
1/2 cup whole kernel corn
1/4 cup finely diced onions
1/4 cup finely diced celery
1/4 cup finely diced red bell pepper
1 tbsp chopped garlic
1/2 cup mayonnaise
1/4 cup Creole mustard
1/4 cup chopped parsley
pinch of thyme
pinch of basil
salt and cracked pepper to taste
Worcestershire Sauce to taste
Louisiana Gold Pepper Sauce to taste
1 egg
2 cups seasoned Italian bread crumbs
oil for frying

METHOD:

In a large black iron skillet, heat oil over medium high heat. In a mixing bowl, combine claw crabmeat, corn, onions, celery, bell pepper, garlic, mayonnaise, mustard and parsley. Using a mixing spoon, blend all ingredients until well incorporated. Add thyme, basil, salt, pepper, Worcestershire and Louisiana Gold. Add egg and stir well into the crabmeat mixture. Fold in lump crabmeat, being careful not to break the lumps. Dust in enough bread crumbs to hold the mixture together and absorb the moisture. Form the crab mixture into round patties, approximately two and a half inches in diameter. Coat the outside of each crab cake lightly with remaining bread crumbs and pan fry on each side until golden brown. Serve with remoulade, tartar or cocktail sauce.

Changes

Poplar Grove Plantation

AND COTTON

Poplar Grove Plantation

"An Oriental Touch"

I remember sitting in Mr. Labat's seventh grade class and hearing for the first time the words "Louisiana architecture." He tried desperately to instill in our young minds the fact that much of our construction was unique to the bayou state. He challenged us to recognize the differences. He went on to say that many of our homes were Greek revival, and we would know these by the large white columns, the plaster and the wide galleries. He told us that the French Creole style could be seen in the simple raised cottages with pitched roofs and wrap-around porches. But my favorite was always the Victorian. He referred to these as Hansel and Gretel houses, always ornate and whimsical in character. That was many years ago, but I never forgot the lesson.

Poplar Grove Plantation was constructed not as a home but as the Banker's Pavilion at the World's Industrial and Cotton Centennial Exposition of 1884 in New Orleans. The building was deliberately styled to be eye catching and was an extremely unusual architectural statement. Designed by the noted New Orleans architect, Thomas Sully, the structure was placed at the disposal of bankers and their families visiting the exposition. The house can best be described as a framed, galleried structure featuring a combination of Chinese, Italianate, Eastlake and Queen Anne elements. The ornate Oriental details are not only unique in Louisiana, but also represent an unusual architectural movement of that period toward Eastern motifs.

Soon after the close of the fair, the building was purchased by Joseph Harris who owned a sugar plantation across the river from Baton Rouge. The building was moved by barge eighty miles upriver to West Baton Rouge Parish. Harris persuaded his cousin, Horace Wilkinson, to leave his holdings in Plaquemine and Jefferson Parishes to manage Poplar Grove. Soon, Wilkinson purchased the 1,438 acre plantation. Today, Ann Wilkinson, Horace's great granddaughter, and her family live here.

To reach Poplar Grove, take I-10 West to Baton Rouge over the Mississippi River to Port Allen. Exit Highway 1 North to Rosedale Road. 504-343-3913.

Ice Cream Making at Poplar Grove

At left, clockwise from bottom left, Chicken and Okra Stew (page 176), Stuffed Artichokes (page 141), and Fig Ice Cream (page 300)

SHRIMP AND BROCCOLI LASAGNA

PREP TIME: 2 hours
SERVES: 6-8
COMMENT:

More and more, we see vegetables taking the place of meats in our recipes. However, this is not new. The Italian gardener at Poplar Grove grew zucchini, eggplant and artichokes and combined all of these in lasagna. In this interesting twist, we not only see broccoli but also shrimp. This combination gives the dish new character.

INGREDIENTS:

2 pounds (21-25 count) cooked shrimp, peeled and deveined
1 head of broccoli, poached
1/4 cup olive oil
1 cup chopped onions
1 cup chopped celery
1/4 cup chopped bell pepper
1/4 cup diced garlic
1 cup fresh tomatoes
1 cup sliced mushrooms
1 can tomato paste
3 (8 ounce) cans tomato sauce
pinch of thyme
pinch of oregano
pinch of basil
1 tbsp brown sugar
salt and cracked pepper to taste
Louisiana Gold Pepper Sauce to taste
1 egg
1 container Ricotta cheese
1 cup grated Parmesan cheese
1 cup shredded Mozzarella cheese
1 package lasagna noodles

Changes

METHOD:

Preheat oven to 350 degrees F. In a heavy bottom dutch oven, heat oil over medium high heat. Add onions, celery, bell pepper, garlic, tomatoes and mushrooms. Saute three to five minutes or until vegetables are wilted. Add tomato paste and sauce and simmer twenty minutes. Season with thyme, oregano, basil, sugar, salt, pepper and Louisiana Gold. Bring to a rolling boil, reduce to simmer and cook thirty minutes. In a stock pot, place noodles in lightly salted water. Bring to a rolling boil and cook noodles until tender. Drain, cool and lay flat on drain board. In a small mixing bowl, combine egg, Ricotta and Parmesan cheeses. Place one layer of noodles in the bottom of a 9 1/2" x 13" baking dish. Spread cheese mixture on top of noodles, then top with even amounts of shrimp, broccoli and tomato sauce. Continue this same format of layering until all ingredients are used. Sprinkle top layer with mozzarella cheese and bake for forty-five minutes or until cheese is bubbly.

FRENCH FRIED FROG LEGS

PREP TIME: 1 Hour
SERVES: 6
COMMENT:

The frog leg, the most rare seafood delicacy, is quite common here in South Louisiana. I have had them prepared in many ways and in many places, but I still enjoy them best beer-battered and deep fried.

INGREDIENTS:

2 dozen frog legs
1 quart buttermilk
1 egg
3 tbsps Creole mustard
1-10 ounce bottle of beer
salt and cracked pepper to taste
granulated garlic to taste
Louisiana Gold Pepper Sauce to taste
Worcestershire Sauce to taste
4 cups seasoned yellow corn flour
oil for deep frying

METHOD:

Preheat oil to 375 degrees F. Place frog legs in a mixing bowl and top with buttermilk. Allow to sit one hour at room temperature. In a separate bowl, combine egg, mustard and beer. Using a wire whisk, stir all ingredients until well blended. Season lightly using salt, pepper, garlic, Louisiana Gold and Worcestershire sauce. Place corn flour in a paper bag. Remove frog legs from buttermilk, coat in beer batter and place in bag. Seal tightly and shake vigorously to coat legs thoroughly. Deep fry until golden brown. Serve with tartar sauce or cocktail sauce (see recipe).

Changes

____

LAGNIAPPE

Buttermilk is used as a tenderizer in this frog leg recipe. Most people realize that buttermilk is a by-product from the processing of butter. But did you know that over 80% of the world's non-white population cannot drink milk? It seems that nature designed milk to nourish babies and thus designed babies to best digest milk. The rich sugar in milk, called lactose, can only be digested with the aid of an enzyme called lactase. This enzyme is produced in the intestines of babies and decreases as one grows older. For some reason, white adults maintain more lactase in their system than non-whites. The American Indians drank no milk before Columbus, because of the absence of milk producing animals, and most still consider it distasteful today. Well, with this bit of information, it is interesting that most of us still love milk. Whether we drink it or not, it is still used in the majority of the dishes we cook.

CAJUN DRUNKEN SHRIMP

PREP TIME: 45 Minutes
SERVES: 6
COMMENT:

I first discovered this technique in Japan where sake was used to steam shrimp. I was amazed to learn that the Germans were combining beer and herbs to steam shrimp in Louisiana over one hundred years ago. When substituting beer for the sake, the dish takes on an interesting flavor and in my opinion, is better than the Oriental version.

INGREDIENTS:

36 (21-25 count), head-on shrimp
6-3 inch links heavy smoked sausage
4-10 ounce bottles of beer
2 cups water
2 carrots, quartered
3 ears of corn, halved
6 new potatoes
1 red bell pepper, sliced
1 lemon, sliced
6 cloves of garlic
1 bermuda onion, sliced
2 bay leaves
1 tbsp green peppercorns
1 tbsp red peppercorns
1 tbsp white peppercorns
salt to taste
Louisiana Gold Pepper Sauce to taste

METHOD:

In a two gallon stock pot, add beer and all remaining ingredients with the exception of the shrimp. Bring to a rolling boil, reduce to simmer and allow vegetables to poach until cooked, approximately thirty minutes. When potatoes are tender, add shrimp and blend well into the vegetable mixture. Cover and allow shrimp to steam approximately fifteen minutes, stirring occasionally. When shrimp are cooked, serve in a large soup bowl with one link of sausage and vegetables. You may wish to use the poaching liquid as a dipping sauce.

Changes

HERBED SHRIMP

PREP TIME: 30 minutes
SERVES: 4
COMMENT:

In South Louisiana, shrimp is normally served in a Creole seafood gumbo or etouffee. However, in this recipe shrimp is quickly sauteed with multi-colored peppers, flavored with herbs and served over white rice or pasta. This dish is Italian in origin and possibly a forerunner to scampi.

INGREDIENTS:

1 pound (21-25 count) shrimp, peeled and deveined
1/2 cup olive oil
1/4 cup sliced green onions
1/4 cup sliced yellow bell pepper
1/4 cup sliced red bell pepper
1 tbsp diced garlic
2 bay leaves
1 tbsp chopped rosemary
1 tsp chopped thyme
1 tsp chopped basil
1 tbsp flour
1 ounce dry white wine
1 cup shellfish stock (see recipe)
salt and cracked pepper to taste
Louisiana Gold Pepper Sauce to taste
1/4 cup chopped parsley

METHOD:

In a ten inch saute pan, heat oil over medium high heat. Add green onions, bell peppers, garlic and bay leaves. Saute three to five minutes or until vegetables are wilted. Add rosemary, thyme and basil, stirring into the vegetable mixture. Add shrimp and stir fry until pink and curled, approximately two to three minutes. Sprinkle in flour, blending well into the mixture and deglaze with white wine. Add shellfish stock. Bring to a rolling boil, reduce to simmer and season to taste using salt, pepper and Louisiana Gold. Once sauce is thickened, serve as an appetizer or over pasta as an entree. Garnish with chopped parsley.

Changes

Cast Iron Dogs Guard the Entrance to Catalpa

CRAWFISH PIE

PREP TIME: 30 minutes
SERVES: 6
COMMENT:

Crawfish etouffee is a simple dish and one that may be served in a variety of ways. Often it is placed on pasta instead of rice, in crepes or in patty shells. A simple but elegant presentation is in a pie shell. With the availability of frozen pie shells, you don't even need to make the crust.

INGREDIENTS:

1 pound crawfish tails
1 cup oil
1 cup chopped onions
1/2 cup chopped celery
1/2 cup chopped bell pepper
1/4 cup diced garlic
1/4 cup diced tasso ham
1/2 cup flour
1/4 cup tomato sauce
2 quarts shellfish stock (see recipe)
salt and cracked pepper to taste
Louisiana Gold Pepper Sauce to taste
1 egg
1/2 cup milk
1/2 cup water
3-9 inch pie shells

METHOD:

Preheat oven to 375 degrees F. In a ten inch saute pan, heat oil over medium high heat. Add onions, celery, bell pepper, garlic and tasso ham. Saute three to five minutes or until vegetables are wilted. Add crawfish and saute an additional five minutes. Sprinkle in flour and using a wire whisk, stir constantly until white roux is achieved (see roux techniques). Add tomato sauce and slowly add stock, a little at a time, until sauce consistency is achieved. Bring to a rolling boil, reduce to simmer and cook thirty minutes. Season to taste using salt, pepper and Louisiana Gold. Remove from heat and allow to cool, preferably overnight. In a small mixing bowl, combine egg, milk and water. Using a wire whisk, stir until all ingredients are well blended. Cut pie shells in half and place a generous serving of the crawfish sauce in the center of each half. Brush the edges of pastry with eggwash and fold over in a triangle shape. Crimp the edges closed with a fork and pierce the top of the pie to create vents for steam to escape during cooking. Brush eggwash over pies and bake until golden brown, approximately twenty minutes.

Changes

BAKED TROUT WITH PESTO SAUCE

PREP TIME: 30 Minutes
SERVES: 6
COMMENT:

Pesto is an ideal sauce to top a fillet of speckled trout. This basil/olive oil mixture was first introduced to Louisiana by the Italians in the late 1800s.

INGREDIENTS:

6-6 ounce speckled trout fillets
1/2 cup extra virgin olive oil
2 cups fresh basil leaves
4 cloves of garlic
1/2 cup chopped pecans
salt and cracked pepper to taste
Louisiana Gold Pepper Sauce to taste
6 lemon slices
paprika for color

METHOD:

Preheat oven to 400 degrees F. Rinse fillets under cold water and dry thoroughly. Place fillets, skin side down, on a large cookie sheet. Season to taste using salt and pepper. Set aside. In the bowl of a food processor fitted with a metal blade, combine oil, basil, garlic and pecans. Process until sauce is pureed. Season lightly with salt, pepper and Louisiana Gold. Spread pesto over fish fillets and garnish with lemon slices and paprika. Bake until fillets are flaky when tested with a fork, approximately ten to twelve minutes. Serve with hot French bread.

Changes

OYSTERS DIABLO

PREP TIME: 1 Hour
SERVES: 6
COMMENT:

The Italians in and around Amite, Louisiana, have created not only an oyster festival, but numerous oyster dishes as well. One of their more famous, Oysters Diablo, has been recreated with hundreds of variations.

INGREDIENTS:

2 cups oysters
1 cup oyster liquor
1/4 cup bacon drippings
1 cup minced onions
1/2 cup minced celery
1 cup sliced green onions
1/4 cup diced garlic
8 slices toasted bread
juice of one lemon
salt and cracked pepper to taste
Louisiana Gold Pepper Sauce to taste
Worcestershire Sauce to taste
24 oysters
24 oyster shells

METHOD:

Preheat oven to 350 degrees F. In a heavy bottom black iron skillet, heat bacon drippings over medium high heat. Add onions, celery, green onions and garlic. Saute three to five minutes or until vegetables are wilted. Wet toasted bread, squeeze dry and break into the vegetable mixture. Using a cooking spoon, chop the bread into the vegetable mixture until well blended. Add two cups oysters and oyster liquor. Continue to chop into the bread mixture until all is well incorporated. Season to taste using lemon juice, salt, pepper, Louisiana Gold and Worcestershire Sauce. Cook twenty to thirty minutes, stirring and chopping occasionally. Add any additional oyster liquor as necessary to retain moisture. Remove from heat and allow to cool slightly. Place one oyster in each of twenty-four shells. Place on cookie sheet and top with stuffing. Bake ten to fifteen minutes or until stuffing is golden brown and oyster is thoroughly heated. This dish may be prepared in advance and frozen.

Changes

Chapter Nine

Wild Game

Houmas House Plantation

Houmas House Plantation

"The Garconniers"

In the 1800s, it was considered common courtesy to provide overnight accommodations for friends and relatives coming to visit your home. Custom demanded that separate quarters be provided for the young bachelors, especially if there were girls in the house. It was for this reason that these beautiful one room garconniers or "gentlemen's quarters" were built. To maintain balance on the property, a similar pigeonaire or pigeon house was built on the opposite side of the mansion. When we stroll around the lawn today, we can only imagine how painful it must have been for the young men to look out of the window of this garconnier over toward the big house. There on the gallery were those beautiful southern belles sipping iced tea and enjoying the cool breeze. Those garcons must have thought, "so near, yet so far away!"

Houmas House Plantation was built on a large tract of land purchased from the Houmas Indians in the late 1700s. The original home has many Spanish characteristics since it was built under Spanish rule in Louisiana. In 1812, the house and surrounding land was purchased by General Wade Hampton, a revolutionary war hero from South Carolina. Though he was a cotton planter, he converted the plantation to sugar production and became one of the first Americans to engage in the growing of this crop. His daughter and son in law, the Prestons, eventually took over the plantation. They constructed the magnificent Greek revival mansion standing today while preserving the original four rooms to the rear. Having come from South Carolina, they added a glass windowed belvedere high at the top of the roof, typical of Carolina seaboard homes.

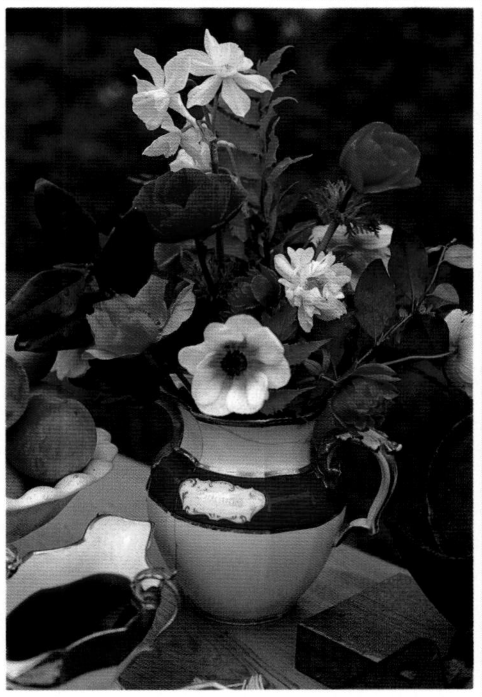

A Personalized, Porcelain Water Pitcher by Edward Honore, the Designer of President Polk's China

In 1858, Houmas House with twelve thousand acres was purchased for one million dollars by John Burnside, an Irishman. Under his direction, the plantation grew to twenty thousand acres with four working sugar mills. Burnside was considered the largest sugar producer in America. In 1940, the home was sold to Dr. George Crozat who restored it beautifully to its original antebellum state.

To reach Houmas House, take I-10 from Baton Rouge east to Exit 179. Follow Highway 44 to the river. 504-473-7841.

At left, clockwise from bottom left, Peach Cobbler (page 291), English Peas with Pearl Onions (page 130), and Breast of Duck with Caramelized Peaches (page 252)

BREAST OF DUCK WITH CARAMELIZED PEACHES

PREP TIME: 1 Hour

SERVES: 6

COMMENT:

Often the breasts of large ducks or small geese were removed for pan sauteing. The plantation cook would quickly sear the breasts to medium rare, remove them from the heat and caramelize fresh fruit in the drippings. You will definitely want to try this modern day version.

INGREDIENTS:

6 Long Island or Mallard duck breasts
2 cups thinly sliced peaches
1/2 cup port wine
1 tbsp cane syrup
1 bay leaf
1 tbsp diced garlic
10 black peppercorns
6 basil leaves, torn
4 sprigs fresh thyme
6 sage leaves, torn
1/4 cup vegetable oil
2 cups game stock (see recipe)
salt and cracked pepper to taste
Louisiana Gold Pepper Sauce to taste

METHOD:

In a large mixing bowl, combine breasts, port, syrup, bay leaf, garlic, peppercorns, basil, thyme, sage, salt and Louisiana Gold. Toss to coat the breasts in the marinade. Allow to sit at room temperature a minimum of four hours. In a large black iron skillet, heat oil over medium high heat. Saute duck breasts, skin down, until lightly browned. Continue to saute, turning occasionally, until internal temperature reaches 140 degrees F or medium rare. Remove and keep warm. Add peaches and saute in the drippings. Reduce heat to low and cook until peaches are caramelized, approximately ten to fifteen minutes. Add game stock, bring to a low boil and reduce to sauce consistency. Season to taste using salt and pepper. You may wish to add a few tablespoons of the marinade for additional flavor. To serve, slice each breast and top with a generous portion of the peach sauce.

Changes

WILD DUCK IN ORANGE CANE SYRUP MARINADE

PREP TIME: 2 Hours
SERVES: 6
COMMENT:

The Spanish brought oranges to Louisiana from South America in the late 1600s. Once sugar cane was introduced into bayou country, these two ingredients were combined to produce a perfect marinade. There is nothing better to my knowledge for tenderizing game than orange juice and cane syrup which are both produced in Louisiana.

INGREDIENTS:

6 small wild ducks
juice of four oranges
1/4 cup Louisiana cane syrup
1/4 cup dry white wine
1 tbsp chopped thyme
1 tbsp chopped basil
1 tbsp chopped sage
1 tbsp diced garlic
1/4 cup vegetable oil
2 cups orange slices
2 cups game stock
salt and cracked pepper to taste
Louisiana Gold Pepper Sauce to taste

METHOD:

In a large mixing bowl, combine duck, orange juice, cane syrup, wine, thyme, basil, sage and garlic. Season to taste using salt, pepper and Louisiana Gold. Toss ducks well in the marinade and allow to sit at room temperature a minimum of four hours. Preheat oven to 400 degrees F. In a large dutch oven, heat oil over medium high heat. Remove ducks from marinade and brown well on all sides. Surround with orange slices and add game stock. Cover and bake until tender, approximately one and a half hours. Uncover and allow ducks to brown evenly. Remove ducks and keep warm. Reduce drippings to a sauce consistency and degrease. You may wish to serve the ducks over dirty rice (see recipe) and top with orange sauce.

LAGNIAPPE

Nothing is quite as satisfying as a perfectly cooked duck full of flavor and juices. Most of the domestic ducks eaten in America today can be traced to China where duck has been an important dish since the 2nd century B.C. Duck was of great importance to the Egyptians and Romans as well. They kept wild birds in pens, always ready for the feast. Nowhere is duck more prominent, however, than here in Cajun country. Wild ducks played an important role in the "swamp floor cuisine" of the early Cajuns. The first Cajun settlement was located at St. Jaques de Cabanocey - an Indian word meaning "where French ducks roost".

Changes

ROASTED CANE RIVER MALLARDS

PREP TIME: 2 Hours
SERVES: 6
COMMENT:

The Cane River runs through the heart of Natchitoches. The early settlers of this Creole town often harvested mallard ducks from this river. There are numerous recipes for the preparation of this delicacy, but I think pot roasting is one of the best. Try substituting a variety of fresh fruit in the place of the apples.

INGREDIENTS:

3 mallard ducks, cleaned
3 medium onions, quartered
2 stalks celery, cubed
2 tbsps diced garlic
2 red apples, cubed
2 green apples, cubed
1 cup andouille sausage, cubed
1/4 cup vegetable oil
4 red and green apples, quartered
1 quart chicken stock (see recipe)
1/4 cup melted butter
4 tbsps Mayhaw or fruit jelly
1 tbsp chopped thyme
1 tbsp chopped basil
1 tbsp chopped sage
salt and cracked pepper to taste
Louisiana Gold Pepper Sauce to taste

METHOD:

Preheat oven to 450 degrees F. Season ducks well inside and out using herbs, salt, pepper and Louisiana Gold. Stuff the cavities of the ducks with onions, celery, garlic, cubed apples and andouille. In a large dutch oven, heat oil over medium high heat. Brown ducks well on all sides, remove from heat and surround with remaining red and green apples and stock. Drizzle butter over ducks and using a pastry brush, paint the breasts well with jelly. Cover and roast the birds for one and a half hours. Check for tenderness, remove cover and allow breasts to brown evenly. When done, remove ducks and keep warm. Reduce the stock over medium high heat until thickened to a sauce consistency. Strain the sauce and degrease. To serve, place one half mallard on dinner plate and top with a generous serving of sauce.

A Brick Slave Cabin, One of Seven at Magnolia

Changes

PAN FRIED QUAIL VON SEYBOLD

PREP TIME: 1 Hour
SERVES: 6
COMMENT:

The bob white and pharaoh quails are the two most popular in the United States. It is the bob white that we in South Louisiana have cherished for hundreds of years. It was the variety that Louise von Seybold, of San Francisco Plantation, often fried or sauteed for breakfast. The dish was so popular that it has become a tradition in New Orleans for jazz brunch.

INGREDIENTS:

6 bob white quail, cleaned
1 cup seasoned flour
1/2 cup vegetable oil
1 small apple, diced
1/4 cup diced onions
1/4 cup diced celery
1/4 cup diced red bell pepper
1 tbsp diced garlic
1/4 cup sliced andouille sausage
1 ounce sherry
2 cups game or chicken stock (see recipe)
salt and cracked pepper to taste
Louisiana Gold Pepper Sauce to taste
1/2 cup sliced green onions
1/4 cup chopped parsley
6 slices of toast

METHOD:

Using a pair of kitchen shears, split quail across the backbone and press flat. Season to taste using salt, pepper and Louisiana Gold. In a large black iron skillet, heat oil over medium high heat. Dust quail lightly in flour and saute until golden brown on both sides. Remove and keep warm. Add apples, onions, celery, bell pepper, garlic and andouille. Saute three to five minutes or until vegetables are wilted. Deglaze with sherry and add stock. Bring to a low boil, reduce heat to simmer and return quail to skillet. Cover and allow to cook until quail is tender and stock is slightly reduced. When done, remove quail and reduce stock to sauce consistency. Season to taste using salt, pepper and Louisiana Gold. Add green onions and parsley and cook two additional minutes. To serve, place quail on toast and top with a generous serving of the sherry sauce.

Changes

WHISKEY BRAISED QUAIL WITH BACON

PREP TIME: 45 Minutes
SERVES: 6
COMMENT:

Cooking with whiskey originated in the hunting camps of South Louisiana. The trappers and hunters, tired of the same old flavors, attempted many combinations in their pots. Some were great, others disastrous. This is one recipe that survived.

INGREDIENTS:

12 quail, cleaned
12 bacon slices
1/4 cup melted butter
3 chopped shallots
1 tsp diced garlic
1/4 cup sliced green onions
1/2 cup sliced mushrooms
1/4 cup whiskey
2 cups game stock (see recipe)
salt and cracked pepper to taste
Louisiana Gold Pepper Sauce to taste

METHOD:

Preheat oven to 375 degrees F. Season the quail inside and out using salt, pepper and Louisiana Gold. Wrap each quail with a slice of bacon, secure with toothpicks and place in a large black iron skillet. Drizzle the quail with butter and cook in oven until golden brown, approximately twenty to thirty minutes. Remove quail and keep warm. Place the skillet over medium high heat and add shallots, garlic, green onions and mushrooms. Saute three to five minutes or until vegetables are wilted. Deglaze with whiskey and add stock. Bring to a rolling boil, add quail and reduce to a sauce consistency. Season to taste using salt and pepper. Serve over wild rice or toast.

Changes

QUAIL EGGS BENEDICT

PREP TIME: 30 Minutes
SERVES: 6
COMMENT:

It was in the white ballroom of this beautiful plantation that this dish was first served. Originally, the dish was referred to as "frog in the hole". Because of the size of the quail egg, this dish is a wonderful hors d'oeuvre. I have used it as an accompaniment to my quail on toast recipe.

INGREDIENTS:

12 fresh quail eggs
6 slices white bread
1/4 cup butter
salt and cracked pepper to taste
Louisiana Gold Pepper Sauce to taste
1 cup hollandaise sauce (see recipe)

METHOD:

Remove crust from the bread and cut into two equal triangles. Using a one inch round pastry cutter or paring knife, cut a hole in the center of each triangle. In a large black iron skillet, melt butter over medium heat. Place triangles in saute pan and crack one egg into the hole of each slice. Cook two to three minutes and using a spatula, turn and brown other side. Continue this process until done. Season to taste using salt, pepper and Louisiana Gold. To serve, top each quail egg with a spoonful of hollandaise and for an extra twist, try a touch of caviar.

LAGNIAPPE

Quail has always been considered the hunter's prize. Most of us, at one time or another, have encountered a covey of quail running along a roadside or open field. The greatest enjoyment, however, is to experience the bird freshly cooked in any fashion. Today, quail is farm-raised in most parts of the country. This trend makes them available to not only the consumer, but also the restaurateur at any time of year. As a young boy, I remember eating quail simply roasted at the end of a long stick over an open fire. Although I have eaten in most of the great restaurants of the world, I don't think I have had a better dish.

Changes

PORT HUDSON SMOKED DOVES

PREP TIME: 1 Hour
SERVES: 6
COMMENT:

It was in the Port Hudson area in St. Francisville that Audubon painted his "Birds of America". This area is also known for the large flocks of doves which come to feed in the corn fields of this parish. Smoked doves were famous at Rosedown.

INGREDIENTS:

12 dove breasts, cleaned
1/4 cup melted butter
1 tbsp lemon juice
juice of one orange
1/4 cup Louisiana cane syrup
1 tbsp chopped sage
1 tbsp chopped basil
1 tbsp chopped tarragon
1/4 cup Worcestershire Sauce
12 strips of bacon
salt and pepper to taste
Louisiana Gold Pepper Sauce to taste
3 cans root beer

METHOD:

Rinse doves under cold running water. Be sure to remove any lead shot from the breasts of the doves. In a large mixing bowl, combine dove breasts with butter, juices, cane syrup, sage, basil, tarragon, Worcestershire, salt, pepper and Louisiana Gold. Allow the breasts to marinate at room temperature four to five hours. Heat homestyle smoker according to manufacturer's directions. Remove doves from marinade, wrap with bacon and secure with toothpicks. Place root beer, marinade and water in water pan of smoker. Place doves on the top rack and cook until done, approximately thirty to forty-five minutes. I prefer to flavor the smoke with fruit wood such as persimmon, muscadine, mayhaw or blackberry. However, pecan wood is a great alternative.

Changes

SQUAB WITH THYME AND ROASTED GARLIC

PREP TIME: 1 Hour

SERVES: 6

COMMENT:

There is a saying in New Orleans that "more is better". Often this is not the case in cooking. When the Italian gardener at Poplar Grove sauteed squab with roasted garlic, not much else was needed in the pot. With the introduction of a bit of thyme and a touch of red wine, this simple dish becomes a delicacy.

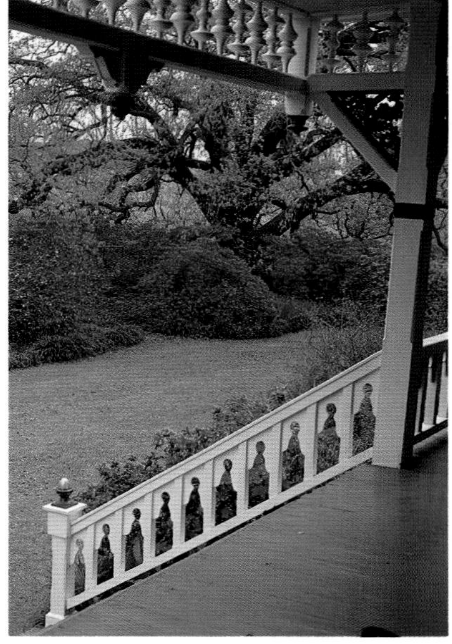

The Entrance Stairway at Poplar Grove

INGREDIENTS:

6 young squabs
24 garlic cloves
6 sprigs fresh thyme
1/2 cup butter
1 cup seasoned flour
1/2 cup dry red wine
2 cups game stock (see recipe)
salt and cracked pepper to taste
Louisiana Gold Pepper Sauce to taste

METHOD:

Rinse squabs under cold running water to clean thoroughly. Season well inside and out using salt, pepper and Louisiana Gold. In a heavy bottom black iron skillet, melt butter over medium high heat. Saute garlic until lightly browned on all sides. Do not scorch or garlic will become bitter. Once browned and tender, remove and keep warm. Lightly dust squabs in seasoned flour, shaking off all excess, and saute until golden brown on all sides. Pour off all but two tablespoons of the butter, return to stove and deglaze with red wine. Add thyme and garlic and reduce wine to one half volume. Pour in game stock, cover and allow squabs to cook until tender, approximately thirty to forty-five minutes. Season to taste using salt and pepper. When tender, remove and keep warm. Reduce stock to a sauce consistency. Serve squab with a generous portion of sauce and roasted garlic.

Changes

POT ROASTED SQUAB WITH KUMQUATS

PREP TIME: 1 Hour
SERVES: 6
COMMENT:

Squabs or young pigeons could be found domesticated in pigeonaires or pigeon houses on any plantation in early Louisiana. The native American Indians found squab to be a delicacy and most tribes had it as a part of their diet. Here, we marry the game flavor of squab with the fruitiness of kumquats for a perfect combination.

INGREDIENTS:

6 squabs, cleaned
1 cup kumquats, whole
1/4 cup vegetable oil
1/2 cup seasoned flour
1 cup chopped onions
1/2 cup chopped celery
1/2 cup chopped bell pepper
2 tbsps diced garlic
2 ounces plum or fruit wine
1 quart chicken stock (see recipe)
1 tsp chopped thyme
1 tsp chopped basil
pinch of file' powder
salt and cracked pepper to taste
Louisiana Gold Pepper Sauce to taste
4 cups cooked popcorn rice

METHOD:

In a large dutch oven, heat oil over medium high heat. Season squabs inside and out using salt and pepper. Stuff the cavity of each squab with onions, celery, bell pepper and one whole kumquat. Dust squabs in flour and brown on all sides. Add onions, celery, bell pepper and garlic. Saute three to five minutes or until vegetables are wilted. Deglaze with plum wine and then add chicken stock. Add thyme, basil, file' powder and kumquats, blending well into the mixture. Season to taste using salt, pepper and Louisiana Gold. Cover and allow squabs to pot roast until tender. Check occasionally as not to overcook because these tender birds will fall apart quickly. When done, remove squabs and keep warm. Reduce the cooking liquid to a thickened sauce consistency. Adjust seasonings if necessary. To serve, place a generous portion of popcorn flavored or wild rice in the center of plate and top with squab and kumquat sauce.

Changes

ROASTED PHEASANT WITH COGNAC AND WILD MUSHROOMS

PREP TIME: 1 Hour

SERVES: 6

COMMENT:

The French brought good cognac and brandies into Louisiana. Naturally, they were consumed at the end of the meal with a good homemade cigar. It didn't take long for the plantation cook to discover the flavor derived by adding an ounce or two of this premium liqueur to a pot of game.

INGREDIENTS:

2 pheasants, cleaned
1 cup cognac
2 cups sliced oyster mushrooms
1/4 cup chopped thyme
1/4 cup chopped basil
1/4 cup chopped sage
1/4 cup diced garlic
1 bunch seedless red grapes
1 cup chopped onions
1 cup chopped celery
1 cup chopped bell pepper
1 cup chopped carrots
6 bacon slices
2 cups game stock (see recipe)
1 cup heavy whipping cream
salt and cracked pepper to taste
Louisiana Gold Pepper Sauce to taste

METHOD:

Preheat oven to 400 degrees F. Wash pheasants inside and out and season completely using herbs, garlic, salt, pepper and Louisiana Gold. Stuff the cavities with grapes and set aside. In a large roasting pan, place mushrooms, onions, celery, bell pepper and carrots. Top with pheasants and place three strips of bacon over each breast. Roast, uncovered, approximately forty-five minutes. Remove pheasants and keep warm. Deglaze roasting pan with cognac over medium high heat. Reduce the liqueur by one half volume and add game stock. Bring to a rolling boil, add heavy whipping cream and reduce to a sauce consistency. Season to taste using salt and pepper. Strain sauce through a fine chinois and degrease. To serve, slice the breasts and legs of the pheasants and top with the cognac cream.

A Rear View of Oak Alley

Changes

STEWED RABBIT WITH WILD PLUMS

PREP TIME: 1 Hour
SERVES: 6
COMMENT:

The Japanese plum or loquat is the perfect flavoring for a wild rabbit stew. Normally, we tend to saute our rabbit in onion gravy. Once again, it was the Native American Indians who instructed the plantation owners in the art of flavoring game with wild fruit.

INGREDIENTS:

2 rabbits
2 cups seeded loquats
1 cup white wine
1/2 cup chopped onions
1/2 cup diced carrots
10 black peppercorns
1 bay leaf
1 tbsp diced garlic
1 tbsp chopped thyme
1 tbsp chopped basil
1/4 cup vegetable oil
2 cups game stock
salt and cracked pepper to taste
Louisiana Gold Pepper Sauce to taste

METHOD:

Cut each rabbit into eight serving pieces. If you can not find loquat plums, use the standard purple variety or any other fruit. In a large mixing bowl, combine rabbit, wine, onions, carrot, peppercorns, bay leaf, garlic, thyme, basil and Louisiana Gold. Toss to coat rabbit well and allow to sit at room temperature a minimum of four hours. In a large black iron skillet, heat oil over medium high heat. Remove rabbit from marinade and brown well on all sides. Add marinade ingredients, plums and game stock. Cover, reduce heat to simmer and allow to cook one hour. Season to taste using salt and pepper. When done, remove rabbit from pan and keep warm. Strain the sauce and degrease. Serve rabbit with a generous portion of plum sauce.

LAGNIAPPE

Rabbit is certainly one of the most widely available game meats. Whether marinated in wine and cane syrup, herb roasted or grilled, rabbit adapts beautifully to any cooking method. Wild hare, or jackrabbit as it is known in America, is widely sought after by the hunter. Young hare is great for roasting but the older ones need long braising or stewing to be considered a delicacy. Domestic rabbit is a great alternative to and is often compared to chicken. This meat is available in most grocery stores and specialty markets.

Changes

Nottoway Plantation

Nottoway Plantation

"Early Conveniences"

It's hard to imagine that a convenience as common as the electric light was not even a thought in the mid 1800s. If you wanted lights in your home, you'd strike up a few candles or possibly ignite a kerosene lamp. However, if you were a wealthy sugar planter building your mansion in South Louisiana back then, there was one other option. You could always go to New Orleans and hire Harvey Giles to construct one of his newly patented gas plants. Harvey would come to your home and bury a metal tank lined with calcium carbide brick. When water was allowed to drip into this tank, acetylene gas was produced. This gas was then allowed to flow through copper pipes into your home and presto...gas lamps. It was Giles who constructed the gas plant for John Hampton Randolph in 1859 when he built his magnificent "White Castle." The original gasoliers purchased by Randolph have been electrified and are still hanging in their original places today at Nottoway. The town of White Castle, located on the west bank of the Mississippi River in Iberville Parish, was named after this imposing mansion standing on the River Road. Boasting 65 rooms and 53,000 square feet, Nottoway is surely the largest plantation home in Louisiana.

A Pianoforte, by Thomas Tomkinson, Circa 1810 at Nottoway

In 1841, Randolph, a descendant of a famous Virginia family, left Woodville, Mississippi to come to this small river town to plan his mansion. It was completed in 1859, ten years after construction began. Henry Howard, the distinguished New Orleans architect, was called upon to design the magnificent Italianate structure which was quite different from the Greek Revival mansions built by other planters in the area.

The impact of Nottoway's grandeur is felt completely in the white ballroom. Here, all appointments are snow white, including the plaster medallions, the carved marble mantles, the Corinthian columns, the curtains and even the floor itself. Seven of Randolph's eight daughters were married in this most famous of all plantation ballrooms.

To reach Nottoway, travel I-10 from New Orleans or Baton Rouge to Exit 182. Follow Highway 70 to Louisiana Highway 1 through White Castle. 504-545-2730.

At left, clockwise from bottom left, Buttered Vegetable Casserole (page 143), Smothered Rabbit with Mushrooms (page 266), and Venison Tenderloin with Blackberry Glace (page 272)

SMOTHERED RABBIT WITH MUSHROOMS

PREP TIME: 2 Hours
SERVES: 6
COMMENT:

The swampland of South Louisiana is the perfect environment for wild rabbit. There's much overbrush for protection and vast quantities of food and water. The swamps around Nottoway provided an ample supply of this game for the dinning room table during plantation days.

INGREDIENTS:

2 young rabbits, cleaned
2 cups sliced mushrooms
2 cups seasoned flour
1/2 cup vegetable oil
1 cup chopped onions
1 cup chopped celery
1/2 cup chopped red bell pepper
1/4 cup diced garlic
1/2 cup chopped tomatoes
2 bay leaves
3 cups game or chicken stock (see recipe)
1/2 cup sliced green onions
1/2 cup chopped parsley
salt and cracked pepper to taste
Louisiana Gold Pepper Sauce to taste

METHOD:

Cut each rabbit into eight serving pieces. Season well using salt, pepper and Louisiana Gold. Dust each piece in flour, shaking off all excess. In a large dutch oven, heat oil over medium high heat. Add rabbit, a few pieces at a time, and brown on both sides. Remove and set aside. In the same pot, add onions, celery, bell pepper and garlic. Saute three to five minutes or until vegetables are wilted. Add chopped tomatoes, mushrooms, bay leaves and chicken stock. Bring mixture to a low boil, reduce to simmer and add rabbit. Cover and braise rabbit until tender, approximately one to one and a half hours. Add green onions and parsley and adjust seasonings if necessary. Serve over white or wild rice.

Changes

ALLIGATOR SAUSAGE

PREP TIME: 1 Hour
MAKES: 25-6 inch links
COMMENT:

The early Cajun trappers of bayou country considered alligator a versatile and tasty ingredient. From sausage to sauce piquant, the white lean meat of alligator found its way into their black iron skillets. Today, this once endangered species is farm raised and available at seafood and meat markets everywhere.

INGREDIENTS:

2 pounds ground alligator
2 pounds ground pork
1/2 pound ground pork fat
1/4 cup chopped onions
1/4 cup chopped celery
1/4 cup diced garlic
1/4 cup chopped red bell pepper
1/4 cup chopped parsley
1/4 cup sliced green onions
1/4 cup chopped sage
1/4 cup chopped basil
salt and cracked pepper to taste
Louisiana Gold Pepper Sauce to taste
15 feet casing for stuffing

METHOD:

In large mixing bowl, combine all of the above ingredients with the exception of the casing. Add one cup of ice water to the mixture and using both hands, blend the ingredients well. Continue to mix in a rolling motion until the fat content of the pork coats the surface of the mixture. This is imperative if the sausage is to be moist and juicy since alligator by nature is quite dry. Once the ingredients are well blended, you may wish to check the seasonings by sauteing a small patty in a frying pan. Correct seasonings if necessary. Stuff the sausage mixture in the hog casing and tie off in six inch links. To cook, poach the sausage in lightly salted water for three to five minutes. Grill over pecan wood or bake in a 375 degree F oven until golden brown, approximately ten to twelve minutes.

Changes

SCALLOPINI OF ALLIGATOR

PREP TIME: 30 minutes
SERVES: 6
COMMENT:

It is interesting that some recipes considered very classical in nature were included on early plantation menus. Scallopini, the pounded, flattened medallions of veal or pork, was certainly one of those European styles. Imagine, in 1860, being served scallopini in South Louisiana.

INGREDIENTS:

12-3 ounce medallions of alligator
1/4 cup chopped basil
1 tbsp chopped thyme
1/4 cup chopped parsley
eggwash (1 egg, 1/2 cup water, 1/2 cup milk, blended)
2 cups seasoned flour
1/2 cup butter
1/2 cup sliced okra
1/2 cup chopped red bell pepper
1 tbsp diced garlic
1 cup white wine
salt and cracked pepper to taste
Louisiana Gold Pepper Sauce to taste

METHOD:

It is best to buy tenderloin of alligator for this recipe. Pound the medallions between two sheets of wax paper until one quarter inch thick. In a large mixing bowl, combine basil, thyme and parsley. Season the medallions using salt, pepper and Louisiana Gold. Dip in eggwash, coat with flour and press into the basil/parsley mixture. In a ten inch saute pan, melt butter over medium high heat. Pan saute alligator until golden brown on both sides. Add okra, bell pepper and garlic. Saute three to five minutes or until vegetables are wilted. Deglaze with wine and reduce to sauce consistency. To serve, place two medallions over angel hair pasta and top with sauce.

Changes

VENISON CASSEROLE SPANISH STYLE

PREP TIME: 2 Hours
SERVES: 6-8
COMMENT:

Once the Spanish and French arrived in Natchitoches, Louisiana, an intermarriage of the two cultures occurred. Within a few years, Creole cuisine emerged from these households. This venison casserole is a typical example of the dishes created in this area.

INGREDIENTS:

3 pounds venison, cubed
1/2 cup seasoned flour
1/4 cup olive oil
1 cup chopped onions
1 cup chopped celery
1/2 cup chopped bell pepper
1/4 cup diced garlic
1-16 ounce can stewed tomatoes
1 tbsp diced jalapenos
1 cup beef or chicken stock (see recipe)
1 tbsp Louisiana cane syrup
1/2 cup sliced green onions
1/4 cup chopped parsley
1/2 cup sliced black olives
salt and cracked pepper to taste
Louisiana Gold Pepper Sauce to taste

METHOD:

Preheat oven to 375 degrees F. Season venison well using salt, pepper and Louisiana Gold. Dust the cubes in flour, shaking off all excess. In a large dutch oven, heat oil over medium high heat. Saute venison cubes until golden brown on all sides. Add onions, celery, bell pepper and garlic. Saute three to five minutes or until vegetables are wilted. Add tomatoes, jalapenos and chicken stock. Bring mixture to a low boil, remove from heat and add cane syrup, green onions, parsley and olives. Season to taste using salt, pepper and Louisiana Gold. Cover and bake until tender, approximately two hours. Serve over pasta or Spanish rice.

One of Two Matching Wings at Melrose

Changes

ROAST OF VENISON WITH CAJUN SAUSAGE

PREP TIME: 2 Hours
SERVES: 6-8
COMMENT:

If venison is known for one unpleasant property, it's the fact that it tends to be dry. Slow roasting methods and protecting the meat with bacon or other fatty meats will help just a little. This recipe uses fresh seasoned sausage in the place of bacon. This not only helps keep the meat juicy, but flavors it as well.

INGREDIENTS:

1-5 pound leg of venison, deboned
1 1/2 pounds fresh seasoned sausage
1/4 cup vegetable oil
1 cup chopped onions
1 cup chopped celery
1 cup chopped bell pepper
1/4 cup diced garlic
4 apples, cubed
1 cup sliced green onions
1/4 cup chopped parsley
2 cups chicken stock (see recipe)
salt and cracked pepper to taste
Louisiana Gold Pepper Sauce to taste

METHOD:

Preheat oven to 375 degrees F. Most grocery stores and meat markets in the South have fresh pork sausage. Here in Louisiana, the fresh sausage is further flavored with garlic, green onions and a mixture of herbs such as thyme and basil. If you cannot find seasoned Cajun sausage, use fresh pork sausage and add the above spices in measurements to your liking. Fill the cavity of the venison roast with bulk sausage. You may wish to truss or tie the cavity shut. Season the roast well using salt, pepper and Louisiana Gold. In a large dutch oven, heat oil over medium high heat. Brown roast well on all sides and add onions, celery, bell pepper and garlic. Saute three to five minutes or until vegetables are wilted. Remove from heat and add apples, green onions and parsley. Add chicken stock and adjust seasonings if necessary. Cover and bake until tender, approximately one and a half to two hours. When done, remove and allow to rest thirty minutes prior to slicing. You may wish to reduce the drippings to a sauce consistency before serving.

Changes

MEDALLIONS OF VENISON WITH CINNAMON AND PEARS

PREP TIME: 30 Minutes

SERVES: 6

COMMENT:

I think the wild cooking pear of South Louisiana is about as versatile a fruit as one may find. Though the plantation cooks tended to can these pears in syrup to serve as a dessert, they were often used in main dishes. The combination of pears with venison and cinnamon shows the creative nature of those early kitchens.

INGREDIENTS:

12-3 ounce venison medallions
1 tsp cinnamon
2 diced pears
1 tbsp pear preserves
1/4 cup butter
1/4 cup diced shallots
1 tsp diced garlic
1/4 cup sliced green onions
1 tsp chopped thyme
1 tsp chopped sage
1/4 cup dry red wine
2 cups game stock (see recipe)
salt and cracked pepper to taste
Louisiana Gold Pepper Sauce to taste

METHOD:

If you are unable to find the wild pears, use the store-bought variety. Any good fruit preserve may be substituted in the place of the pears in this recipe. In a large black iron skillet, heat butter over medium high heat. Season medallions using cinnamon, salt and pepper. Saute until golden brown, approximately three to five minutes on each side. Venison is best when served medium rare. Remove and keep warm. Add shallots, garlic, green onions, thyme and sage. Saute three to five minutes or until vegetables are wilted. Add pears and preserves and deglaze with red wine. Add game stock, bring to a rolling boil and reduce to sauce consistency. Return the venison medallions to the sauce and heat thoroughly. Place two medallions in the center of a ten inch serving plate and top with strained sauce.

Changes

SAUTEED TENDERLOIN OF VENISON IN BLACKBERRY GLACE

PREP TIME: 1 Hour
SERVES: 6
COMMENT:

Tenderloin is considered the "king of meats". Whether the game or domesticated variety, tenderloin is always in demand. In plantation days, this particular cut was reserved for a very special guest and an equally impressive recipe.

INGREDIENTS:

2 venison tenderloins
1 cup Zinfandel wine
2 tbsps sugar cane syrup
1/4 cup chopped thyme
1/4 cup chopped basil
1/4 cup chopped tarragon
1/4 cup chopped garlic
1/4 cup butter
1 cup fresh blackberries
1/4 cup Zinfandel wine
2 cups Louisiana hunter sauce (see recipe)
salt and cracked pepper to taste
Louisiana Gold Pepper Sauce to taste

Fall Front Late Empire Mahogany Desk in the Smoking Room at Nottoway

METHOD:

Place tenderloins on a large baking sheet with one inch lip and top with wine and cane syrup. Using your hands, rub the syrup into the tenderloins. Season with thyme, basil, tarragon, garlic, salt, pepper and Louisiana Gold. Continue to rub the seasonings thoroughly into the meat. Allow to sit at room temperature a minimum of four hours, turning occasionally. In a heavy bottom black skillet, melt butter over medium high heat. Cut tenderloins into twelve equal medallions and saute until golden brown on all sides or medium rare. Remove and keep warm. Add blackberries and deglaze with wine. Allow mixture to reduce to one half volume and add hunter sauce. Bring to a low boil and season to taste using salt and pepper. Return medallions to sauce and allow to heat thoroughly. To serve, place two medallions in the center of a ten inch plate and top with blackberry glace. You may wish to use two cans of beef consomme in place of the hunter sauce. If so, reduce the consomme to approximately two cups and thicken with a blonde roux (see roux techniques).

Changes

ROASTED LEG OF VENISON BAYOU BLUE

PREP TIME: 2 1/2 Hours
SERVES: 6-8
COMMENT:

Bayou Blue is a small body of water that runs through the Coushatta Indian reservation. Venison was a primary ingredient in the Native American diet. The Coushattas combined the pine nuts of the long needle pine forest with the venison to create a dish that was often served on the tables of our Louisiana plantations.

INGREDIENTS:

1 3-5 pound venison leg roast
1/4 cup vegetable oil
3 cups oyster or button mushrooms
2 cups sliced bermuda onions
10 cloves garlic
4 sweet potatoes, cubed
2 cups muscadines or red grapes
3 cups chicken stock (see recipe)
1 cup pine nuts
pinch of thyme
pinch of basil
salt and cracked pepper to taste
Louisiana Gold Pepper Sauce to taste

METHOD:

Preheat oven to 400 degrees F. Season the roast well using herbs, salt, pepper and Louisiana Gold. In a large dutch oven, heat oil over medium high heat. Brown the venison well on all sides. Surround roast with mushrooms, onions, garlic, potatoes and muscadines. Pour in stock and pine nuts and bring to a rolling boil. Remove from heat, cover and bake until roast is tender, approximately one and a half to two hours. Check for tenderness and when done, remove roast and keep warm. Reduce the cooking liquid to a sauce consistency. If you prefer, thicken with a light roux (see roux techniques). Adjust seasonings if necessary. When ready to serve, slice venison roast and top with sauce.

LAGNIAPPE

Here in South Louisiana, we were raised on venison. During hunting season it was common to see a hunter's bike or truck carrying a carcass of venison. Most of our hunting camp suppers featured venison in some fashion as the main ingredient. Today, however, with domesticated venison available through mail order houses and specialty stores, anyone may savor the flavor of venison. This farm-raised game tends to be milder and less tough and gamey than its wild cousin. If you have strayed away from venison because of its strong flavor, try the domesticated variety. I think you'll change your mind.

Changes

CASSEROLE OF VENISON AND SQUASH

PREP TIME: 1 1/2 Hours
SERVES: 6-8
COMMENT:

With a state motto like "Sportsman's Paradise", is it any wonder that many combinations of wild game and vegetables appear in our black pots? Here, we see the influence of the Spanish with the blue corn dumplings and the native American indians with the squash, corn and pumpkin. It was the innovative Cajuns, however, who put them all together.

INGREDIENTS:
3 pounds venison stew meat, cubed
2 cups zucchini, cubed
2 cups summer squash, cubed
2 cups yams, cubed
2 cups pumpkin, cubed
1/4 pound butter
1 cup chopped onions
1 cup chopped celery
1 cup chopped bell pepper
1 tbsp diced garlic
3/4 cup flour
3 quarts chicken stock (see recipe)
1 tbsp chopped thyme
1 tbsp chopped basil
pinch of rosemary
2 bay leaves
1 diced jalapeno pepper
salt and cracked pepper to taste
Louisiana Gold Pepper Sauce to taste
12 blue corn muffins (see muffin recipe)

Changes

METHOD:

In a dutch oven, melt butter over medium high heat. Add venison and brown on all sides. Add onions, celery, bell pepper and garlic. Saute three to five minutes or until vegetables are wilted. Sprinkle in flour and blend well into meat/vegetable mixture. Add stock, bring to a rolling boil and reduce to simmer. Add thyme, basil, rosemary, bay leaves and jalapeno peppers. Continue to cook until venison becomes tender, approximately thirty minutes. Add all cubed vegetables and cook fifteen to twenty minutes longer or until yams and pumpkin are tender. Add a little stock or water to the pot, if necessary, to retain volume. Season to taste using salt, pepper and Louisiana Gold. When ready to serve, ladle a generous portion of the stew into a bowl and top with blue corn muffins. The cornbread muffin recipe is perfect for this accompaniment, however, substitute blue corn meal in place of the yellow corn meal.

Chapter Ten

Desserts & Breads

Loyd Hall Plantation

Loyd Hall Plantation

"Legacy of A Wayward Son"

When Frank and Virginia Fitzgerald purchased this piece of land on Bayou Boeuf in Central Louisiana, they knew the property was complete with row crops and out buildings. What they didn't know was the secret that lay covered with over-brush and twenty-five years of neglect. While flying over the property one day to survey their acreage, they spotted the shell of a structure. Upon careful investigation, they discovered the remains of a plantation home built over 150 years before. History and legend had it that the home was built by a wayward son of the famous Lloyds of London family. It seemed the son had fallen out of favor and was banished to America. He was given a sum of money to start a new life which included changing the spelling of his name. Though the new found structure was in terrible disrepair, when reconstructed, it would become their family home.

This six hundred forty acre working plantation has been in continuous operation since 1800. Visitors to the home will get a hands-on look at Louisiana agriculture with current crops of corn, cotton, soybeans and cattle. You may even be lucky enough to meet Clarence the donkey, who will certainly steal your heart, or be serenaded by the mysterious violin player, who often appears at midnight on the balcony. The home is impeccably furnished with priceless antiques and art. The plaster ceilings and suspended staircase truly give this three story home a one-of-a-kind look. Downstairs, the rooms are twenty by twenty with sixteen foot ceilings. They are elaborately detailed with plaster, cornice moldings and ceiling medallions. The doors are cypress and the beautiful floors are polished heart of pine. Twenty-eight large shuttered windows are symmetrically situated in the sixteen-inch thick walls. The home is Georgian in style and is constructed of bricks handmade on the property.

1800s French Mahogany Fournier Clock in the Entrance Foyer at Loyd Hall

Union troops discovered the home on their way to the Battle of Mansfield. While there, they discovered the owner, William Loyd, trading secrets to the South. He was hung as a spy. Over the years, the plantation had over twenty different owners. Today, the son of the owners, Frank, Jr., and his wife, Ann, run a bed and breakfast on the property.

To reach Loyd Hall, take I-49 North from Lafayette. Take exit 61 at Highway 167 to Loyd Bridge Road. 318-776-5641.

At left, Praline Icebox Cheesecake (page 278)

PRALINE ICEBOX CHEESECAKE

PREP TIME: 30 Minutes
SERVES: 6-8
COMMENT:

Although ice box style cheesecakes aren't as popular as the baked varieties, personally I think they are a life saver. Not only are they quite flavorful, but they can certainly get you out of an emergency.

INGREDIENTS:

1-8 ounce package cream cheese, softened
1/3 cup sugar
1 cup sour cream
2 tbsps vanilla
1 tbsp praline liqueur
1/2 cup chopped pecans
1-8 ounce container frozen whipped topping
1 graham cracker pie crust
8 pecan halves

METHOD:

In a large mixing bowl, whip cream cheese until smooth. Gradually add sugar until well blended. Add sour cream, vanilla and praline liqueur, continuing to whip into the cream cheese batter. Sprinkle in chopped pecans and fold in the whipped topping. Make sure all ingredients are well incorporated. You may wish to add additional praline liqueur if a stronger flavor is desired. Spoon the mixture into the prepared graham cracker crust, smooth and chill a minimum of four hours. Place the eight pecan halves at equal intervals around the outer edge of the cheesecake for garnish. Serve with your favorite fresh fruit or additional whipped cream.

Changes

STRAWBERRY SHORTCAKE

PREP TIME: 1 Hour
SERVES: 6-8
COMMENT:

Ponchatoula, Louisiana, is the strawberry capital of the world. It certainly makes sense that this very English dessert was first created in this area of our state. There is dispute over the exact shortcake recipe, however, most agree with this version.

INGREDIENTS:

4 cups sliced strawberries
1/2 cup sugar
1/2 cup water
2 3/4 cups flour
2 1/2 tbsps sugar
1 1/2 tbsps baking powder
1 tsp salt
7 tbsps butter
1 cup heavy whipping cream

METHOD:

Preheat oven to 375 degrees F. In a large mixing bowl, combine strawberries, sugar and water. Blend thoroughly, cover and chill a minimum of three hours. In the bowl of a food processor fitted with a metal blade, combine flour, sugar, baking powder and salt. Pulse to blend thoroughly. Add butter and continue to pulse until consistency of fine meal and pale yellow in color. The tenderness of the shortcake depends on the flour and butter being thoroughly mixed. Slowly pour in cream until mixture comes together in one mass. Turn dough out onto a floured surface and knead gently three to four times. Do not over-work. Roll the dough to three fourths inch thickness and cut into three inch circles. Before baking, brush with a little cream and sprinkle with sugar. Bake twenty to thirty minutes or until golden brown. To serve, split the biscuits horizontally and top with strawberry mixture. You may wish to garnish with a spoon of heavy whipping cream and drizzle with strawberry liqueur. Dust with powdered sugar prior to serving. I prefer to serve the shortcake while the biscuits are still warm.

LAGNIAPPE

Strawberries, or Alpine berries as they were called, were a rarity in home gardens and markets in early America. They were considered wild and so perishable that hunters and trappers sought after them in the early 1800s. It soon became fashionable to grow strawberry gardens in the cities and to eat the delectable berries off of the vine. In 1840, Martin Van Buren was attacked publicly during his presidential campaign because he used public money to raise strawberries for his own table. The largest fruit frenzy in America took place in June of 1847. A milk train brought 80,000 baskets of fresh strawberries to New York City where they were quickly sold within a few hours.

Changes

CANE RIVER POUND CAKE

PREP TIME: 1 1/2 Hours
SERVES: 10
COMMENT:

Though there were very few exotic flavors popping up in the kitchens of early Louisiana, one that seemed to be ever present was coconut. Due to the busy Port of New Orleans, many of these "different" fruits did make their way into bayou country and eventually to the rest of America.

A Cypress Hall Tree on the Gallery at Magnolia

INGREDIENTS:

2 1/4 cups sugar
8 ounces butter
6 whole eggs
2 1/4 cups all purpose flour
1 tsp baking powder
1/2 cup milk
4 tbsps vanilla
2 tbsps praline liqueur
1 ounce rum
1/2 cup chopped pecans
1/2 cup shredded coconut

FOR ICING:

2 tbsps butter
1/8 cup milk
1 cup sifted confectioner's sugar
1 tbsp praline liqueur

METHOD:

Preheat oven to 325 degrees F. In a large mixing bowl, combine sugar and butter. Whip until light and fluffy. Add eggs, one at a time, beating after each addition. Sprinkle in flour and baking powder, a little at a time, until all is incorporated. Continue to whip until ingredients are well blended. Add milk, vanilla, praline liqueur, rum, pecans and coconut. Continue to whip until all ingredients are well blended. Oil and flour a tube or angel food cake pan and fill with the cake mixture. Bake in center of the oven for one hour fifteen minutes or until a tester comes out clean when inserted into the cake. Remember that many ovens cook at varying temperatures, so check cake often. Remove the cake and allow to cool. In a small sauce pan, combine remaining butter and milk over medium high heat. Bring to a rolling boil, remove from heat and add confectioner's sugar and praline liqueur. You may wish to add a drop of your favorite food coloring. Remove the cake from the baking pan and paint with the praline glaze. Continue until all is used up.

Changes

PRECIOUS PEAR CAKE

PREP TIME: 1 1/2 Hours
SERVES: 8-10
COMMENT:

Wild pears of many varieties were available in South Louisiana in the mid 1800s. These pears were used mostly for canning and were enjoyed as a preserve for breakfast or supper. Today, however, these wild pears are used in dishes ranging from wild game to ice cream. If wild pears are not available in your area, just use the store-bought variety.

INGREDIENTS:

1 cup cooked pears
1 cup butter, softened
3/4 cup sugar
5 eggs, separated
1 tsp baking soda
1 cup buttermilk
2 1/2 cups flour
1 tsp cinnamon
1 tsp ground nutmeg
1 tsp ground allspice
1 cup chopped pecans

METHOD:

Preheat oven to 350 degrees F. NOTE: You may wish to make your own pear preserves by cooking four cups of diced pears, along with one fourth pound butter, one cup sugar, pinch of cinnamon and nutmeg and one half cup water. Allow this mixture to simmer until softened and the consistency of any fruit preserve. Ripe pears are preferred for this technique. In a large mixing bowl, cream butter and sugar, beating until fluffy. Add the egg yolks and continue to beat until pale yellow and creamy. Dissolve baking soda in buttermilk and add to the egg mixture. Slowly sprinkle in flour, stirring constantly to guarantee a smooth batter. Add spices and continue to blend until well incorporated. Fold in pecans, pear preserves and additional flour, if necessary, to stiffen the batter. Make sure that all ingredients are well incorporated. Whip egg whites until stiff peaks form and gently fold the whites into pear mixture. Grease and parchment line three 9-inch cake pans. Pour equal amounts of batter into each pan and bake thirty-five to forty-five minutes or until cake tester comes out clean. Cool in pan for fifteen minutes and spread with your favorite frosting both between the layers and over the cake. A cream cheese or caramel type frosting is wonderful with this cake.

Changes

POACHED BRANDIED PEARS

PREP TIME: 1 1/2 Hours
SERVES: 6
COMMENT:

There are many pears on the market that are perfect for poaching, such as Bartletts, Boscs, Kiefers and even the numerous wild varieties found here in Louisiana. In bayou country, we tend to slice, cook and jar the pears for use later as a dessert topping or pie filling. I have come to really enjoy a cold poached pear better than the sweet preserves we are used to in Louisiana.

INGREDIENTS:

6 hard pears, peeled and scored
2 cups water
2 cups red wine
3 1/2 cups sugar
1 tbsp vanilla
1/4 cup lemon juice
pinch of cinnamon
pinch of nutmeg
1 ounce brandy
1 tbsp corn starch
6 mint leaves
1 cup fresh whipped cream

METHOD:

When scoring the pears, you may wish to use a channeling tool, found in any gourmet or cutlery shop, to carve a design into the meat of the pear. If you cannot find one, a paring knife will do just fine. In a heavy bottom stock pot, place water, wine and sugar. Bring to a rolling boil while stirring constantly to thoroughly dissolve the sugar. Add vanilla, lemon juice, cinnamon and nutmeg. Reduce to just below simmer and add pears. Place a very clean dishcloth or small plate over the pears. Cook thirty to forty-five minutes or until pears are completely tender, but not mushy. Once tender, remove from heat and allow to rest in the poaching liquid, preferably overnight. This additional time will allow the pears to absorb the color and flavor of the poaching liquid. When ready to serve, place one and a half cups of the poaching liquid in a saute pan. Add brandy and bring to a rolling boil. Thicken the liquid with one tablespoon of corn starch dissolved in an additional one fourth cup of the cold poaching liquid. To serve, place cooled brandy sauce on the bottom of a ten inch plate. Garnish the pear with chopped mint leaves and a dollop of whipped cream.

Changes

Catalpa Plantation

JENNY LIND

Catalpa Plantation

"A Will to Survive"

I am often amazed to learn of the tragedies many of our Louisiana plantation homes had to endure just to be here with us today. This home was built by the Fort family near St. Francisville in the early 1800s. It is a perfect example of a plantation's will to survive. The house was nearly destroyed by the invading Union Army during the Civil War. Even the china and silver of the home were wrapped in burlap for protection and thrown into a nearby lake only to be retrieved years later. It was in the late 1800s that a tragic fire totally consumed the home but luckily most of the original furnishings were once again spared. The Fort family quickly rebuilt on the original foundation and most of the family treasures are here on display today because of their persistence and fortitude.

William Fort came to Spanish Feliciana to establish his cotton plantation. His strong sense of continuity and reverence to the past is exemplified in the home. The current owner, Mamie Fort Thompson, is quick to point out that the home is not a museum.

John James Audubon Painted this Soup Terrine at Catalpa

It is lived in and loved. Fine portraits, exceptional antiques and beautiful old china, porcelain and silver are on display daily. These artifacts are either original to Catalpa or from the famous Rosedown Plantation, home of Mamie's mother.

In addition to its elegant furnishings, the home was known for its grounds. A park-like atmosphere was created using exotic plants, flowers and fruit trees that were developed and nurtured in a large hot house on the property. These extensive gardens included a pool, deer park, peacocks, pigeons and other exotic animals. The invading Union troops destroyed the beautiful house and its gardens. Everything edible was foraged by the hungry army. Fort's widow, Sally, held onto the property and rebuilt it to its original grandeur.

Catalpa is quite a treasure in St. Francisville. One of the most interesting aspects of this home is Mamie Thompson herself. She represents the sixth generation of Forts who have lived in the home continually since its construction.

To reach Catalpa, take US 61 North from Baton Rouge five miles past St. Francisville. 504-635-3372.

At left, Port Hudson Buttermilk Pie (page 286), and Creamy Potato, Green Onion and Sausage Soup (page 76)

PORT HUDSON BUTTERMILK PIE

PREP TIME: 1 1/2 Hours
SERVES: 8-10
COMMENT:

Once a by-product of the churning of milk or cream to make butter, this "sour flavored" milk today has many uses. It is perfect as a main ingredient when making salad dressings and soups, but my favorite use is in desserts.

INGREDIENTS:

1/2 cup buttermilk
3/4 cup sugar
1/4 cup flour
1/2 cup melted butter
3 eggs
2 tbsps lemon juice
1 tbsp vanilla
pinch of salt
pinch of cinnamon
pinch of nutmeg
1-9 inch unbaked pie shell

METHOD:

Preheat oven to 350 degrees F. In a large mixing bowl, combine sugar, flour, buttermilk and butter. Using a wire whisk, whip until a smooth batter forms. This is very important because the flour may have a tendency to form lumps in the batter unless it is blended smooth. Add eggs, lemon juice and vanilla, continuing to incorporate all of the flavors into the batter. Finish with a pinch of salt, cinnamon and nutmeg. When blended, pour into a nine inch pie shell and bake for approximately one hour. The pie will be perfectly baked when lightly browned and a light crust has formed on the top. Allow the pie to cool prior to serving.

Changes

BEAUREGARD SWEET POTATO PIE

PREP TIME: 2 Hours

SERVES: 6-8

COMMENT:

Irv Daniels, of The Oaks Plantation in St. Francisville, has been in the sweet potato business for many years. Today, he grows the Beauregard sweet potato exclusively. This smooth-skinned, rose-colored yam is by far the best variety in Louisiana.

INGREDIENTS:

6 Beauregard sweet potatoes
juice of 1/2 lemon
1/4 pound butter
1 cup sugar
1 tbsp vanilla
2 tbsps flour
3 ounces cream cheese
1/4 pound butter
1 cup flour

METHOD:

Preheat oven to 350 degrees F. Peel sweet potatoes, split lengthwise and cube. Place in a four quart stock pot with lightly salted water to cover by one inch. Bring to a rolling boil over medium high heat and cook until potatoes are tender and water has been completely absorbed into the potatoes. Remove from heat and allow to cool slightly. During this process, ninety-nine percent of the water should be absorbed into the potatoes. Discard any remaining liquid. Using a fork, mash potatoes and place in a large mixing bowl. Add lemon juice and butter, mashing well into the vegetable mixture. Add sugar, vanilla and flour. Continue to blend until all ingredients are incorporated into the potatoes. Set aside. In a separate bowl, blend cream cheese and remaining butter. Sprinkle in flour while mixing thoroughly. Turn out onto a floured board and knead three to four times. Roll pie crust to one eighth inch thick, place in a nine inch pie pan and fill with the sweet potato mixture. Bake approximately one hour, remove and allow pie to sit two to three hours prior to serving.

Changes

SWEET POTATO ORANGE SPICE CAKE

PREP TIME: 1 Hour
SERVES: 12-15
COMMENT:

This recipe is often prepared using pumpkin in place of the sweet potato. I find that either way is great. You may wish to serve this spice cake as a breakfast item or in the place of traditional coffee cake.

INGREDIENTS:

1 cup cooked sweet potato or yams, mashed
3/4 cup butter
2 cups flour
3/4 cup sugar
1 tsp baking soda
2 tsps pumpkin pie spice
1/4 cup orange zest
1 egg, beaten
1 1/4 cups buttermilk
1 cup golden raisins
1/4 cup chopped pecans
1/3 cup chocolate chips, chopped

METHOD:

Preheat oven to 375 degrees F. In a large mixing bowl, combine butter, flour and sugar. Using your hands, rub the flour between your palms to create a crumb effect. Add baking soda, pumpkin pie spice and orange zest, blending into the flour. Add sweet potato, egg and buttermilk. Blend into dry ingredients and when well mixed, add raisins and pecans. Gently stir into the batter to incorporate liquid but do not over-mix. Grease a 10"x 15" jelly roll pan and spread mixture evenly into pan. Sprinkle on chocolate chips and bake twenty five to thirty minutes or until cake springs back when touched.

The Master Bedroom at San Francisco

Changes

SWEET POTATO PONES

PREP TIME: 1 Hour
SERVES: 6-8
COMMENT:

The term "pone" normally refers to a baked cornbread or biscuit stick. These four to six inch sticks are baked in a special pan and served hot with butter. Here, the pone is more of a turnover and the name was given to this dish over 100 years ago, so who are we to change it!

INGREDIENTS:

3 sweet potatoes
1/4 pound butter
1 tsp salt
1 cup brown sugar
2 tsps cinnamon
1/4 cup lemon juice
2 sticks butter

2/3 cup sugar
1 egg
1 tbsp vanilla
2 tsps cinnamon
1 tsp salt
2 1/2 cups flour

METHOD:

In a one gallon stock pot, boil potatoes until soft enough to mash. Peel and place in food processor with butter, salt, sugar, cinnamon and lemon juice. Blend on high speed until all ingredients are well incorporated. Remove and set aside. Preheat oven to 350 degrees F. In a large mixing bowl, cream together butter and sugar. Beat one egg with vanilla, cinnamon and salt. Add to the sugar mixture and blend well to incorporate. Add flour and mix well to form dough. Knead three to four times to blend all ingredients thoroughly. Once the dough ball has formed nicely, cover with clear wrap and chill for up to three hours or overnight. Remove and roll out one eighth inch thick dough on a floured surface. Cut into five inch circles. Place a generous spoonful of potato mixture in the center of each circle and fold in a turnover fashion. Seal the edges with a fork, prick to allow steam to escape and bake until golden brown, approximately fifteen to twenty minutes. Serve either hot or cold. The pones work well as an accompaniment to any entree or as a late night snack.

LAGNIAPPE

Cooks often ask, "What's the difference between a sweet potato and a yam?" Well, a lot! Early historical records state that the Choctaw Indians introduced the Cajuns and Creoles to the sweet potato upon their arrival in the 1600s and 1700s. This yellow, wild root vegetable has been growing in the subtropical regions of the Western Hemisphere for thousands of years. The white yam, indigenous to Africa and Asia, was brought to this country and around the world during slave trade. Records show that this African yam was cultivated in Colonial Virginia in the very early 1600s. Today, Louisiana sweet potato growers use the marketing term "yam" to promote their superior variety of sweet potatoes for the world market. So now we can all agree that sweet potatoes are indigenous to Louisiana and yams are a gift from Africa.

Changes

LOUISIANA FRUIT TRIFLE

PREP TIME: 1 Hour
SERVES: 10-12
COMMENT:

Fruit trifle, the layered fruit and custard dessert, was brought to Louisiana by the English many years ago. The abundance of fresh berries and other seasonal fruit made the creation of this dish simple in bayou country. Try substituting a variety of mixed fruit.

INGREDIENTS FOR CUSTARD:

2 cups half and half cream
4 egg yolks
1/2 cup sugar
1 tbsp vanilla
pinch of cinnamon
pinch of nutmeg
3/4 tbsp corn starch
1 tbsp water

Changes

METHOD:

Place the cream in a sauce pan over medium high heat and bring to a low boil. In a mixing bowl, whip eggs, sugar, vanilla, cinnamon and nutmeg. In a measuring cup, combine corn starch and water. Dissolve well and set aside. Once cream begins to boil, remove from heat and pour approximately one cup into the egg mixture. Using a wire whisk, whip constantly. Pour the egg and cream mixture back into the pot with the remaining one cup of milk and continue to stir. Return the sauce pan to heat, pour in corn starch and stir until custard begins to thicken. Remove from heat and continue to stir three to five minutes. Set aside.

INGREDIENTS FOR TRIFLE:

1-9 inch loaf pound cake
1/4 cup brandy
1 cup sliced strawberries
1 cup sliced blueberries
1 cup sliced bananas
1 cup blackberries or raspberries
2 cups prepared custard sauce (see above)
1 cup sweetened cream, whipped

Changes

METHOD:

Cut pound cake into one inch squares. Place squares in large mixing bowl and sprinkle with brandy. In a large footed trifle dish, layer the cake, fruit and custard sauce until all is used. Top with the whipped cream and garnish with a sprig of fresh mint and a sprinkle of cinnamon.

PEACH COBBLER

PREP TIME: 1 1/2 Hours
SERVES: 8
COMMENT:

Houmas House had many visitors back in the mid 1800s and often they would write of their experiences at the plantation. One such visitor wrote about the wonderful peas that were grown in the garden and eaten day after day. He mentioned the mint juleps served before breakfast and the fabulous peach cobbler that ended every meal. Here is a rendition of that dish.

INGREDIENTS:

6 cups sliced fresh peaches
1 1/2 cups sugar
1/4 cup water
3 tbsps flour
1/4 cup sugar
pinch of salt
pinch of cinnamon
pinch of nutmeg
pinch of allspice
1 cup all purpose flour
1/2 cup sugar
2 tsps baking powder
3/4 cup milk
1/2 tsp salt

METHOD:

Preheat oven to 400 degrees F. In a heavy bottom sauce pan, combine peaches, sugar and water. Bring to a rolling boil, reduce to simmer and allow fruit to cook until softened. In a measuring cup, blend flour, sugar, salt, cinnamon, nutmeg and allspice. Pour into the peach mixture, stirring constantly until mixture thickens. Remove from heat and pour the mixture into a nine inch black iron skillet or cobbler pan and allow to cool slightly. In a mixing bowl, combine flour, sugar, baking powder and milk. Using a wire whisk, whip until well blended. Season with salt. Pour the batter in an irregular shape over the center of the cobbler and bake for approximately forty-five minutes or until golden brown. NOTE: You may wish to garnish the cobbler with fresh sliced peaches, powdered sugar and a sprig of mint.

LAGNIAPPE

The Romans were the first people to write about peaches. The Chinese buried their dead with a bowl of peaches in the 2nd Century B.C. Louisiana was named for Louis XIV who was a glutton for peaches. Louis shared this fondness for the fruit with the American Indians and it is said that he gave peaches to both the Creeks and Seminoles. The Natchez Indians were so fond of peaches that they named one of their thirteen months after them. Passed from tribe to tribe, the peach tree spread through the American Indian nation faster than the white man did. In fact, William Penn wrote in 1663 that the peaches grown by the Indians in the Philadelphia area were every bit as good as those in England.

Changes

PECAN AMBROSIA

PREP TIME: 30 Minutes
SERVES: 6-8
COMMENT:

Flavored fruit salads have many variations throughout the country. Often they simply call for only one or, at the most, two main ingredients. In Louisiana, we tend to use all that is at hand to create an ambrosia unlike any other.

INGREDIENTS:

1-20 ounce can sliced peaches
1-20 ounce can crushed pineapple
6 mandarin oranges, peeled and sectioned
1 cup sliced strawberries
1 diced red apple
1 diced green apple
1- 3 1/2 ounce can flaked coconut
1/2 cup sliced maraschino cherries
1 cup chopped pecans
1-8 ounce carton Cool Whip

METHOD:

In a large mixing bowl, combine all of the ingredients except the strawberries and Cool Whip. Toss the ingredients well to ensure that they are thoroughly mixed. Cover with clear wrap and place in the refrigerator for a minimum of four hours, allowing ingredients to marinate. Immediately prior to serving, fold in the sliced strawberries and the Cool Whip. Blend until the fruit is well coated with the "dressing". You may wish to serve a spoon full of the ambrosia in a slice of butter lettuce and garnish with grated cheddar cheese for added affect.

A Rear Garden at Layton Castle

Changes

Shadows on the Teche **Plantation**

Shadows on the Teche Plantation

"A Diary Recovered"

When David Weeks built his plantation home on Bayou Teche in 1834, little did he realize that the home would remain in his family throughout its history. The Weeks family proved to be great record keepers and wrote diaries and journals on everything imaginable. They wrote about life-styles in the 1800s, the evolution of medicine and agriculture on the plantations and even fashion. It is because of the over 17,000 handwritten manuscripts found in the attic of the home that, today, we have a better understanding of life and times on a Louisiana plantation.

The Main Gate at Shadows

Bayou Teche is the main waterway flowing through Iberia Parish. It was on the bank of this bayou that David Weeks built Shadows. Under construction from 1831 to 1834, it was built as a townhouse for his wife, Mary, and their six children. After David's death, Mary lived on at the Shadows, and took responsibility for raising and educating her children, as well as running the plantation. In 1841, she married Judge John Moore. The plantation prospered and their lavish life-style lasted until the Civil War. The Union army marched into New Iberia and the Shadows became its headquarters. Mrs. Moore, seriously ill at the time, remained in her second floor bedroom until she died, a prisoner in her own home.

The architecture here is a blend of Georgian, French Creole and Anglo-American styles. The walls are constructed of coral colored brick produced on the plantation. Most of the main rooms are located on the second floor and can be reached only by an outside staircase. The home was lived in only intermittently after the war and didn't thrive again until the early 1920s. Weeks Hall, the builder's great grandson, returned from Paris and spent the rest of his life restoring the home. Hall was a talented artist with many friends in the artistic, literary, political and entertainment fields who visited him often. Shadows gained national fame and became a focal point of literary and photographic works. Hall lived in the house until his death in 1958. The house has been featured in many movies and on television. Today, it has become the property of The National Trust for Historic Preservation.

To reach Shadows, take I-10 to Lafayette. Follow Highway 90 to Louisiana Highway 14 at New Iberia. 318-369-6446.

At left, Orange Cane Syrup Pecan Pie (page 296) and Crabmeat Stuffed Breast of Chicken (page 175)

ORANGE CANE SYRUP PECAN PIE

PREP TIME: 1 Hour 15 Minutes
SERVES: 8
COMMENT:

Though there are hundreds of variations of the Southern Pecan Pie, I have tried diligently to come up with my own rendition that is lighter and less sweet. The addition of orange juice in the place of brown sugar makes this recipe more appealing.

INGREDIENTS:

1/4 cup fresh squeezed orange juice
1 tbsp grated orange peel
3/4 cup chopped pecans
5 whole eggs
1/2 cup sugar
1 cup light Karo syrup
1 tbsp sugar cane syrup
1 tbsp flour
1-9 inch unbaked pie shell
16 pecan halves

METHOD:

Preheat oven to 350 degrees F. In a large mixing bowl, combine eggs and sugar, whipping well with a wire whisk. Do not over beat. Add Karo and cane syrup, and blend into the egg mixture. Pour in orange peel and orange juice and sprinkle in flour. Blend until all is well incorporated. Add chopped pecans, fold once or twice into the mixture and pour into pie shell. Place the pecan halves in a circular pattern on the outer edge of the pie. Place on a cookie sheet and cover with parchment paper. Bake approximately one hour and check for doneness. It is best to cool the pie overnight. Slice into eight equal portions.

Changes

FELECIANA FRUITCAKE

PREP TIME: 2 Hours
MAKES: 4 loaves
COMMENT:

Here in South Louisiana, fruitcakes are a must at Christmas time. There is no gift more cherished than a homemade fruitcake from an old family recipe. These cakes may be made in the early summer, drizzled with liquor and aged for that special Christmas gift.

INGREDIENTS:

6 cups flour
2 tsps baking powder
2 tbsps cinnamon
1 tbsp nutmeg
1 tbsp ground cloves
1 tbsp allspice
1 pound butter
2 cups sugar
10 eggs, separated
1 cup whiskey
8 cups chopped pecans
2 pounds currants
1 pound raisins
1 pound chopped dates
1/2 pound chopped candied cherries
1/2 pound chopped dried figs
1 cup fig preserves

METHOD:

Preheat oven to 300 degrees F. Place all of the chopped dried fruit into a mixing bowl with one cup of flour. Blend to coat the fruit and set aside. In a large mixing bowl, combine flour, powder and dried spices. Blend well. In a separate bowl, cream butter and sugar, whipping until fluffy. Add egg yolks, one at a time, incorporating well after each addition. Beat egg whites until fluffy and fold into egg mixture. Add flour and stir until well blended. Add whiskey and chopped fruit, stirring well into the batter. Mix thoroughly to ensure that all ingredients are incorporated. Oil four loaf pans and line with parchment paper. Fill to three fourths volume with the batter. Bake for one and a half hours or until tester comes out moist but not wet. Once cakes are cooled, cover tightly with aluminum foil and place in the refrigerator. You may wish to add one tablespoon of whiskey every few weeks to "season the cakes".

Changes

JELLY ROLL

PREP TIME: 45 Minutes

SERVES: 6-8

COMMENT:

I love jelly rolls and my mother made the best. I remember those Saturday afternoons when she would whip up the batter as we children scraped the blackberry jelly from the jars. After completing the jelly rolls, she would trim the ends square prior to slicing. These trimmings were our reward for hard work.

INGREDIENTS:

1 cup blackberry jelly
3 eggs
1 cup sugar
1/4 cup cold water
1 tbsp vanilla
3/4 cup flour
2 tsps baking powder
pinch of salt
1/4 cup powdered sugar

METHOD:

Preheat oven to 300 degrees F. Line a 15"x 10" cookie sheet with lightly oiled parchment paper. Make sure to oil the sides of the pan. In a mixing bowl, cream eggs and sugar. Using a wire whisk, whip until smooth and fluffy. Add water and vanilla and continue to whip. Blend flour, baking powder and salt into the egg mixture. When all is incorporated, pour onto the cookie sheet and spread out evenly. Bake ten to fifteen minutes but do not over-cook. When done, remove and allow to cool slightly. Place a large dish towel on the counter and cover with parchment paper. Sprinkle powdered sugar evenly over the paper. After cake has cooled five to six minutes, turn out onto the sugared paper. Beginning at the ten inch end, roll the cake, jelly roll style using the towel and parchment. Allow to sit ten minutes. Unroll, spread evenly with the jelly and roll again, this time using only the parchment paper. When set, slice into one quarter inch pieces, sprinkle with powdered sugar and serve.

Changes

CHALMETTE SUGAR COOKIES

PREP TIME: 1 Hour
MAKES: 12-14
COMMENT:

There weren't many desserts available for the soldiers at the Battle of New Orleans. It seems, though, that the simple sugar cookie made its way to the battlefield and was considered a fabulous treat. There are many variations, but this is my favorite.

INGREDIENTS:

1 cup butter, softened
1 1/2 cups confectioner's sugar
1 egg
1 tsp vanilla
1/2 tsp almond extract
2 1/2 cups all purpose flour
1 tsp baking soda
1 tsp cream of tartar
1/2 cup brown sugar

METHOD:

In a large mixing bowl, combine butter and confectioner's sugar. Using a wire whisk, whip until well blended. Add egg, vanilla and extract and stir well. Combine flour, soda and tartar, blending well into butter mixture. Form dough into a ball, cover and chill a minimum of two hours. Preheat oven to 375 degrees F. Place dough on a floured surface and roll to one quarter inch thick. Cut into desired shapes and sizes and sprinkle with brown sugar. Place on a lightly greased baking sheet and cook seven to eight minutes or until edges of cookies are light brown. You may also wish to frost the cookies with your favorite colored icing.

Changes

A Militiaman at Rene Beauregard

FIG ICE CREAM

PREP TIME: 2 Hours
MAKES: 3 Quarts
COMMENT:

Figs certainly are a versatile fruit in Louisiana. It was the Indians who first showed us uses for the fig in cooking. However, the Italian immigrants gave us the fig ice cream recipe.

INGREDIENTS:

2 cups fig preserves
1 1/2 cups sugar
1/3 cup flour
4 cups cream
5 eggs, beaten
5 cups half and half cream
1 tbsp vanilla extract
1/4 cup Louisiana cane syrup

METHOD:

In a large mixing bowl, combine sugar and flour. Stir well and set aside. In a one gallon sauce pan, bring cream to a low boil over medium high heat. Gradually add the sugar mixture, stirring constantly until well blended, approximately five to eight minutes. In a mixing bowl, stir one cup of the hot mixture into the eggs, whipping constantly. Add egg/cream mixture into the sauce pot, stirring constantly. Cook one minute longer and remove from heat. Allow to cool while stirring occasionally. Add half and half, vanilla, cane syrup and fig preserves. Blend well and chill for two hours. Pour chilled mixture into a homestyle ice cream freezer and freeze according to manufacturer's directions. Place in freezer approximately two hours prior to serving.

Changes

Rosedown Plantation

Rosedown Plantation

Fruitcake, Candied Fruit and Port in the Gentleman's Parlor at Rosedown

"A Portrait of the Past"

I have often wondered about the difficulty of furnishing one's home in the early days of our country. There were no furniture stores or showrooms, so you had to be a bit more creative. Many people simply built their own furniture. Others, the wealthy, travelled to New Orleans or abroad and had their furniture specially designed, built and delivered. One specially designed bedroom set is located at Rosedown Plantation. It was designed for Henry Clay and was destined for the White House. But when he lost the presidential election, the furniture was purchased by the Turnbull family and shipped to Rosedown. Two matching wings had to be added to the home just to house the furniture.

Rosedown was built in 1835 by Daniel Turnbull, a descendant of George Washington, as a home for his new bride, Martha Barrow. On their honeymoon trip to Europe, the couple purchased magnificent furnishings for their new home. On a brief stop in New York, they attended a play called *Rosedown*. In one scene, a rose colored mansion painted on a stage curtain reminded Martha of her Louisiana home. She immediately decided to name her plantation Rosedown.

The central part of the house is constructed of cypress which is painted white. Six simple Doric columns support the roof and double galleries across the front. Georgian sidelights of leaded glass accent the front doors at each level. Two stuccoed brick Greek revival wings were added in the 1840s. One of these wings houses the Henry Clay bedroom. Today, Rosedown is furnished with over eighty-five percent of the original Turnbull furniture.

The Civil War ravaged Rosedown the same way it crushed most of the grand Louisiana plantations. The Turnbulls persevered and fought adversity as it arose. Daniel died during the first year of the war. But Martha, along with her daughter and son-in-law, refused to relinquish the property. An ivory button was eventually placed on the newel post of the entrance staircase to show friends and guests that the mortgages had all been paid.

Rosedown is known for its magnificent gardens, which were patterned after European gardens visited by the Turnbulls on their honeymoon. Today, the home is owned by Mr. and Mrs. Milton Underwood of Houston.

To reach Rosedown, take US 61 North from Baton Rouge to St. Francisville. 504-635-3110.

At left, Garlic Stuffed Leg of Lamb (page 208) and Louisiana Style Hunter Sauce (page 30)

CANDIED FRUIT

PREP TIME: 30 Minutes
MAKES: 1 Cup
COMMENT:

One can only imagine how hot the old plantation kitchens could be while baking. Fires were burned to produce coals to heat the brick ovens. When the ovens were sufficiently warmed, baking could begin. There was certainly a need to create beautiful desserts that didn't require baking. Glazed fruit was not only popular, but was certainly a solution to the problem.

INGREDIENTS:

1 cup sliced mixed fruit
1 cup sugar
3/4 cup water
1/4 tsp cream of tartar

METHOD:

In a heavy bottom sauce pan, combine sugar, water and cream of tartar over medium high heat. Bring to a rolling boil, cover and cook without stirring three minutes. This will allow the steam to wash down any sugar crystals that may have formed on the sauce pan. Uncover, lower heat to simmer and cook to the hard cracked stage, 300 degrees F. Remove pan from heat and place over very hot water. Dip a few pieces of fruit at a time into the mixture and quickly remove them with a toothpick or fork. Place on a wire rack until the coating hardens. Should the syrup begin to solidify, reheat over hot water and repeat the dipping process. It is best to glaze fruit in small batches for best results.

LAGNIAPPE

Glazed fruit was not only beautiful to look at on the table, but it was also quite tasty and prepared with minimal effort. The success of this confection depends on sparkling dry weather and last minute preparation. They must be eaten the very day they are prepared because they will not keep. Remember to use only fresh fruit and when glazing a large quantity, divide into several small batches. Fruit must be at room temperature prior to dipping and it is always best to dry the fruit on paper towels four to six hours prior to dipping.

Changes

HONEYED APPLE RINGS

PREP TIME: 30 Minutes
SERVES: 6
COMMENT:

It is difficult to determine whether this recipe is a salad, vegetable or dessert. In fact, it could be any one of the three. I have always served this dish as an accompaniment to my smothered sausage and apple cider recipe. However, I know friends who serve it hot over mixed greens as a salad, and others who eliminate the vinegar and put it on ice cream. Why don't you decide.

INGREDIENTS:

2 red apples, cored and sliced
2 green apples, cored and sliced
2 cups honey
1 cup red wine vinegar
pinch of cinnamon
pinch of nutmeg
pinch of salt

METHOD:

It is important to leave the peelings on the apples in this recipe for better presentation on the plate. You must remember that apples oxidize and turn brown quickly when exposed to the air. It is always best to submerge the sliced apple rings in a bowl of water with one half cup lemon juice to prevent this oxidation process. However, you must drain the apples well on a paper towel before sauteing or poaching. In a heavy bottom black iron skillet, combine all ingredients over medium high heat. Using a wire whisk, stir until all is well incorporated and the liquids are slightly simmering. DO NOT BOIL. Cook the apple rings a few at a time in the simmering liquid until they are very tender, but not mushy or overcooked. Remove and keep warm. Continue until all the apples have been "poached" in the honey/vinegar mixture. Once all the apples have been cooked, arrange them around the edge of a large platter and serve with smothered pork sausage (see recipe).

Changes

____

____

____

____

____

BUZZARD'S PRAIRIE DROP BISCUITS

PREP TIME: 30 Minutes
MAKES: 12 Biscuits
COMMENT:

The name buzzard's prairie was given to the land surrounding Chretien Point by the Indians of the area. The large number of crows or buzzards flying in the area after the discovery of the carcass of a mastodon probably contributed to this name.

INGREDIENTS:

1 3/4 cups all purpose flour
3 tsps baking powder
1/2 tsp salt
6 tbsps softened butter
1 cup buttermilk

METHOD:

Preheat oven to 450 degrees F. In a large mixing bowl, combine flour, baking powder and salt. Mix thoroughly and, using a fork, blend in butter until dough is formed. Make a well in the center of the dough mixture and pour in buttermilk. Stir the dough one to two minutes or until buttermilk is well blended into the mixture. Using a large mixing spoon, drop twelve equal amounts of the mixture onto an ungreased baking sheet. This procedure will create inconsistent shapes which will look more homemade than a cut biscuit. Bake for fifteen minutes on the center oven rack or until the biscuits are evenly browned. Remove from oven and brush with melted butter before serving. Here in bayou country, we mix one half cup softened butter with one tablespoon of Steen's cane syrup for a great topping for hot drop biscuits.

Changes

STRAWBERRY PECAN MUFFINS

PREP TIME: 30 Minutes
MAKES: 12 Muffins
COMMENT:

In many ways, muffins are like biscuits, but they are usually made with a loose, sweet dough. Mixing of the muffin batter should be held to an absolute minimum. Even a light stirring of ten to twenty second intervals is enough. This will keep the muffins moist and tender. Many variations can be made by adding fruits or nuts.

The Portrait of Celestine Cantrelle Hangs over the Mantle at Chretien Point

INGREDIENTS:

3/4 cup chopped strawberries
1/4 cup finely chopped pecans
2 cups flour
2 tsps baking powder
1/2 tsp salt
2 tbsps sugar
pinch of cinnamon
pinch of nutmeg
1 cup milk
1 egg, beaten
3 tbsps oil

METHOD:

It is always best to sift the dry ingredients to give the muffins a lighter texture, however, this is not mandatory. Preheat oven to 425 degrees F. In a large mixing bowl, sift the flour, baking powder, salt, sugar, cinnamon and nutmeg. In a separate bowl, add milk, egg and oil. Using a wire whisk, whip until all ingredients are well blended. Fold in strawberries and pecans. Pour the liquid ingredients into the flour mixture and stir with a fork gently until well moistened. DO NOT beat this batter. Once well blended, drop equal amounts of the batter into well greased muffin tins until approximately two thirds full. Bake on center oven rack twenty to twenty five minutes or until done. NOTE: You may wish to saute the strawberries in the three tablespoons of oil to render the liquid from the berries, prior to adding them to the milk-egg mixture. This will ensure that your muffins are not watery or soggy, especially if you use overripe berries.

Changes

SWEET POTATO PUMPKIN BREAD

PREP TIME: 1 1/2 Hours

SERVES: 6

COMMENT:

Both sweet potatoes and pumpkins are indigenous to South Louisiana and are most often cooked in desserts or sweetened casseroles. Here, the two are combined with a simple bread mix to create a quick and easy bread recipe that is sure to please.

INGREDIENTS:

3/4 cup cooked cubed pumpkin
3/4 cup cooked cubed sweet potatoes
3 cups sugar
4 eggs
1/2 cup oil
2 tbsps cinnamon
2 tbsps nutmeg
3 1/2 cups all purpose flour
1 tsp salt
2 tsps baking soda
1/2 cup water
3/4 cup raisins
1 cup pecans
pecan halves for garnish

METHOD:

Preheat oven to 350 degrees F. Par boil sweet potatoes and pumpkin cubes until tender. Remove, mash and set aside. You may wish to use eight ounce cans of cooked sweet potatoes and pumpkin, rather than fresh. In a large bowl, mix sugar and eggs until creamy. Add oil, sweet potatoes and pumpkin. Mix on high speed until creamy, reduce to low and add dry ingredients alternately with water. Beat until well blended. Stir in raisins and pecans and pour into a large greased cake pan. Bake for one hour or until top is golden brown. Garnish with pecan halves. For an added touch, glaze with Louisiana cane syrup.

Changes

CORNBREAD MUFFINS

PREP TIME: 1 Hour
MAKES: 16 Muffins
COMMENT:

Cornbread can be made into every shape and size imaginable. I've seen it served in skillets, stick pans and muffin tins. It has been referred to as skillet bread, hushpuppies, spoon bread and corn sticks. Whatever you call it and however you cook it, it is still good ole' Southern cornbread.

INGREDIENTS:

1 1/4 cups yellow corn meal
3/4 cup all purpose flour
2 1/2 tsps double acting baking powder
2 tbsps sugar
1 tsp salt
1 egg
3 tbsps melted butter
1 cup milk
1/4 cup whole kernel corn

METHOD:

Preheat oven to 425 degrees F. Grease two eight-hole muffin tins and set aside. In a large mixing bowl, combine flour, baking powder, sugar and salt. Mix well, add corn meal and blend until the ingredients are well incorporated. Add egg, butter and milk and continue to blend ingredients well. Fold whole kernel corn into the cornbread batter. Pour the batter into muffin tins and bake twenty to twenty-five minutes or until golden brown.

LAGNIAPPE

If you grow up in South Louisiana, you certainly know what good cornbread is all about. It always has that slightly browned crust but is light, sweet and gritty to the bite. It is hard to make a good cornbread without a heavy black iron skillet or muffin pan. The old folks say that the pan should always be heated to about 400 degrees F in the oven before the batter is placed in the pan. They also say that a little bit of crackling or bacon, and always whole kernels of corn, should be added for better flavor. Yes, if you grow up in South Louisiana, you know exactly what they're talking about.

Changes

PLANTATION DIRECTORY

Index

Roux, Stocks, Sauces, etc.

Appetizers

Soups

Salads

Vegetables

Poultry

Meat

Beef

Lamb

Pork

Seafood

Wild Game

Desserts and Breads

The Company Store

When cooking the cuisine of South Louisiana, numerous specialty products such as cast iron pots, crawfish tails and andouille sausage are utilized. Most of these unique items are grown or manufactured here in our state.

At Chef John Folse & Company, we are able to make these unique items available to you. If you are interested in purchasing or obtaining information on any of the products featured in this cookbook or on our PBS series, "A Taste of Louisiana with Chef John Folse," please write or phone:

Chef John Folse & Company
2517 South Philippe Avenue
Gonzales, LA 70737
(225) 644-6000
FAX (225) 644-1295
or
Visit our Company Store online at
http://www.jfolse.com